Sincerely,

Virginia Laur Burns

FIRST
FRONTIERS

Christopher J. Stringer, M.D.

F.A.C.S. — F.A.C.P.

Diplomate

American Board of Thoracic Surgery

and

Virginia Law Burns

ENTERPRISE PRESS
8600 S. Fenner Road
Laingsburg, MI 48848

Cover design by artist-illustrator Max Altekruse of Franklin, Michigan from photographs provided by the authors.

ISBN 0-9604726-2-2

Library of Congress Catalog Card Number 85-081071

INTRODUCTION

There are two opposing views regarding the value of knowing history — medical history, included. One holds that "those who do not learn from history are doomed to repeat it." The other that, "the only lesson history teaches, is that no one ever learns a damned thing from it." I mention this because longtime Lansing resident Dr. Christopher Stringer has written a memoir, a lively recounting of his fifty years as a chest surgeon, that I heartily recommend you read — not because you might know him or be curious to learn what he has to say, good and bad, about his fellow Michigan physicians, but because it is thoroughly fascinating and enjoyable reading.

When recently asked to explain his remarkable success as a best-selling crime novelist, Elmore Leonard said, "I guess, because I leave out of my books, those parts a reader usually skips." Chris Stringer and Virginia Law Burns know how to do this, too; they write in short, suspenseful bursts that keep you turning pages.

In an early chapter, Dr. Stringer states that his Uncle Lew, an admirable physician from Monroe, Louisiana, influenced him greatly in his choice of careers — and I've no reason to doubt this. But after reading about all the high-risk surgery Chris Stringer undertook, the deadly diseases he exposed himself to, the wild airplane rides to the Upper Peninsula he somehow survived, I think he's had a guardian angel to guide and protect him from boyhood on.

I've always believed that medicine is — or should be — more of a calling than a profession. Evidently Chris Stringer does, too, considering that he went to medical school in the 1920's when only two truly therapeutic drugs, digitalis and quinine, existed and the practice of medicine had reached such a low estate that a medical student was reputed to be "the only son of a family who was too lazy to farm, too stupid for the bar, and too immoral for the pulpit." Medicine has, of course, improved immensely since then, but to have been "at the creation" of so many of these changes, to have actually brought about some yourself — as Chris Stringer has done — and to be able to look back now and know they were right, must be a surpassing thrill that we can share, in part, through his writing.

In his opening chapter, Dr. Stringer describes the successful surgical repair of a coartation of the aorta in a twenty-seven year old female that he performed in 1951 — one of the first such operations in the State of Michigan and certainly one of the most complicated ever (by extremely elevated blood pressure and previous sympathectomy.) And if this hair-raising tale doesn't rivet your attention, there's much more to come. Just imagine treating a pulmonary abscess in a young female by plunging a white-hot soldering iron through her chest wall into the abscess cavity to drain it!

In one of his best chapters, Dr. Stringer describes some of his wilder adventures with an endoscope, especially the times he went fishing for coins lodged in youngsters' gullets. Since we more or less know in advance that these fishing expeditions will have happy outcomes, they make very funny reading.

In short, Chris Stringer has not only led an extraordinarily interesting and useful life but is a natural story-teller. Never mind your interest, or lack of it, in medical memoirs; for no better reason than the sheer entertainment it offers, spend a free afternoon reading this book. I guarantee that you won't want to put it down until you've finished it.

by

Marshall Goldberg, M.D.
Chief of Endocrinology
Hurley Medical Center;
Professor of Medicine
Michigan State University
College of Human Medicine

PREFACE

I have based this narrative on the most memorable events of a 50 year career in chest surgery and have included a sprinkling of specific surgical experiences.

The first chapter is an example of such an experience.

The episodes have been pulled from my records and when these were not available, gleaned from my memory and the recollections of others. In some cases the dates are approximate. I have also used ficticious names where it would have been insensitive not to do so.

I am particularly indebted to Ruth, my wife of 50 years. In addition to her memory of events, Ruth has edited the manuscript and allowed liberal quotations from her journal.

I am also grateful to Mr. Earl Snodgrass and to Mrs. Bettie Cannon and Mrs. Carolyn Hall for their helpful critique of the book.

Mrs. Elvi Trethewey, my long time secretary, with her marvelous recall has contributed valuable information, particularly in regard to names and dates.

Dr. LeMoyne Snyder, famed medicolegal expert and author of the text, *Homocide Investigation,* graciously assisted me on the Michigan State Police chapter. Dr. Snyder's comments have been most encouraging and helpful.

As I look about my study and assess the stacks of pages of notes I made as one recollection made me think of another, I recall one telephone conversation with Dr. Snyder from his home in Paradise California, when he suggested that there is enough material for two books. Co-author Virginia Burns, who originally encouraged me to collect and record the many events of fifty years, has more recently urged me to stop and finish this one first!

Virginia has become a close and valued friend of both my wife Ruth and myself. She has met our sons and daughters-in-law and grandchildren. Without Virginia as co-author, this work would not have been possible.

DEDICATED TO MY FAMILY
MY MOST VALUED ASSET

FRONTIERS IN CHEST SURGERY
TABLE OF CONTENTS

Chapter	Page

CHAPTER 1

AN EARLY FRONTIER

On a spring day in 1951, I stepped from the Chest Hospital's surgical scrub room into the operating room. For ten minutes I had scoured my hands and arms, then rinsed with alcohol. I stood, forearms raised and dripping, until a nurse handed me a sterile towel. I dried and slipped into the green cotton gown she held; thrust my hands downward into the surgical gloves she presented. The floating nurse padded up and, carefully circling, tied the strings at my neck and back.

I paused, appreciating the cool air and absolute cleanliness of the place. Our operating rooms were the first to be air conditioned in Lansing; probably the first in Michigan.

It was a more fresh than antiseptic smell—a little like the iodine we used so much those early years. I took the sterile towel offered, wrapped my hands in it and waited. This stance enabled me to avoid contact with others and remain germ-free.

I contemplated the task before me. Surgery is always an emotional experience for the patient and the patient's family. If the surgeon isn't also concerned for the patient and the family he should not be operating. The patient being put to sleep on the operating table presented me with more than the usual challenge. I would need not only my own expertise but the undivided attention and cooperation of

1

well trained surgical assistants, skilled surgical nurses and luck for the several hours operating time that would be required for this case.

The surgical team worked fast and efficiently on my patient, positioning her (left chest up) on the stainless steel table. Two nurses fastened heavy, fiber stabilizing straps across her legs and hips.

I thought back to the patient's doctor, a conscientious and skillful neurosurgeon, who had already operated on her, for very high blood pressure—a sympathectomy (surgically dividing the sympathetic nerves—the accepted procedure for essential hypertension). The surgery was unsuccessful. The neurosurgeon had observed not only that his patient's blood pressure had remained high, but the lower portion of her body had become cyanotic (bluish in color denoting poor circulation and therefore inadequate oxygen). This had not been present before the sympathectomy. That's when he asked me to see the young woman. Her name was Loretta Strong.

"Let me put this all together for you," I had said, after examining her. "Your doctor is a competent surgeon. He thought you had essential hypertension, and so he severed the sympathetic nerves along the spine. This procedure removes the body's natural control of blood pressure and in essential hypertension the blood pressure will often fall to normal. Unfortunately, in your case the problem is one that is not relieved by a sympathectomy."

She glanced quickly at my face for a clue to what was coming next. I hurried on.

"Fortunately, the neurosurgeon recognized this at once and called me, Miss Strong. I'm a chest surgeon and you have a severe cardio-vascular disability—a constriction of the aorta. The aorta is the large blood vessel which delivers oxygenated blood into the circulation. The more the vessel is pinched, the more the blood pressure is elevated."

Loretta reached up, nervously smoothing her auburn hair.

"I want to take a chance on living a normal life, Dr. Stringer," she said. Her brown eyes looked straight into

2

mine and she made a tight, sad little smile. "I'll die soon anyway. I was an invalid before I saw either the neurosurgeon or you, and without an operation, I'll be an invalid right up to the end. I'd just as soon gamble on it."

"Do you really understand how great the risk is?" I forced myself to return her direct gaze. "I must tell you that when I remove the aorta's constriction, since you no longer have the stabilizing effect of the sympathetics, your blood pressure may drop too low to maintain life and the operation itself is not without risk."

Her eyelids flickered. "Yes, I understand."

What she didn't know was that aortic resection was a fairly new operation and I was sure no surgeon had ever done it following a sympathectomy. Her situation put me on the fringe of a medical frontier. A frontier I hadn't sought; it's circumstances had found me.

Chest surgery is a bloody business even without getting into the vital major vessels. It would be even more so in this case of very high blood pressure. The blood vessels above the constriction would likely be enormously enlarged and bleeding could be profuse.

After Loretta left I called two of my chest surgeon friends, Dr. William Tuttle, one of my former teachers at Herman Kiefer Hospital and at Wayne State University, and Dr. Cameron Haight, Professor of Surgery at the University of Michigan. One said "Don't operate" and the other said, "I would be sure her family understands she might not survive". I hung up feeling increased concern. That it was risky, I already knew. Pushing back my anxiety, I got going.

I scheduled Loretta's surgery, gathered two resident surgeons and with them spent many hours the following week resecting and grafting animal aorta in our laboratory at Michigan State University. The more finely honed my technique, the better her chances of survival.

****

3

The team, I realized, was waiting for me to give the starting signal.

I nodded.

Dr. Lawrence Towne, the anesthesiologist, passed an intratracheal tube down her throat, which had been previously sprayed with cocaine. This tube gave him better control of the anesthetic and the amount of pressure inside the lungs. I waited uneasily while Lawrence opened valves and adjusted dials. Certainly no doctor welcomes the challenge of untried surgery under unusual circumstances. Besides, the congenital constriction should have been operated on in childhood, when it would have been safer. Loretta was 27 years old; older than any recorded case of aorta resection at that time.

She lay strapped firmly to the table; Dr. Towne pressed the hydraulic lift which adjusted the table to my height. It was a luxury I appreciated, after using the monstrous, immobile, ratchet-controlled tables in the 1920's and 1930's. The new surgical light system loomed over the table like a spaceship, an overhead contrivance on a long rod which could be deftly raised and lowered. The main portion of the lamp resembled an old-fashioned deep sea diver's helmet, with the top sprouting a mushroom-shaped globe, the bottom open to shine downward. From the ends jutted stainless steel arms holding four mirrors the size of large round cake tins; these served to intensify and focus light wherever the surgeon willed.

Stepping up to the table I glanced at Lawrence over the sheet-draped metal hoop. The patient's head and shoulders lay under the small tent, visible to Lawrence, but not to me. It separated, in effect, his "turf" from mine. He nodded. I turned to my assistants. They were ready.

I scanned the Mayo Table (an instrument table designed at the Mayo Clinic many years ago). It extended over the patient's hips, below the surgical field. On it lay a sterilized synthetic graft section about ten centimeters long. The surgical nurse placed a scalpel in my hand and I made an incision beneath the third rib and carried the ten-inch cut throught the skin and subcutaneous tissue. I cut the chest

4

wall muscles transversely and opened the chest cavity, clamping and cauterizing the bleeding vessels en route.

An assistant, using sponges on large forceps, lifted and held the left lung forward and out of the way while I cut through the parietal pleura over the aorta. There it was!

A definite narrow and severe constriction, exactly as I had imagined, but it involved only a small portion of the aorta length. My own heart fluttered with new hope. Maybe there was a better chance for this cheerful, courageous young woman. The aorta is normally pinkish red, but the constricted portion of this aorta was white. All of the blood supply to the arterial wall had been squeezed out.

Gently, I freed the vessel from adjacent tissue. One of my assistants, Dr. Arthur Stanley, leaned forward and marvelled. "Look at the size of those intercostal arteries."

I had expected this condition. The human body is an exquisite machine, usually ready to compensate for injuries or ravages of disease. In this case, the five to six millimeter arteries were more than double normal size, as a result of the cardiovascular system's efforts to increase the blood supply beyond the constricted aorta. Apprehensive, yet hopeful, I suture-ligated and cut these intercostal arteries. This helped to provide access to the aorta, which was now well exposed. I freed the artery from its bed, and applied Potts' clamps at right angles to the aorta above and below the constriction and exactly parallel with each other. I cut out the coarctated area of the great artery.

Dr. Towne's voice came from behind the arch and draped sheets.

"Pressure too high to record, Doctor."

"Yes, yes . . ." my voice trailed off. I glanced at the wall clock. I had already been operating for three hours! I must hurry!

The lumen of the protruding vessel ends looked full and healthy. Good! I should be able to bring the two ends of the aorta together for suturing and avoid the need for an artificial graft and the extra risk involved.

I placed a ratchet at right angles on the handles of the

Potts' clamps and gradually drew the cut ends of the great vessel together.

"Watch it, Stanley!" I gently took hold of Stanley's hand and moved it away from the aortic clamps.

Inadvertantly, my assistant had pushed against the handle of a clamp. If one of these were knocked loose, we would lose the patient. I went back and tied the handles of the clamps together. That should work as an additional safeguard. But I could feel the murmuring and tension of my team as I returned to the suturing. I waited a few seconds for everyone to settle down and continued.

With the healthy portion of the aorta brought together in the jaws of the clamps, I reunited the cut ends with fine silk sutures.

"O.K., Lawrence, watch for a big fall in blood pressure."

This was the most crucial moment. The pressure might fall too low to save her.

I removed the anchoring ratchet and slowly released the clamps. Blood rushed in from the released proximal aorta. I prayed and watched for tension and bleeding at the suture line. The seal was holding!

"We've lost all blood pressure!"

Dr. Towne's alarm brought me back from the edge of victory. What I had feared most was happening!

I had released the clamps entirely when I knew the seal was good, but they were still lying in place near the reconstructed aorta. I swiftly closed the clamps and the blood pressure rose to 200/80. Dr. Towne relaxed. I didn't. It was an acceptable level, but I was not at all sure I could get it to stay there. I wondered, too late, if I should have attempted this case.

We waited five minutes . . . the longest five minutes of my life.

I gradually released the clamps again. Another dive in pressure, but not as far. This was encouraging. I repeated the process three times and finally the pressure stabilized at 160/80. I let out my breath slowly, removed the clamps completely from the aortic bed and closed the pleura. Dr. Towne expanded the lung. I felt a warm wave of relief wash over me. We had outplayed death.

I realized suddenly, that I was exhausted. My legs felt like tree stumps and my arms tingled with fatigue.

I looked at the clock. We had been working on Loretta for five hours.

"Fellows," I said, motioning toward my three assistants, "close it up". This case wasn't the first of my several forays into medical frontiers. But it was the most memorable because of Loretta's faith in me. She had taken the risks with a quiet courage I'll aways remember.

****

The patient, now Mrs. Loretta Abraham, has raised a daughter and has three grandchildren. Now, after more than thirty years, her blood pressure is still normal, except for an occasional transitory drop. She phones me periodically, just to let me know she's well, and I always hear from her at Christmas time and on my birthdays.

CHAPTER 2

GETTING STARTED

I was 9 years old in 1913 when the idea of being a doctor was planted by my Uncle Lew Newsom who practiced medicine in Monroe, Louisiana. Before that I had spent many long, Louisiana summer days of childhood happiness at the Oak Grove farm of Grandfather Christian James. I was named for him. After a doctor had delivered me at home, my parents found that he had written my name as Christopher instead of Christian. They let it go. I suppose they felt I would be called "Chris" anyway, whichever name was on the birth certificate. Actually, I have been called C.J. by my family all my life.

Grandmother James had died before I was born. Grandpa had a cook, Ma Green, who ran the household with a firm, kindly hand.

Throughout Louisiana's West Carroll Parish and beyond, Grandpa Christian James was known simply and with respect, as Uncle Chris. Miraculously, he had made it through the Civil War without injury. He'd been a Confederate officer, and after the defeat, he was riding along a dark trail towards home in Oak Grove when he fell asleep in the saddle. He was dragged as his foot caught in the stirrup and was permanently crippled.

To this quiet, burned out land, Grandfather's two brothers also returned. Somehow they borrowed money enough to rebuild their comfortable homes and barns. I suspect Federal Banks had a hand in my family's reconstruction—certainly their Confederate money was worthless.

The James brothers' plantations spread. Grandpa once tried to create a better cotton market by buying up the Northern Louisiana production and holding the cotton. He built mammoth barns, stuffed them, then stored the excess cotton bales on the ground. It didn't work. The price of cotton plummeted and Grandpa lost a bundle of money.

I was about three when my Dad and Mother first allowed me to go to Grandpa's house to stay the night. I was overjoyed. Grandpa spent the evening entertaining me. Ma Green tucked me in and I went to sleep in a joyful haze. In the dead of the night I awoke, succumbing to a noisy case of home-sickness.

"Get him dressed," Grandpa ordered over my howling and Ma Green's vigorous attempts to rock me back to sleep. "I'll have the buggy hitched up and take him home."

One time when I was about seven, Grandpa became interested in Florida land. The idea was that it would be easier to clear since the forests were not as dense down there. He sold some Louisiana land, and Dad and an uncle made a trip to Florida to determine for him what could be bought and at what price, and also to learn about the fertility of the land. They boarded a train to Delray, Florida, which was as far as Flagler's railroad went. There they rented a buggy and drove the remaining fifteen miles to the place Grandpa had marked on the map. (It is now called Ft. Lauderdale.) After kicking around in the sand, they decided the land was worthless for farming. The sun was getting hotter on their backs as they climbed in the buggy and headed back for Delray and the train north to West Carroll Parish.

There Grandpa bought back the previously sold land for twice the price ($2.00 an acre). This was timber land which was considered a liability because it had to be cleared. (They could have bought all of where Ft. Lauderdale is now for as little as $10,000.) However, when World War I erupted, the oak timber on the Louisiana land was sold for ten times what the land cost and they still had the land.

We called Grandpa James' plantation the Home Place. The house rested on a hill flanked by three tenant houses, one at each side of the big house, a third across a lane in front.

The tenant farmers and single farm hands were all white. The unattached men roomed in a wing on the main house and they took their meals at a long table in the big kitchen.

In back of the main part of the Home Place was a long row of bee hives—there must have been dozens. About a hundred yards west of the main house there was a large, rough-hewn smoke house where Grandpa had meat cured for family use and for the commissary.

This rural, almost backwoods, store provided farm neighbors from many miles distant a place to buy supplies—and often Grandpa financed more than their food and household needs.

Many Southern children were taught to ride as soon as they could walk. Ma Green's son, one of the farm hands, taught me, and Grandpa, greatly pleased, gave me a horse. By the time I had seen six summers, I was trotting my horse, Spot, to the post office. There was a short cut across one expansive cotton field. The hitch was that a gate was planted at the end of the lane on each side of the field. That meant I had to jump off my horse, open the gate, lead the horse through, close the gate and use it as a ladder to clamber back on my horse.

Once, while concentrating on re-mounting my horse at the gate, I dropped the letters I was supposed to mail. I didn't miss them until I was almost half way across the field.

Greatly distressed, I swung off the horse, ran back to the gate and retrieved the letters. It wasn't until I was walking back that I gave my horse any thought. I ran faster and faster, clutching the envelopes, toward the place where I had abandoned my horse. He waited patiently; I stood panting a moment, gratitude washing over me. But it was a short-lived thankfulness. I realized that I had no way of getting back on that tall animal.

Sheepishly, I led the horse back to the gate and climbed

on the horse, hoping no one had seen me. But a field hand had watched the whole scene. That evening at dinner, Grandpa reached across and tousled my hair.

"How's my mail rider today?" he said, winking.

"Couldn't be better, sir," I said.

Mother was not well during these early years of the 1900s. Eula, my sister, and I spent time with her at a health resort in Hot Springs, Arkansas, and Dad was there when he could get away from his hardware business in West Carroll Parish.

Hot Springs had a reputation as a curative place. The hot water, which flowed from the ground, was said to restore health to persons having all kinds of ailments—mainly arthritis and rheumatism sufferers. Our house had a hot spring in the back yard, with a clapboard bath house close by. Mother's illness, I learned later, was a peptic ulcer, so, of course, the baths helped her not at all.

I was in the third grade in Oak Grove when Mother died. I felt a terrible sense of loss and Eula was devastated. She drooped and become very quiet after the funeral. The family petted and fussed over her and finally sent for a doctor. She had contracted typhoid fever and lay critically ill for many days. I stood at the foot of her bed and worried. Why didn't the doctor do more? The light went out of my young life—my sweet, gentle mother gone and my only sibling about to join her in death. The days crept by and one day, to my great joy, Eula began to look at me and talk. Slowly, she recovered.

Dad managed pretty well. One Sunday morning he came into my room and patted me awake.

"Get dressed, C.J. We're going for a ride."

Awake with curiosity, I rolled out of bed and put on my next-to-Sunday-best clothes. After all, Dad wouldn't say where we were going and I did not intend to struggle into a starched shirt and stiff shoes for nothing.

After breakfast, Eula and I hopped around the yard waiting for Dad to hitch up the horse and buggy.

"Up you go," he grunted. With his help, we scrambled onto the slippery leather seats.

We turned onto a street going out of town to the less prosperous section—in fact—the Negro area. Dad slowed the horse and we suddenly knew our destination. The Colored church! We were aghast, but kept our mouths shut and sat very still. The sweetest singing I'd ever heard floated from the sagging open door and windows of the little unpainted frame church.

The harmony was pure; the syncopated hand-clapping and foot-stomping was perfectly timed.

These people, not long out of slavery, had found a creative release that was acceptable. We returned many times and the memory of those precious hours we spent eavesdropping outside the little church will be with me always.

Within a few months after I lost my mother, Grandfather James died. How I missed them! No more sitting beside Grandpa evenings on the long verandah of the Home Place as he relaxed in his huge chair and surveyed his lands.

"It's all mine as far as you can see in any direction," he used to say, "and further".

No more lazy days with Ma Green. I had little time to brood, though, for my father's West Carroll Hardware Company became part of the Monroe Wholesale Hardware Company and we moved to Monroe, Louisiana.

I finished the third grade, then, in a new school in Monroe.

Before we moved to Monroe Dad married again. His second wife was Clara Eakin. She was from Elletsville, Indiana, and Dad had met her while she visited her brother. Eula and I were still grieving our mother's death. Some years later after his second wife died our father married an English woman. I never knew her well.

Uncle Lew Newsom was to become a most important member of my family. He had never married, but he was blessed (or burdened) with dozens of nephews, nieces, grand-nieces and grand-nephews. I was one of the latter and particularly favored because I was the only child-relative who lived in Monroe.

A successful doctor and prosperous he was, but I didn't see that as a nine-year-old. I saw only a big, mild-mannered, kindly man who earned the respect and admiration of everyone. He certainly had my respect. I worshipped him. The times he had to make house calls near the school, he would drop into the principal's office, chat a bit and I would be summoned. The messenger was a waste—I was watching for him from the window of my classroom and would be loitering quietly near the office door before the messenger got ten steps down the hall.

Onto that hard black leather seat I'd hop and we would clatter off. My family never worried when I didn't come home from school on time—they knew I was with Uncle Lew. He would tell me about his patient's illness and injuries as we dashed smartly from one house to another—sometimes in Monroe (population about 50,000), sometimes out in the parish farmlands.

I asked innumerable questions and he always answered patiently. If he picked me up at home, we took along my little black bag with make-believe medical supplies inside, and pretended that I was a doctor too, doing my work exactly as Uncle Lew did.

My school was a first through twelfth grade institution, and Professor Hayes, the chemistry teacher, was also the principal all my years in Ouachita Parish High School. I did well when I studied chemistry, partly because I was fond of Professor Hayes but mostly because he was a gifted teacher. And I knew he liked me. Once I overheard him saying as much to one of his teachers and he finished off with "and he's Doctor Newsom's nephew". I was prouder of being Lew Newsom's nephew than being in good favor with the school principal. I wanted to be so like Uncle Lew that I gladly basked in the light of his eminence.

Uncle Lew had one of the first automobiles in Monroe—a Stanley Steamer. The twins, Frances and Freeland Stanley, had produced their first steam-driven car in 1897 and it was successful enough to stay on the market for several years. When Uncle Lew purchased one, hoping to reach patients more quickly and easily, the Louisiana roads were unprepared for this mechanical contraption, which could and did blow itself to bits on occasion, taking the occupants

13

with it. Uncle Lew was spared that fate though he did have one problem with the steam vehicle that I knew about.

I had accompanied him one morning, on a trip down a rutted Louisiana logging road. Approaching us on the trail was a logging team, loaded higher than the horses' heads with southern pine, stripped and ready for the mill.

"Oh-oh," Uncle Lew grumbled. "One of us is going to have to give." He knew, as well as I, that wagon and team only had one gear—forward. What he didn't know was that the Stanley Steamer propelled itself backwards as fast as forward. He shifted the gear, our necks jerked wildly, and we flew back along the narrow, tree bordered trail, Uncle Lew screwed around in the driver's seat looking backwards, clutching desperately at the steering stick, while the lumps and holes beneath us threatened to overturn the car each time the wheels touched down to earth again. With a magnificient show of courage and reverse steering skills, Uncle Lew wheeled onto a side trail. I opened my eyes, uncrimped my hand from the dashboard and let out my breath.

We waited while the wagon lumbered past. The driver tipped his hat.

****

One time, as a teenager, I was hanging around Uncle Lew's office when he said, "Don't leave before I'm done seeing patients today, C.J. I have something for you."

Intensely curious, I sat around and tried to read an anatomy book. When the last patient had left, he motioned me up to his desk.

"I think you should go to pre-medical school at the same place as you take medical training," he said. He never even considered that I wouldn't be a doctor. "It will be less fragmenting for you. Here's a copy of Zinser's classification of medical schools. It's yours."

I almost snatched it from his hand. Thanking him over my shoulder, I jogged for home and the privacy of my room.

There I poured over the pages until I knew certain sections by heart.

It showed Iowa as tops in the pre-clinical years for medical training and Harvard was considered best in the clinical years of medical school.

I graduated from high school, applied to the University of Iowa and waited. In the meantime, I got a job in the Louisiana gas fields working for Union Carbide Company at $4.50 an hour. This was an outstanding wage for a teenager in 1923—until you understood what had to be done to earn the money. I collected carbon black from metal troughs underneath burning gas jets. The temperature inside was 160 degrees. I worked 30 minutes of each hour inside those blistering hot tin structures. It seemed cool to step outside to a humid 90-degrees-plus temperature.

When I reached 18, three years away from my majority and concerned that Eula's and my inheritance from our mother and grandfather James was dwindling, I went to Oak Grove and asked our banker for an accounting of our late mother's estate. Our father was trustee. They probably shouldn't have legally given me the information, but it was a small town. There were few secrets.

With a sinking heart I found that our assets from Grandfather's estate, which had been substantial, were nearly gone. Our father and his new wife had been using our inheritance funds. Immediately I petitioned the court for early emancipation, which was granted. I was then able to claim the remaining money. It was adequate for Eula's and my college years, if I found work for the summers and all vacation times. As far as medical school, I'd have to tackle that issue when the time came.

When summer ended, I went away to the University of Iowa in Iowa City—and found myself very much alone. For the first time in my life there were no encircling family and friends close by. Most of all I missed my frequent visits with Uncle Lew.

I joined a fraternity, Phi Kappa Rho, and began new friendships. These college mates from many geographical areas made up my social life the first year.

That first summer vacation, and subsequent vacation periods, my closest friend, Russell (Doc) Lundy and I got together and worked out a formula for treating the bindings of leather books. We contracted for more work than the two of us could produce, so we hired other boys to do the labor. We went broke. Somewhere along the line we hadn't figured pay for ourselves.

We scurried around and with only three weeks left before college classes began, we got a job treating books at the Chicago Law Library. We returned to school with $600.00 each in our old pants' pockets.

My Phi Kappa Rho friends, particularly Doc Lundy, and I, all worked hard to bring a new chapter of the oldest southern fraternity to the Iowa campus. Phi Kappa Rho was the founding group and became Gamma Nu chapter of Pi Kappa Alpha. Some of us are still corresponding and the fraternity is also still flourishing.

During my third year at Iowa, I applied for admission to Iowa's medical school and planned to transfer to Harvard for the last two years. Harvard had been my first choice for the clinical years, but my teachers and friends had became so much a part of my life I could not break away from what was successful and happy for me.

Studies during those college years came easily and I had the time to date, but not much money. I did meet a girl from Carroll College I liked. She was a striking, brown-haired thing, full of fun. That budding romance wilted when she moved to California with her parents. For a time I saw a young nurse, then a young woman named Ruth, who married a hometown boy after her sophomore year.

I entered Iowa Medical School in 1927. Uncle Lew loaned me tuition money at the beginning of each term thereafter and I was left with the responsibility of earning the balance. I opened a checking account at the First National Bank in Iowa City and when it closed its doors in 1930, it took my money for that term's expenses with it.

I was morose for a while, but I had plenty of company. The Great Depression was upon us.

I phoned Uncle Lew back in Monroe. His bank was still solvent and he promptly sent me the $800.00 I requested. His bank did shut down during the 1933 bank holiday, but quickly reopened, so I doubt if Uncle Lew lost much. During my senior year at medical school, my professor and later good friend, Dr. N. G. Alcock, asked me to serve as an extern in the Department of Genito-Urinary Surgery. He was chairman of the Department and I was greatly pleased at being singled out. Actually, there were three other fellows asked to extern in other departments and we did the work of interns; that is, first-year doctors receiving experience.

My life style changed. I had to move out of my fraternity room and into the hospital staff quarters. The hospital was brand new, having been opened in 1929 across the Iowa River from the old hospital. Funds had been provided by the Rockefeller Foundation and the State of Iowa. The staff quarters were in the central tower above the main entrance and were large and adequate. The rooms opened off a lobby that served as a living room for the resident staff.

My meals were provided in the staff dining room and the uniforms were furnished. There was no pay. I don't remember signing any kind of an agreement concerning this arrangement, but there was an understanding that we would not be required to attend any more medical school classes. I did, however, go to lectures whenever I could. There was also an understanding that we would be excused from having to take final examinations that senior year. Yet, when May rolled around, I received notice, along with all the other seniors, of the time and place of exams.

Appalled, I hurried to Dr. Alcock.

"Just hold your horses, Chris. We have a few days grace. I'll work out something."

I stewed. The three other externs fretted and we all crammed. Within a few hours, we heard from Alcock.

"I've arranged for several members of the faculty to meet with the four of you for tutoring. Be at the library at 7:00 p.m."

Thus, we put to work the 90 percent of our brain experts say we humans don't ordinarily use, and we passed the subsequent examinations.

There was to be one other stumbling block this year of 1931—the state medical board examination. The fee for applying to take the examinations was $25 and very few of us had the money.

That month of May, Dr. Alcock sent a notice out saying all who needed a loan for the fee were to meet him in his office at a given time.

Self-consciously, we assembled. Dr. Alcock opened a bank bag and began stacking up 5, 10, and 20 dollar bills on the table. He had drawn it from his own funds.

"Come and get it," he said and we filed past and received the money, his best wishes and a hearty hand shake. We thanked him, stumbling over the words to express our appreciation. God only knows where else all of us could have gotten the money.

Several years later I returned to Iowa City and made tracks to visit my teacher and benefactor.

"How much money did you get back?" I asked, secure in the knowledge that I had returned the loan from my first earnings.

"As you know, Chris, I didn't keep a record of who I gave it to—except that I remember the total amount," he said, grinning at the memory. "I've already gotten back more than I loaned—as I knew would happen."

CHAPTER 3

RUTH

I saw her swishing down the hospital hall and was smitten. I'd had only the quickest glance at the young woman, but I'd taken in the rich chestnut hair and incredibly long, dark eyelashes which framed her blue eyes. She was small and trim and chic.

I wheeled around and caught the sleeve of my colleague, Dr. Tipton.

"That girl you just spoke to—will you introduce me to her?"

Dr. Tipton looked at me, surprised.

"Sure," he said laughing. "She is Ruth Hibbs. Her father is Dr. Hibbs over in Carroll. Come on."

We dashed in the direction she had gone, and slightly out of breath, caught up with her.

"Oh, Ruth," Dr. Tipton called. "Wait up. I'd like you to meet a friend of mine."

She turned and smiled. It was a wide, friendly smile. She's not stuck up, I thought happily. We were introduced and chatted for a few moments. She said she had graduated from Iowa State College, Class of 1931. Since her name was Hibbs she was obviously still single! I'd have a chance with this intelligent, pretty girl!

I was still figuring ways to see her again when Dr. Tipton asked me to take her as a patient. What unbelievable good

19

luck for me. But for Ruth Elizabeth Hibbs, it wasn't so fine. She had a severely ingrown fingernail which had resulted in a perinychial infection. Some distortion was already apparent and the grossly swollen index finger made her small hand look even smaller.

"It will certainly need corrective surgery, but we'll have to wait for a few days for the infection to subside."

"Whatever you say, doctor," She looked into my eyes and I knew I loved her.

****

Within the week it was safe to operate so I scheduled surgery.

It was a delicate procedure—actually, plastic surgery. After the initial incision along the side of the finger above the nail root and elevation of the nail, I had to take great care not to damage the nail-bed when I removed the half-nail down through the root. As I cut down the middle of the nail to the root with a heavy scissor, it made a loud crunching noise, like cutting through bone. I glanced quickly at Ruth; if she flinched, it was inwardly. I completed the amputation by sharp dissection using a fine surgical scissor.

Carefully, I sutured the full thicknesses of tissues back together. If the sutures are tied too tightly, they cut into the flesh and could cause an ugly scar. I didn't want that on this brave little lady.

I dressed and splinted the small hand and gave her some pain medication to get her through the night. This surgery was on a most sensitive area and when the anesthetic wears off it can be more painful than other post-operative cases.

The following morning I stopped in to see Ruth and change the dressing. She had, indeed, spent a sleepless, painfilled night and wasn't interested in seeing anyone, much less the person who had been the cause of it. My best bedside manner went unappreciated. She put her hand out to me to work on, turned her face away and lay silently.

When I finished, I tried to chat. She didn't respond. During the following days I took good care of her, and she did thaw out. After she recovered, I made a lot of trips to her home in Carroll and got to know her family. Her little sister, Juanita, who was five years old that year, liked to sit on my lap and dig in my coat pocket for little wrapped candies. Without my asking, little sister would give me a thorough run-down on Ruth's other suitors. But I won out.

On the day of our wedding, one of Ruth's former boy-friends stopped by to see her, not knowing what had happened.

"She married Chris Stringer," her mother said. "They just left."

"What!" he cried. "Which way did they go?"

I wonder if someone else had operated on Ruth and caused her so much pain—would it have taken a year for me to talk her into marrying me?

Today, 1983.

I asked Ruth to show me the finger I operated on more than 50 years ago.

"I'm not sure which one it was, honey," she said, peering first at one index finger, then the other.

I took the little hands and looked at them too. There wasn't even a hairline scar.

"Not bad plastic surgery for a chest surgeon, eh?" I said, fishing a little.

"No, not bad," she teased, smiling.

CHAPTER 4

IF IT'S MONDAY,
SHE DIED OF PNEUMONIA

Cherokee Hospital

Growing up in Louisiana and being educated in the great depression years programmed me not to expect an easy life. Yet, what I found in the way of supplies and equipment and surgical facilities in 1933 at the Cherokee Iowa State Hospital was so inadequate and meager that the smallest improvement had immediate positive impact.

I had agreed to do general surgery for the pathetic, under-cared-for people in this mental hospital. During the two years I spent there, I did everything from simple appendectomies to complete gastric resections, gall bladder surgery and amputations.

But I didn't start at once operating on these suffering, forgotten people. I couldn't. The ancient operating room in the old, creaking 2,000 bed hospital had never been used; it had stood there for 32 years while the new white plaster turned grey. The old white painted iron operating table sat on two pedestals, each with a manual lift, the likes of which I had never seen before or since. The paint had flaked off, exposing the rusty metal beneath. One bow-legged instrument cabinet squatted beside a wall. It had also felt the brush and white paint but I doubt that it had ever harbored any instruments.

A young woman named Ruby Pash assisted me as surgical nurse. Ruby was a slim, vivacious redhead whose intelligence and knowledge of mental patients lifted me many times out of some bad situations. She was "streetwise" in her psychological insights of the neurotic and insane. What a strong, willing co-worker she was. Ruby ordered attendants to scrub the entire operating room walls and ceiling and its spartan contents with strong soap. After everything dried, she saw that the room was painted. White, of course.

On weekends, Ruby and I labored to make or convert necessary supplies for the operating room. One Sunday Ruby and I were working away, with Ruth, then my fiancee, generally getting underfoot. I loved having her nearby anyway. I was trying to fashion a water trap for surgical suction. This involved forcing two pieces of glass tubing through two holes in a rubber stopper.

Pushing the stopper onto the tubing with my right hand, I held it steady with my left. Suddenly, the glass shattered and the end of it cut through my right hand near the base of the index finger. I felt the glass grate on the bone.

When I jerked the tubing out and blood spurted everywhere, I exclaimed with surprise and pain. The two women sprang into action.

"You take care of him, Ruby!" Ruth dashed from the room.

Ruby whipped out some heavy, sterile gauze and applied pressure with it over the cut. It took ten minutes for the bleeding to slow.

"It will need suturing," I said as we waited for the bleeding to abate. The pain and throbbing of the wound was little compared to the anger I felt at my own carelessness. This could put me behind in my surgical plans for days, maybe even weeks.

"Doctor Stringer, I can't do it," Ruby said. "Shall I call the psychiatrist on duty? Maybe . . ."

"He wouldn't know which end of the needle to use," I snapped. "I'll have to try suturing it using my left hand."

Without a word, Ruby set to work and I instructed her as to the instruments I would need. She put out medium-sized

23

silk sutures with swedged-on cutting needles, a needle holder, forceps and scissors. She drapped the ancient operating table with a sterile sheet and I sat on a stool at the end of it.

I held my wounded right hand over a pail and Ruby poured iodine over all of it, up to the elbow. Then she went to the other side of the table and scrubbed my good left hand with a brush and soap, rinsed it with alcohol and dried it with a sterile towel. She held out a rubber glove and I pushed my hand down into it.

I saw she had a sterile syringe and needle prepared for the novocain. I was as ready to operate on myself with my left hand as I would ever be.

I got as comfortable as possible on the stool and injected the anesthetic into the two edges of the cut. I directed Ruby to put on a pair of sterile gloves, although I really didn't know how I was going to use her. I waited two or three minutes for the local anesthetic to take effect and began sewing. The pain was pretty bad; the anesthetic had mostly run out of the wound. I went ahead and put in ten sutures, securing the ends of the suture material with small hemostats. After they were all in place, I removed the hemostats one at a time and tied with my left hand, with Ruby pulling one end of the suture material as the knots were tied. I discovered I could use my left palm and remaining fingers to hold the knot while tying the sutured ends with the thumb and index finger.

It was done. Ruby, in immense relief, applied a dressing four times as large as needed and Ruth ventured back into the room.

By the time we had returned to the main building, word had preceded us. "Doctor Stringer is operating on himself."

The wound healed in about a week, leaving a hairline scar, which is still visible.

****

We kept plugging away in our free time and ten days later I began operating on patients.

Those were depressing times. There was not even marginally acceptable medical care for patients committed to mental hospitals. True, mental patient treatment is more difficult, but I believe this was not the reason. No one cared enough about the pathetic souls to do anything about the snakepit conditions. Their physical problems went mainly undiagnosed, and even if a name were given to a specific physical ailment, the patient went untreated.

The hospital was pitifully understaffed. The psychiatrists made rounds by simply walking the halls and depended on the nurses, or more often the attendants, to report anything unusual.

"Filling out death certificates is easy," a nurse told me facetiously. "If a patient dies on Monday, death was due to pneumonia, if it is Tuesday, we put down heart disease, if the patient expires on Wednesday, it was caused by gall bladder disease, if..."

One evening after we were married, Ruth and I were playing bridge with one of the physicians and his wife. Doctor and Mrs. Love had quarters in the hospital administration building, as we all did. The rooms were huge, high ceilinged bedroom-sitting room combinations with a screen at one end for dressing and a fireplace at the other. Each morning during cool weather, an attendant (a trusty patient) would kindle a blaze in the fireplace. There were no connecting bathrooms . . . only two big rooms at the end of one hall marked "Men" and "Women".

This night, Dr. Love was on call. The phone rang.

"One of the patients has died," he said, putting on his coat. "I'll be right back."

He was back in moments. "He was alive when I got there," he said looking puzzled.

We resumed the bridge game and about a half hour later another phone call came. The same patient had died. Dr. Love left for the ward again and found the patient breathing when he got there. He stayed a short time; the man seemed to be steady, so Dr. Love returned to the bridge table.

It was probably thirty or forty minutes later when the

nurse phoned again saying the patient had died. By this time Dr. Love was beginning to wonder if the nurse could tell if a patient was alive or dead.

"Are you sure?" he said a little testily.

The nurse was just as testy. "Could YOU hold your breath for thirty minutes!"

****

The director of the hospital, Dr. Leonard Ristine, called me to his office many times. Among other things, he wanted to talk about the problems of granting furloughs to mentally retarded patients.

Most of these patients were male; many were married and had large flocks of mentally retarded children. The offspring were, of course, also being cared for with public funds and their numbers were increasing. With each furlough granted, it seemed the patient impregnated his wife or someone else.

At length, Dr. Ristine devised a plan stipulating that a male, mentally retarded patient in the hospital must be surgically sterilized before being allowed a furlough. We were careful in all cases to obtain written permission of the patient (which meant nothing) and the spouse, which should have meant something. Sometimes neither the patient nor the spouse could write, so they would simply make a cross mark which we would have witnessed.

The plan worked fine. I operated dozens of these unfortunates, and felt pleased that I was instrumental in cutting down on the supply of children whose only birth right seemed to be poverty, deprivation, and the pity and scorn of those who were more fortunate. Incidentally, the operation did not impair the patient's sexual performance, only his ability to propagate.

I guess it was bound to happen.

I sterilized a man whose spouse was not his legal guardian. The legal guardian was a high ranking officer in the American Legion Post in the town in which the patient had lived.

26

The officer (and his entire post) became inflamed, not because of the surgery but because he, as guardian, had not been consulted. It was a clerical error, but we were in trouble.

The Legionnaire and his men wrote the Governor, Legislators, and state board of medical licensure, and the Des Moines Register Newspaper. The newspaper published their complaint on the front page, with considerable embellishment.

We talked to the Iowa Attorney General and did what we should have done before starting the sterilization program. We researched the law and found we were too late. There was a statute—an old one from 1910, stipulating that before anyone could be surgically sterilized, there had to be approval by the State Eugenics Board.

"What's the State Eugenics Board?" I asked.

The Attorney General was mystified.

"Hell, I don't know."

We kept digging and found that the board was to consist of the Attorney General, the State Health Commissioner, the Secretary of State, two state senators, the dean of the college of medicine, two lawyers, and two ministers. Not one of these persons knew he was on the board, or even that there was such a board. In fact, there had never been a meeting nor had the legislature provided funds for a staff or other expenses.

Since I was the most active law breaker, I proposed a new statute to the incumbent state senators and to Governor Herring. After input from several other sources, including Dr. Ristine, they prepared a statute decreeing briefly, that a mental hospital medical superintendent could order a person sterilized.

Strictly interpreted, this meant that the doctor heading any Iowa mental hospital could walk out on the street, point his finger at anyone and say, "Come on, we're going to sterilize you."

Naturally, this was going too far in the other direction. But I left Iowa soon afterwards and do not know if the law was ever used or even if it existed very long.

****

At times, results of my surgery were rewarding and I would see the patient as quiet and cooperative. In rare cases, some recovered mentally. Then I would go to sleep at night feeling that I was making a difference for the better.

Ruby and I labored long and hard to make these differences, but I could see these pitiful creatures needed more than my single efforts as a surgeon. I persuaded the medical director that hiring another doctor would alleviate some of the problems we were encountering.

There was no internist or diagnostician on the staff. This need was apparent for all of the patients but I particularly needed help for the pre-operative study of my surgical patients. Actually, the hospital was staffed by psychiatrists. Some of them had a one year general internship a long time ago. I talked with the administrator, Dr. Ristine. He agreed, and asked if I knew of a trained internist we might get.

I had, of course, just the man in mind for the job. I phoned my good friend and medical school colleague, Mark Wheelock, in Sioux City, Iowa, where he practiced internal medicine. Actually, I had already talked to him and he had visited me at the hospital. He readily agreed to join us, and when I told Ruth the good news, she beamed. It meant I would not be quite so burdened with patient responsibility and there would be another young wife for Ruth to spend time with. Ruth and Mary Lou Wheelock became close friends.

The administrator of the hospital was pleased and flattered that a successful, practicing internist was willing to join the staff. Early mental hospitals did not enjoy a decent status in the medical world. I suspect we were at the lowest pecking order.

The year, 1934, wound down. I had done some serious thinking about what branch of surgery I wanted to train for specifically. The preceding year, Dr. Evarts Graham had done the first lung resection, and when I discussed my future with my teacher, Dr. Howard Beye, back at the University, he suggested I look into this new surgical area.

In the early 1930's, almost 50 years prior to this writing,

a doctor had little choice in his search for training in chest surgery. Especially scarce were qualified training centers where the trainee could receive some recognition for his work.

My decision concerning training in chest surgery had been influenced by my high regard for Dr. Beye. He in turn believed I had the capacity and discipline to carry through—perhaps become a mentor for others. I was touched and began scrounging about seeking possible training centers.

Dr. Beye was right. The field was not only wide open, it seemed to be empty. The office of the National Tuberculosis Association (now the American Lung Association) came up with one name—The Gallenger Memorial Hospital in Washington, D.C. This sounded prestigious enough and I was anxious to get on with my life's work.

Gallenger accepted my application for a residency in thoracic surgery. In the very depth of the great depression, Ruth and I probably had less money than any one we knew, unless it was other people in the same educational bind.

After discussing my plan with Dr. Ristine, it was agreed that Ruth would remain in Cherokee using our quarters and the staff facilities until I could arrange for suitable living quarters in Washington.

Ruth helped me pack for the trip to Washington and assumption of my new responsibilities. The set-up in Cherokee had been comfortable with the fringe benefits; the rooms were large and sunny, we took our meals in the staff dining room, and even our laundry was taken care of. It hardly made up for the abysmal patient-care conditions and lack of equipment, however.

Thank God I had Ruth. She was the bright light in my uncertain world, a tiny thing, but solid, supportive and affectionately critical. I depended upon her good sense when I had to make career (and other) decisions all my active years. I still do.

Ruth was straightening and putting bits and things into my suitcase. The staff had given us a farewell party the night before and I had tickets for the afternoon train to Washington.

The phone rang. It was Mark Wheelock.

"Chris—I need you at once. A patient is in pretty bad shape over here."

"I can't come, Mark. We're just about to leave for the station."

Mark knew that, of course. He'd had a rather good time at our party.

"You can't," he said flatly. "I'll be right over."

In moments he was standing in our doorway holding what looked like a ring out of a human windpipe.

"The man tried to kill himself by cutting his throat. He missed the artery, though, and cut through the trachea. He must have made several passes to cut a ring out."

"Gee whiz, is he alive?"

Vaguely, I saw Ruth leave the room.

"He was when I left to come here," he said. Mark's eyes were popping with disbelief at the bloody piece of cartilage he held. "He was breathing through the distal severed end of the trachea—it's sticking out from his neck."

I had little choice. To refuse to go to the victim's aid would have doomed the poor soul to a horrible death.

"OK, Mark, let's go."

We took off running. In the operating room, faithful Ruby had already prepared the patient. She had no doubt that I would come, Washington or no Washington. The patient lay face up on the operating table, very still, but breathing. Air swished in and out through the windpipe that protruded from the hole in his neck. The three of us stared a moment at the sad sight—the poor fellow could not have botched things much worse. The only sound in the room was his life's breath sucking in and expelling.

I quickly scrubbed and gowned but I was not at all sure I could get the severed ends of the trachea back together, let alone surgically repair the injury and re-establish the airway. If I could not the patient would certainly die in a very short time.

"Mark—you'll have to help me."

He blanched.

"I'm no surgeon, Chris . . ."

"You are now," I said, hoping I didn't sound as grim as I felt. "Start scrubbing."

While Mark was preparing, I looked my patient over. General anesthesia was out of the question, since the airway to deliver the anesthetic was cut off. He didn't need putting under anyway, I thought, he's too far gone.

However, I injected the edges of the jagged wound with novocain. I remembered my own wound of two years previous, and wondered if the pain killer would be as ineffective.

In order to elevate the ends of the trachea, I passed two penrose drains around the protruding sections. This was touchy, because the distal end had retracted downward into the neck. Fine Allis forceps could ordinarily be used, but the trachea was already fragmented and I couldn't risk damaging additional tracheal wall.

With the ends thus ready, I placed a row of fine, silk sutures in the membraneous back wall. I left these sutures untied until they were all in place. I used a round swedged-on needle to reduce the risk of further damage to the wall of the trachea, extended the row to the beginning of the hyaline cartilage, and at this point included a ring of cartilage above and below using heavier sutures as an anchor. I put tiny hemostats in place and made sure the ties came outside the lumen.

"Now, Mark," I said, indicating the ends of the anchor suture on his side, "Pull on that suture while I do the same on this side. It will reduce the tension on any one suture."

Mark tugged, gingerly. I tied the two heavier sutures. They held and served to approximate the severed trachea, at one point on each side. Next I tied the sutures in the membraneous wall. They held and didn't cut through the fragile tissue. My gamble had paid off! There was now an anchor to relieve the tension. The most difficult part was done.

The tracheal opening became smaller as the suturing was carried forward. The sound of the air passing in and out of the wound became more shrill. As I united the last portion of the trachea, the whistle abruptly stopped.

Mark looked over at me, raised his eyebrows and let his breath out slowly, as if he'd been trying to breathe for the patient. I sighed with relief and thankfulness that the unusual procedure had gone so well.

I stepped back from the still form. I needed the moment for my mind to go forward to the post-operative period.

"A size 8 tracheostomy set, Ruby," I said. To Mark, I explained what I intended to do next.

"I'm going to make an opening in the trachea—right here—below our repair through the area of the fifth cartilageneous ring. See—I'll incise the cartilage on each side and the membrane above the cartilage and turn it down like the flap over a window."

Mark looked puzzled.

"But, he can breathe normally now that his trachea is reconnected."

"Yes—but this is another tension-reducing technique until healing can take place. It ought to be accomplished in a week or so," I said. "Then all you have to do is withdraw the trachestomy tube and the small defect will fill in spontaneously."

I instructed Ruby and one other nurse in the specialized care of the tracheostomy. The inner metal tube which is inserted through the tracheostomy tube must be removed at least every six hours, cleansed and replaced. Also, the lower trachea must be suctioned every three hours, or more often if there is gurgling, indicating the presence of secretions.

Mark nodded uncertainly.

If this suction is not promptly done, and it usually is not in general hospitals, the patient is better off without a tracheostomy because then he can make some effort on his own to raise the secretions. We did not want our patient to have to make this effort because of the risk of stress on the suture line.

"You two can do it. You were both excellent assistants," I said, including Ruby in my praise. Certainly I couldn't have done it without both of them.

I stepped forward and quickly did the tracheostomy. I had done my first teaching and my first chest surgery. Fate had taken over, giving me the assurance I needed that I had chosen what was right for me—the new and virtually untried field of thoracic surgery. I never researched the subject of whether or not any surgeon had ever reunited an attempted suicide's trachea with one ring cut out but so far as I know this was another personal surgical frontier.

I missed the train to Washington that day. We unpacked my pajamas, and I caught the train to Washington the next day after checking on my attempted suicide patient. Ruth and the Wheelocks took me to the train.

A dust storm, the result of three decades of over-cultivating the rich prairies, alternately blasted and whirled around us as we stood on the dirty platform. Heads down, huddled close, we tasted, smelled and felt the grit and heat of displaced soil. I shook hands with good friends, Mark and Mary Lou, and gave Ruth a hug and a kiss as the tears washed two little paths down her cheeks. I swallowed hard and clambored inside the day coach. All the way to Washington, D.C., the minute particles of dust chased us and sifted through the window casings of the train cars. I was not surprised the following morning when newspapers in the capitol city reported that "dust from the mid-west is invading our city." I phoned Ruth that night and among other things she said that Mark had reported that my surgical case, the severed trachea, was doing well. The man did recover.

The only certainties that 30th year of my life were that I had the best wife in the world and I wanted to be a chest surgeon. And I was lonely and apprehensive. What kind of a place would Gallenger Hospital be.?

CHAPTER 5

WHERE I COULD HAVE
BECOME A CHIEF

The next morning, July 1st, 1934, I hailed a cab and found myself being rushed through early Washington traffic. In a few minutes we arrived at Gallenger Hospital and the taxi driver lifted my bags from the trunk and set them beside me. I paid him and stood, disappointed at the scene which lay before me. So this was the "prestigious" Gallenger Hospital! I saw a main building of dirty white bricks. There was an uncared-for look about it, likely due to the ragged lawn and sparse, wild-looking vegetation. On either side, unconnected and sitting slightly behind, were two decrepit frame buildings. They, too, were a grayish-white, but their color was due to the peeling paint. There were cracks in the walls, and an orange crate served as a step up to the front door of one of the buildings. I was soon to discover that these run-down buildings were for tuberculosis patients—one was for blacks and the other for whites.

I shook off a feeling of apprehension and went inside the main structure. I found my way to the office of the superintendent, a man named Babcock, and introduced myself.

"Welcome," he boomed. "I know you're going to be one of us right away. Your resume is excellent—and we need a good surgeon."

"But I'm not a complete surgeon yet—at least not a thoracic surgeon and . . ."

"You're unduly modest, Dr. Stringer—but come I'll show you to your quarters. They're not much—but you won't have a lot of free time anyway. There's just so much to be done."

Babcock wheeled out of his office carrying my luggage and I followed. He kept up a running monologue of the virtues of the place; the dimmer the recesses we approached, the more glowing his description.

"Well, here we are," he said, dropping my bags. "Dinner's at 6. We could put you to work right this minute, ha-ha, but you probably need a rest after your trip. See you at dinner."

I nodded and tried to smile convincingly. The resident's quarters were hot, airless and humid, yet I felt myself shudder with a sudden chill as I unpacked.

****

I went to work with enthusiasm—there was more than enough to keep me off the streets. I scrutinized x-rays and patient charts, made rounds and scribbled notes to myself. My meager knowledge and lack of formal chest training became painfully apparent to me as I tried to sort out the various chest diseases. Babcock sought me out many times, inquiring about my progress and chanting praises of Gallenger Hospital.

The morning of the fourth day there, I spent a little longer than usual at breakfast. I'd have had to be stupid not to notice the absence of other doctors in my new "training area". I decided to go no further until I was given some answers to questions that were jumping out at me. I stepped into his office.

"Mr. Babcock, I'll come straight to the point," I said. "I've been here three days and have yet to meet the senior staff surgeons. If I'm to start training, I should know who my chiefs in chest surgery will be."

Babcock put down his pencil and gazed at me in great seriousness.

"My boy. YOU are the staff."

"This is hardly what I expected. I will have to think about it."

All the other questions I had intended to ask flew from my head. I was speechless. I turned and left.

I went about my duties the rest of the day in a daze. By evening, when my head had cleared, I had found a Medical Journal which had an article in it on pulmonary diseases. The author was a doctor from Washington, D.C.

I hurried to the telephone and reached this Dr. Winthrop. He was not only courteous, but extremely helpful. He arrived the next day at my pathetic little infirmary, lugging his own pneumothorax apparatus. This consisted of two one-half gallon bottles on a rack with a manometer. Our facility did not own such a device, as simple as it was. He looked at some x-rays and helped me start two patients on pneumothorax. Later, when I saw my new friend to the door and shook hands, I was grateful.

"Let me know whenever you think I can help,"he said.

That same afternoon a notice came to me from the chief of the general surgical staff. I was asked to attend a conference with them at 4 o'clock.

When I came into the large room, I got my first glimpse of the whole surgical staff. They sat around a long conference table, many of them smoking. The air felt damp and impure. The only other furniture was a tiny bookcase which stood against a far wall; it was covered with a thick film of dust.

I sat quietly through the preliminaries wondering why I was there. After all, they were general surgeons and I was only interested in thoracic surgery. Maybe they were going to announce they were bringing in specialists in chest surgery on sort of consulting basis. I'd stay to find out, of course. I thought back to some of the bizarre aspects of the past week. Babcock was sparing no tricks in his hard-sell technique aimed at getting me to join the Gallenger team. Disgusted, I had refused all his bait. The only reason I hadn't walked out of the place was that I needed time to plan what to do next. Hospitals and hospital chiefs weren't exactly flocking to the doorsteps of young hopefuls seeking training.

Babcock's last ditch effort at keeping me had been a mind-boggler.

"Dr. Stringer," he had said grandly, "if you'll stay on our staff, I'll see that you're made director and chest surgeon of one of the tuberculosis hospitals under construction here in Washington. They're due to be finished soon."

I was so overwhelmed by the absurdity, I don't remember what, if anything, I said. This man was willing, even anxious, to place me, totally inexperienced in all but the most basic thoracic surgery, as director and surgeon of a chest hospital! I would have killed any number of unsuspecting patients in the operating room, no matter how conscientiously I tried.

I brought my mind back to the conference room. The Chief of General Surgery, Dr. White, was addressing me.

"Dr. Stringer, I'd like to start doing thoracoplasties. You've been here for several days. Will you prepare a list of tuberculosis patients suitable for thoracoplasty?"

I sat stunned. Responses tumbled around in my head, all relatively polite, but I rejected them. The man must be insane.

"Dr. White," I said angrily, "I have no idea what criteria to use for selecting such patients. That's precisely what I came here to learn, among other things." Before he could recover, I plunged on.

"Furthermore, you shouldn't, as a general surgeon, attempt to do thoracic surgery."

Dr. White came to life.

"I am more than capable, sir, and all of us have to start somewhere . . ."

I stalked back to my quarters, sat on the narrow, lumpy bed and pondered my next move. I had said the unthinkable. I had berated a senior—maybe I had burned my bridges. But surely there were others to cross. I must get cracking. The phone rang. It was Babcock.

"Dr. Stringer, it's just come to my attention that you invited Dr. Winthrop to assist with your patients this afternoon. He is not welcome in this hospital."

I remained perched on the miserable bed, but I wanted to jump up and fling that big, black telephone straight through the filthy windowglass.

"I'm sorry to hear that," I said struggling to keep from shouting, "but I guess it doesn't make any difference to me. I'm leaving this place.

"You do," he shot back, "and I'll see that you never obtain training anywhere.

"You've misrepresented Gallenger and the training program from the beginning," I said. I also suggested what he could do with his hospital, which wasn't very nice of me, but I meant it.

Hastily, I made more telephone calls. No use wasting time being angry. I called the National Tuberculosis Association in New York with a choice, descriptive report of their Gallenger recommendation. The officials there took me seriously and I believe, learned from this mistake.

Years later when I was a member of the Board of Directors of the National, Gallenger was no longer listed as an approved residency.

One of my calls proved to be incredibly good luck. I dialed a prominent pulmonary physician in New York City, whose references I'd ferreted from the American Review of Tuberculosis.

It developed, as we discussed my dilemma, that this outstanding doctor was on the board of Stony Wold in Saranac Lake, New York, the only hospital within hundreds of miles, that had its own chest surgery program.

"Can you get to New York tonight? I will go up to Saranac Lake with you tomorrow."

"Yes, sir. I'll phone you when I arrive." Anger and depression turned to jubilance. I would leave this place immediately; whatever I found in Saranac Lake could not be worse. I got train reservations without difficulty, but I would have hitchhiked, if necessary.

CHAPTER 6

STONY WOLD

After Robert Koch discovered the cause of tuberculosis, the tubercle bacillus, more than 100 years ago, the accepted treatment for tuberculosis was bed rest and climate. Every environment known to man was advised at one time or another. Doctors in Colorado sent their tuberculosis patients to the hot, dry climate of Arizona, and doctors in Arizona sent their patients to the cold, dry climate of Colorado. Other victims were advised to move to the hot, wet climate of Florida and Floridians were advised to go to the cold, dry climate of the Adirondack Mountains in New York State.

My first experience with the extremes of this type of treatment was at the mecca for tuberculosis at Saranac Lake, New York, where Edward Livingston Trudeau had built the first tuberculosis hospital—a small frame cottage for two patients, still standing and known as "Little Red".

The hospitals were constructed so the beds with the patients in them could be rolled out onto "cure porches" for the afternoon rest and for the night. In cold weather, and sometimes the temperature plunged to 40 degrees below zero, the patients were bundled up so heavily they couldn't have gotten up to move around even if they were permitted.

The development of Saranac Lake in the Adirondack Mountains was largely the work of this one man, Trudeau.

Dr. Trudeau had had pulmonary tuberculosis himself and often made trips to the Adirondacks for game hunting. After each of these excursions, he thought his own symptoms from tuberculosis were less severe, and he reckoned this was due to the fresh air and exercise.

Because of this belief, he moved his medical practice and his family to Saranac Lake, New York, which at that time was a very small mountain village. He later built "Little Red". This was followed by numerous facilities for the treatment of tuberculosis, some of them in private homes.

Former patients and interested corporations often assisted Dr. Trudeau with their concern and their money in the development of the increasingly popular Trudeau Sanatorium.

Mrs. Elizabeth Newcombe, the widow of a wealthy New York otolaryngologist, had been one of Dr. Trudeau's patients. She was an ordinary-appearing woman—not tall, a bit overweight, with wavy gray hair and conservative but very expensive clothing.

Mrs. Newcombe approached Dr. Trudeau with an offer to finance the building of a substantial addition to the Trudeau Sanatorium to provide a facility for the treatment of under-privileged New York City girls. She also offered to underwrite the cost of treating these patients. It is said in Saranac Lake lore that this offer and discussion came at the end of a busy day for Dr. Trudeau. He was tired, and having coped with a number of similar projects said, somewhat irritably, "Why don't you build your own hospital!"

She did! And wasted no time.

Mrs. Newcombe first acquired a large tract of land on Lake Kushaqua near the Trudeau spread. She assembled architects, contractors and hospital designers and oversaw the construction of a large, modern brick hospital which she named Stony Wold. It rose on the shore of beautiful Lake Kushaqua in the wilds of the Adirondack Mountains. The hospital was larger and better equipped than any other in the Saranac Lake area and it was the only one with its own surgical facilities.

In addition to the main hospital, there were several other buildings: Two to house medical staff, a nurses' residence, and a building for the other employees. Mrs. Newcombe also built a large summer home for her own use on the shore of the lake near the hospital. The late Dr. Newcombe must have been as good in business as he was in medicine.

When Ruth and I came to Stony Wold, the hospital administrator planned to remodel a cottage on the hospital grounds for our use. In the meantime, we were provided adequate living quarters in the hospital. Mrs. Newcombe also had an apartment there which she used while her summer home was being prepared for the season. The patients who were able to be out of bed for meals, ate in a large dining room with the professional staff. Mrs. Newcombe also dined there when she was living in the hospital. The table reserved for her and her guests was on a platform at one end of the dining room about a foot above the rest of the dining area.

When Mrs. Newcombe entered, the waitresses stood at attention and the staff and patients rose at their tables until she and her guests were seated at her special table.

Ruth had driven out from Iowa to join me and while we were occupying the temporary quarters in the hospital, a duplex unit which was more adequate than the cottage, became available, and we moved in. Ruth added to the basic furnishings already there by making silk pongee curtains and laying down the handsome braided rugs made by patients in the Iowa mental hospital. (The materials were old worn gray and blue blankets.) We scrimped and bought blue willowware dishes and sterling silver flatware. We were happy and proud of our first real home, even if it was a sanatorium duplex.

Ruth's first attempts at cooking were at Stony Wold. (Meals didn't always turn out as we anticipated.)

I am fond of deer hunting and sometimes I'd bring home an animal. I restricted myself to the legal deer season in the mountains. Adirondack natives did not accept this limitation. Frequently, we would hear a noise on the porch in the early morning and by the time I got down stairs all I could see was an unidentified native retreating down the road. On the porch would be a nice package of fresh venison. The giver had been hunting out of season and he wanted us to have the venison, but he didn't want us to be able to identify him. Ruth became an excellent wild game cook.

Mrs. Newcombe had no problems with the preparation of meals. She had a superb cook and she entertained lavishly for the hospital staff at her palatial summer "cottage".

In addition to her interests in the treatment of tuberculosis, Mrs. Newcombe became concerned about the health and living standards of the often impoverished Adirondack natives. It is said that this beautifully dressed, dignified and proper matron was sometimes seen holding a local kid under a water pump while she scrubbed his teeth with a brush. She was capable of using the brush in other places too.

None of the other wives of medical staff presumed to entertain Mrs. Newcombe since they could not reciprocate on such a lavish scale. Ruth had no such inhibitions. After we were entertained twice by this gracious lady, Ruth announced to me that it was her turn and invited Mrs. Newcombe and her companion for dinner at our little duplex. Exactly on time, the lady's long, chauffeured, Packard limousine pulled up in front of our little place. The vehicle was almost as big as our house. Her chauffeur escorted her up the steps, followed by her lady companion.

"Would you like something to drink?" I asked after they were seated in our living room. Obviously we had no household staff such as she was accustomed to.

"A Tom Collins, if you please."

I was shocked. "Mrs. Newcombe, do you really think you should?" After all, she had been a tuberculosis patient, and she was a diebetic with a heart problem.

"Well," she snapped back, "you asked me what I wanted. Have I ever questioned your choice at my place?"

I backed down. "You shall have your Tom Collins," I said and escaped to the kitchen.

In this duplex, there were no doors between the downstairs rooms. She could see me mixing her cocktail in a fruit jar. Before dinner was ready, our guests had another drink. It was a highly successful dinner party. Ruth's cooking was superb and I was unabashedly proud of my bride.

The following week, Mrs. Newcombe asked Ruth to go shopping with her. They drove off in the limousine and came back to present me with a cocktail shaker, compliments of Mrs. Newcombe. I still have it.

Ruth and Mrs. Newcombe became friends and corresponded long after we had left the Adirondacks to pursue further training. When we started our family, Mrs. Newcombe remembered the children's birthdays as long as she lived.

CHAPTER 7

HERMAN KIEFER
HOSPITAL TIMES

I had set my objectives—one was a year's study in pulmonary diseases. I needed the Saranac Lake stint to be followed by 3 years of intensive training in chest surgery in preparation for a practice in thoracic surgery associated with teaching responsibility. But first I had to know what medical men were doing as the basis for training in chest surgery. Not many surgeons agreed with me. Their view as surgeons seemed to be that we should cut and sew and leave the treatment of disease to others. I didn't believe that was a good basis for becoming a thoracic surgeon. Any chest surgeon worth his salt should have a basic knowledge of thoracic diseases.

But, of course, such a philosophy might work a surgeon right out of a job, sort of a diminishing return. This certainly proved to be the case with tuberculosis. I have often thought that in many cases of surgery—perhaps in most—there ought to be a better way.

During my year in New York, I made plans for the years of additional training I wanted.

I phoned Dr. Howard Beye, professor and Chairman of Surgery at the University of Iowa.

I had long considered Dr. Beye to be a model surgeon and a great teacher so it was natural for me to seek his advice. He was always responsive.

Dr. Beye, upbeat and energetic, had an invigorating effect on those around him. He was an unpretentious man, always thinking of others and always with a project underway. For this reason he was constantly in the middle of some kind of a controversy. He was not a large man physically but he had a superb mind, and often served as a mediator.

As an example, when the University of Iowa was kicked out of the Big Ten, he served as chairman of the committee to decide what to do, and almost singlehandedly mediated the problem. He said, "So we've made some mistakes. We recognize these mistakes, we apologize and we will rectify them." Some supporters wanted to forget the Big Ten and thought the action against the school was unjustified. Dr. Beye told them all, "No use trying to go it alone—we belong in the Big Ten"—and the University got back in the Big Ten.

Another time Dr. Beye, Dr. N. G. Alcock, Chairman of Urology, and Dr. Fred Smith, Chairman of Internal Medicine, ran the school for several months because the dean suddenly left.

When Dr. Beye became Chairman of Surgery at the University of Iowa, he was the youngest Chairman of Surgery of all the medical schools in the country.

When I called him, he said, "Let me think about it for a few days and I will write or call you."

He did call back the next day.

"I think training under Hedbloom in Chicago would be excellent," he said, "and if you want me to I'll contact him."

I wrote immediately to Dr. Hedbloom, and after some swift exchanges of mail and telephone calls, I arranged to study with him for three years in Chicago. I was then to return to the University of Iowa where I would help start a division of thoracic surgery.

But in one shattering moment, my goals were crushed. Dr. Hedbloom died. I had met him only once, yet he had become part of my life.

The following week someone phoned me from Dr. Hedbloom's office saying briefly that he had died—they would keep in touch. But they didn't. There probably was nothing that could be done anyway. At that time, with Dr. Hedbloom gone, there was a great void in Chicago so far as training in chest surgery was concerned.

What do I do now, I thought. I felt sorrow and displacement that spring, as I neared the end of the Saranac Lake commitment.

After the dust settled I called Dr. Beye and Dr. Woodruff, the leading chest surgeon in Saranac Lake. I guess I was using them as a sounding board. They both suggested that I call Dr. E. J. O'Brien in Detroit. By the time I got Dr. O'Brien, he knew my story and that Dr. Hedbloom had died. There was no position immediately available, but Dr. O'Brien suggested that I contact Dr. Bruce Douglas, the Medical Director of Herman Kiefer Hospital in Detroit, and in the meantime, he would talk to Dr. Douglas and to Dr. Beye. When I called Dr. Douglas, he asked me to come to Detroit for an interview and he would see what could be worked out.

I went to Detroit for the conference. Dr. Douglas was a tall, gangling man, a Quaker by religion, soft spoken, and quietly intelligent. As I came to know him through the years, I never heard him raise his voice in anger. He was the exact opposite of Dr. E. J. O'Brien, but they respected each other and were close personal friends.

Two days after I returned to Stony Wold, Dr. Douglas called and asked if I would accept a staff appointment to one of the medical sections in Herman Kiefer for one year and then transfer to surgery. I knew I wanted to do this but, of course, I had to talk it over with Ruth before accepting. When I went home that evening, we discussed Dr. Douglas' proposal.

Ruth said, "You will never be satisfied until you are

back in a large teaching hospital." I wired Dr. Douglas that I would be there July 1. This was 1935.

I spent the remaining time tying together the work I had started at Stony Wold, including the finishing of scientific material I was publishing.

We were to leave on a midnight train. It stopped at the little station at Stony Wold, only if there were passengers to get off or on. This meant that boarding passengers were supposed to advise the agent during the day so he could have the train stop that night. In the hustle-bustle of the final day, I forgot to do this and the agent did not stay at the station that night.

Mrs. Newcombe had a marvelous going-away party for us the evening of our departure. About 11:30 a friend asked me if I had made the necessary arrangements for the train to stop. He knew by my guilty face I hadn't. Dashing out the door, and over to the railroad tracks, he flagged the train down. Our bags were already at the little station, with cartons and crates to follow. There was much laughing and jostling as our friends hurriedly escorted us to the train. We had no trouble getting to sleep.

The following morning we took separate trains from Utica. Ruth went to Iowa to visit her family and I transferred to the Detroit train.

I lived in the residents' quarters at Herman Kiefer until I found a suitable apartment near the hospital.

Ruth joined me after about a month. The following is taken from her journal:

"Chris sub-leased a nice sunny apartment where he could go by streetcar or walk to the hospital. After the first year, the original leasees moved their furniture out. We bought our first furniture and loved every minute of the shopping. We got most of it at Sears, Roebuck and we carefully spread out the precious $500.00 of the budget. Our prize purchase was a red brocade reclining chair that a Sears executive had ordered and not taken—a real bargain for us. We added a blue davenport, Lord Winthrop desk and Windsor chair. It looked wonderful with our braided rugs made by former

patients at Cherokee, Iowa. The dining room and bedroom pieces were maple. I was particularly fond of a handmade afghan a patient had given us."

The first year at Herman Kiefer proved to be one of my busiest. After the first month, Dr. Douglas came up to my floor and told me (he didn't ask) they were extending my responsibilities to include all the orthopedic and urological cases in the hospital. I was to take care of them, keep up the records, arrange for surgery for the indicated cases and assist the consulting surgeons in surgery!

Dr. William Tuttle had joined the senior surgical staff as an associate of Dr. O'Brien about the time I came and he found that I was often needed in chest surgery even before I was on the chest surgery service.

I was doing about three jobs at the same time that first year.

CHAPTER 8

PNEUMOTHORAX!

Chest surgery for tuberculosis patients was still very risky while I was a resident in training at Herman Kiefer Hospital from 1935 to 1938. Drugs effective against the tubercle bacillus were not yet available. We used various forms of surgical collapse to put the involved lung at partial rest.

In 1905 the first procedure to partially collapse tuberculous lungs to promote rest of the diseased organs was introduced and developed by Carlo Forlanini, an Italian physician. He, thus, initiated the era of collapse therapy, which was to be the accepted mode of therapy for forty years.

Pneumothorax is accomplished by instilling air into the pleural space around the lung through a needle in the chest wall.

At first, Forlanini used nitrogen gas but as the procedure evolved, it became apparent that room air filtered through water was equally effective.

Unfortunately for some patients, the tuberculosis had produced adhesions between the pleural surfaces preventing adequate collapse of the diseased lung. Chest surgeons would then have to either abandon the pneumothorax or surgically open the chest and cut the adhesions under direct vision.

This procedure was drastic. As a less extreme alternative, a closed method was developed by a German chest surgeon. It involved two small incisions in the chest wall—one opening to admit a trocar (a sharp pointed instrument used to provide a channel for introduction of a thoracoscope for examination). The thoracoscope has a light and a lens system. The second incision admitted a Bovie cautery knife to cut the adhesions.

O'Brien disapproved of the two incisions. Using his tremendous experience in chest surgery and his facile mind, he devised an instrument still using the Bovie knife but positioning it in the sheath directly along side the thoracoscope. This eliminated the extra opening in the chest.

The tension on these adhesions could and sometimes did cause a tear in a blood vessel producing severe hemorrhage and death.

Cutting the adhesions through the thoracoscope, called a pneumonolysis, was not without risk. Any time a doctor entered a patient's chest—either double entry or with the O'Brien thoracoscope, there was danger. Tension on the adhesions could pull a blood vessel down into the adhesions. There it was easy prey for the cautery (Bovie knife) and once cut, the vessel would hemorrhage uncontrollably with death following in minutes. Since the chest was unopened, the surgeon believed in those mid-1930's that he could not get to the source of the bleeding quickly enough to save the patient.

There could be trouble if the adhesions were left uncut and there could be danger if they were surgically cut. During my residency training I witnessed fatal hemorrhage without surgery and also during surgery. There had been no such tragedy reported in the medical literature but I wonder if that might have been because cut or torn arteries as the cause of death went unreported. Two such patients were on my service and I was responsible for their care. I was the one then who had to tell the family the terrible truth.

I raged inside that these tragedies happened. We should not have so little control. I was aggrieved, angry and frustrated. I wondered if it might be wiser to abandon the pneumothorax in such cases and allow the lung to reexpand and use some other type of treatment. Unfortunately, during that era other treatment might not be suitable either.

In later years I was to meet this problem head on in one shattering moment in my own surgical practice.

CHAPTER 9

O'BRIEN AND LAFERTE

Dr. Pat O'Brien was a stickler for fast surgical time. He was an effective teacher too, but he had a reputation among surgeons for being a champion thoracoplasty speedster.

"Accuracy first," he would bellow as he incised, clipped, clamped, and sewed, "BUT BE FAST".

The awed residents and interns and other potential chest surgeons wondered if they could ever learn those skills.

Speed surely was an asset in those early days. It prevented long periods of anesthesia from ether and nitrous oxide. Nitrous oxide is actually an anoxia anesthesia—it replaces oxygen in the body, bringing on unconsciousness. It is a dangerous anesthetic and isn't used much any more.

Pat had intense loyalty—God help anyone who criticized any of his team. (A privilege he reserved for himself and used well). But he had a broad Celtic sense of humor.

Once, after assisting with surgery, I was in the doctor's dressing room, cleaning up. Pat was putting on his street clothes. I freshened up in hospital whites. I caught him looking at me edge-wise, a gleam in his Irish eyes.

Finally, he said, admirably straight-faced, "I hear you told off White in Washington when you were there."

I jerked to attention. He had hit my past too unexpectedly. How was I to answer for the insubordination I had been forced into those three years ago? Was it really only three years! It seemed like a decade.

Pat dropped into a chair, laughing uproariously, probably as much from my discomfort as his discovery.

"I happened to see old man White in Washington and when he tried to tell me about it, I cut him off. I told him that you are my resident now and you're going to stay in practice with me when you finish. NOW DON'T MAKE A LIAR OUT OF ME."

Dr. O'Brien and Dr. Bill Tuttle and Dr. Claude (Dutch) Day played important roles in my training. Bill was as adamant in his belief that residents should publish as Pat was about surgical speed.

I heeded both, especially my mentor Bill Tuttle, and set out to research a presentation for a scientific meeting. Subsequently, and to my great satisfaction, my material would be published. Although it was the depression era, the hospital, Kiefer, allowed me a modest budget for charts, graphs, and slides.

Fifty years ago, slide projectors could take only large glass slides. The glass covering protected the printing, x-ray, or whatever. They were expensive and before I realized it, I'd run over the budget by a lot of dollars.

Once, after surgery, I'd retreated to my office on the surgical floor next door to the nurses' station.

I was poring over some records when Pat came striding down the long hall and sat down across from me in the one rickety little chair. Any other big-wig-doctor-in-charge would have sent for me and I would have scurried to respond.

"The hospital administrator tells me you have exceeded the budget for the preparation of aids for the material you plan to present and publish," he said. There was a dispassionate air about him.

Oh, oh, I thought. I'm either going to have to come up with the extra money or cut back on my visuals. I detested the idea of doing either.

"I guess I got carried away . . ."

"Don't worry," he said, "your stuff is worthy of publication. Keep up the good work."

He rose and I walked to the door with him. In the hall, I stood and stared at Pat's retreating figure.

I decided not to worry—there was nothing I could do about it anyway.

****

Years later I was to learn quite by chance that Dr. O'Brien paid for my over-run out of his own pocket and told no one.

****

As the resident-in-charge of orthopedic cases, I grew to know and admire Dr. A. L. Laferte, who served gratis as a consultant orthopedic surgeon. Always amiable, kind, and resourceful, this honorable man taught me a great deal.

I was still in my first year at Kiefer when Dr. Laferte operated on and removed a wrist bone from a young professional baseball player. Dr. Laferte confided in me one day that he had taken the wrong wrist bone from the athlete.

"What will you do?" I was horrified, but Dr. Laferte was so depressed and humble, I felt a strong, almost paternal rush of compassion for this capable and honest man. He was in the deepest shaft of despair and self-recrimination.

"I told his family immediately," he said. "Then I wrote him a letter apologizing and admitting my mistake. I don't know how I could have made such an error."

"But they'll sue you, won't they?"

I saw the family's side—they would probably claim that a promising career was cut short by a careless surgeon. Most doctors had very little liability insurance in those times.

"I'll take the responsibility."

He was resigned. For a time Laferte continued to operate at Kiefer. There was a lot of tuberculosis of the spine in that era and many of these patients required a fusion operation.

The radiologist, hearing of Laferte's plight, reread the after-surgery x-rays. He found that Dr. Laferte *was* mistaken. He had misread the post-operative x-rays. Dr. Laferte again studied the x-ray films. Yes! The proper bone had been removed—the ball player would have a full range of motion and his career could go forward as soon as the wrist healed.

Tremendously relieved, Laferte contacted the patient with the good news. Not only did the ball player disbelieve Dr. Laferte, he had already started litigation against him, which ultimately won the ball player a huge settlement— $300,000! It was an inordinately large amount, 50 years ago, and Dr. Laferte worked long and hard to pay the judgment.

Dr. Laferte and his friends and patients and his several expert witnesses wondered how such an injustice could be allowed. However, the ball player was popular and the jury accepted his claim that he would be unable to play again. The big mistake was writing the letter.

Interestingly, this "crippled" baseball player became a professional football player within a year after he received the settlement!

My heart went out to Laferte. Eventually, he recovered his self esteem and outgoing personality. I know he relied exclusively upon the expertise of radiologists during the remainder of his career.

One morning after the baseball player incident, he phoned the hospital where I was setting up an operation for him.

"Chris, I can't be there. The baseball case has taken too much of a toll—you just go ahead with the surgery."

Puzzled, I hung up, dizzy with surprise and apprehension.

With some trepidation, I did as he ordered. From that time on, I scheduled and did all the orthopedic surgery. I had to sandwich this additional chore between my numerous other duties.

****

Hospital life had a lighter side. It wasn't all gloom and tragedy. We had parties—and Pat O-Brien loved to give a fine party. For weeks we all anticipated his Christmas gathering for staff and their families and close friends.

For those occasions, Pat believed that alcoholic beverages were a must. But finding spirits during Prohibition posed a problem that most moderate drinkers didn't want to grapple with. Not Pat. He always managed to have enough booze for everyone at his famous Christmas party.

No one could get him to reveal the source of his contraband. He'd just grin and say "Wouldn't you like to know."

We suspected a former patient of Dr. O'Brien's was his supplier, but it was years before it was confirmed. And how it came about was so funny that the story is still being told around Detroit.

Pat's former patient, whom I'll call Mr. Ex, was observed making several trips to the O'Brien home in Palmer Woods just before the Christmas season. Mr. Ex went in the house carrying no luggage or parcels of any kind and emerged a few minutes later.

Windsor, Canada, Mr. Ex's home, is across the Detroit River from Detroit. Canada was not bending under the weight of Prohibition. Alcohol flowed freely there and many border Americans only had to cross the bridge or drive through the tunnel to find a friendly Canadian tavern.

Mr. Ex always motored from Windsor across the Ambassador Bridge for these special forays. At the Detroit end of the bridge, border officials checked only every fifth or sixth auto for smuggled goods. There wasn't enough staff to inspect every car.

Mr. Ex's number finally came up. He was asked to step out of the car for inspection. Nonchalantly, he did as directed, hauling his more than ample girth from behind the driver's wheel.

He was about to straighten up when he felt something snap and give way under his overcoat. It was a wide belt, patterned like a cartridge belt, with pockets sewn just large enough to hold pint bottles of liquor. Mr. Ex didn't have time to wonder if it had broken or just become unhitched. With both elbows he grabbed the sides of the belt, still under the great wool overcoat, and began screaming.

"Chest pains! My heart! I was on my way to see Dr. O'Brien at Herman Kiefer Hospital. Oh, oh, oh!"

The sight of this huge man crying in pain was more than the guards could handle. They called a police officer and while he arranged for another officer to drive Mr. Ex's car, the big rum runner managed to reach inside his coat and rehitch the belt.

Off he went in a patrol car, wailing louder than the siren, and pleading for someone to call Dr. O'Brien at his home to tell him his patient from Windsor was being brought to the emergency entrance of Herman Kiefer Hospital.

"Be sure to tell him the good border police are bringing me in," he whined.

O'Brien, suspecting the truth, and hoping it was not a real attack, instantly called the hospital and arranged for two orderlies to meet the caravan with a stretcher.

When the two cars arrived, it took all four men to hoist Mr. Ex onto the stretcher cart. Down the long hall they went, orderlies trotting, Mr. Ex groaning. An officer parked the man's car and left the key with a clerk, and the two policemen departed.

O'Brien met Mr. Ex in the hall. As the orderlies gaped, the patient stopped hollering, jumped off the cart, and dashed outside with Dr. O'Brien to his big car.

The party that year was especially festive. And even though the word had gotten around the hospital about the scam, no one said a word. I can't even say how I got the inside story. You don't look a gift horse in the mouth.

****

Pat O'Brien was unusually quiet the next day. We were in surgery and the worry picked at me that maybe something was wrong with my work. True, Pat had gone to bat for me, yet that was characteristic of him. The operation was routine, but I forced myself to push away the anxiety and concentrate on my role as assistant. Now was no time to cut the wrong vessel.

Nearing completion, Pat suddenly laid aside the instruments and stepped back.

"Chris, you close up. I'm going to the dressing room and I'd like to see you when you're finished."

I nodded and held out my hand for the sutures and needles. I didn't dare look up, fearing everyone would see the alarm in my eyes. What was Pat doing? Was I being tested? Did he know something about my work that I didn't know?

Somehow, I completed the operation and both drawn and repelled, I pushed the doors open to the dressing room.

Pat sat, quietly, his shoulders slumped, his broad, handsome features frozen.

"Chris," he said, "Dr. Beye was killed last night."

"My God!" I felt the blood drain from my face. I sat down opposite him. "How? What happened?"

"Auto accident." He rubbed a big hand across his forehead. "I don't know the details."

I leaned back, stunned. What a terrible waste! The premature death of two fine surgeons, Doctor William Hedbloom and now Doctor Howard Beye, changed the course of my career. Ruth wrote in her journal:

"Doctor Beye was killed in an automobile accident and Chris is naturally upset. He was such a good teacher and friend. They still want Chris to start the University of Iowa thoracic surgery department, but sources of income that Doctor Beye planned to use for this are no longer available."

CHAPTER 10

ON BEING AN
EXPERT WITNESS

My long-time friend, Dr. Charles Bailey, a renowned chest surgeon in New York, had the right idea. He became so concerned about the courts, the lawyers and the legal process that he went to law school and became a lawyer. He is now an internationally known chest surgeon and a lawyer. I suspect Charley did this in order to provide some degree of protection for himself and his colleagues from the unpredictability of the legal process. It's a complete puzzle to me—and as the years have passed, legal proceedings have sometimes become downright irritating.

Attorneys have asked me for help and advice. I've also been subpoenaed. Either way, they make a point of cautioning me to tell the truth. I find this annoying for two reasons. One, if a lawyer has any doubt about the honesty of his witness, why is he or she seeking his help? Two, the same attorney who reminds his or her witness to tell the truth will often try to prevent the opposing witness from doing so. I've been told this is called the adversary process. Whatever that means.

There is also testimony considered "inadmissible evidence" and the frustrated witness who has sworn to tell the "whole truth and nothing but the truth" is often prevented by the lawyers and the court from doing so if the testimony is considered inadmissible. I've never been able to under-stand or even extract a definition of what kind of evidence is inadmissible from a lawyer.

Worse, there is the spectacle of two opposing lawyers yelling in apparent anger at witnesses and at each other, and walking out arm in arm at recess, evidently in high spirits at the prospect of lunching together and replaying conversationally the morning's session.

During my training years in chest surgery, I was respon-sible for the care of a patient with advanced tuberculosis. Somehow this unfortunate man fell into the clutches of a labor lawyer named Andrews, who brought suit against the patient's former employer, Chrysler Corporation, alleging that the man had silicosis, an occupational disease. This was before the enactment of our present compensation law and a litigant could claim any amount he and his lawyer wanted to. Andrews phoned and asked for my help, so I arranged to meet him in my sparse little office. I wasn't very high in the hospital echelon and this cubicle, which had a wash basin, a battered old desk, desk chair and one creaky straight chair in front of the desk for visitors, was tucked away on the fifth floor of Detroit's Herman Kiefer Hospital. The toilet was discriminatory. Once inside, a fat person could not have shut the door. Everything needed a coat of paint. I directed lawyer Andrews to the straight chair across from where I sat.

Andrews was eager.

"Dr. Stringer, your patient and my client can use your expertise in presenting his case to a court jury."

"I'll do what I can," I said. "How do you plan to proceed?"

He licked his lips. "I intend to prove that a certain opera-tion at Chrysler is an occupational hazard. As a chest doc-tor, you would be my expert witness."

"I understand that part," I said. "On what grounds do you intend to build your case?"

"That my client is ill because Chrysler has been negli-gent in providing a safe environment for workers." He warmed to the vision of sympathy he hoped to evoke. "I figure my client is so ill from silicosis because of his work exposure, he should not have to appear in court but, since he should testify on his own behalf, I would order a stretcher for him."

I was beginning to dislike the man.

"No, you won't!" I heard myself speaking too loudly. "That would be unfair—and unsafe for the patient and people with whom he would come in contact."

"Dr. Stringer," he said, putting on a pious face, "just think of all the other workers being subjected to these same hazards—there must be 200 or 300 men in that department who could be sick with this very same lung disease. I could get for them what's due them."

"No, Mr. Andrews." I was emphatic. "My patient does not have silicosis. He has tuberculosis."

He seemed not to hear.

"As an expert witness, you can help." He indicated my barren little office with a tossing gesture as if he were already throwing bribe money my way.

"You staff physicians can always use extra cash, and there would be plenty if I can win this case."

I could feel blood rush to my face.

"Mr. Andrews, you aren't interested in the truth or you would have heard me the first time." I strained to keep my voice level. "You're only interested in winning—right or wrong. I'll say it again—my patient does not have silicosis, or any other occupational disease. There is no way I can help you."

It sank in this time. Pressing his lips into a thin line, he slammed his briefcase shut and stomped out. The heavy footsteps were the last I heard of Andrews until months later.

* * * *

"Dr. Chris Stringer?" The stranger in the dark business suit stood in the doorway of my office, one hand in his pocket.

I identified myself and his hand emerged from the pocket holding a subpoena. It had been issued by Chrysler's attorney, a man named Collins. I had not choice; I was bound to be a witness in the "Chrysler Case".

I got busy and assembled information about my patient, then summarized it all. It took considerable time and energy. There was so much material, including x-rays, that it needed two clerks from the hospital record room and myself to carry it.

The three of us trundled down to the federal building in Detroit. Later, when I was called to the witness stand, I handed over the remaining medical charts, nurses' records, x-rays and correspondence to my two helpers.

"You are not to release these to anyone but me unless you are ordered to do so by the court," I instructed the clerks.

The trial had been in progress for more than a week and I had sat in the audience part of the preceding day to observe what evidence the crafty plaintiff attorney Andrews presented. He had found three former fellow employees of my patient who testified primarily about conditions in their working area at the Chrysler factory. Andrews did have a medical doctor witness whom he finished direct-examining just before noon recess. This man testified that my patient did not have tuberculosis but did have silicosis, an occupational disease.

Lunch hour came and the court recessed. I made my way over to Attorney Collins.

"You should further explore this doctor's qualifications," I suggested to him. "I know or know about every qualified medical person connected with chest diseases in the area, and I've never heard of this man."

"Good point." Collins made quick notes on his yellow-pad. "Anything else?"

"Yes—ask him to tell the court what kind of dust was alleged to permeate the air in the factory."

Collins went to work when the court reconvened. In moments, he had discredited the "expert witness". When asked if the dust in the air was due to silicon dioxide particles, the witness said no. He didn't even know that silicon dioxide has to be present in the dust to cause silicosis. That is where the disease gets its name.

Antagonistic Andrews was able to see his evidence for silicosis was close to destruction so he switched tactics. He tried to prove that the patient's tuberculosis was due to working conditions. This was a more reasonable consideration but still a discredit to the truth.

"When you cross-examine the doctor again," I whispered to Collins, "ask him to name the germ that produces tuberculosis."

Collins nodded. Shortly he re-cross-examined the doctor-witness.

No, the "expert" witness couldn't name the exact organism and said there were several.

I knew this would be his answer, yet I felt embarrassed and sorry for the fellow. At the first opportunity, I leaned towards Collins. "Lay off—the poor guy just isn't qualified and obviously the court realizes this."

"I did prove my point, didn't I?" Collins said smugly.

At 4 o'clock court adjourned.

"I have other witnesses to call, Your Honor," Andrews said.

Judge O'Brien recognized his petition and set the court time for the next morning.

I stayed on the job at the hospital that next morning and was eating lunch when Collins phoned.

"Court reconvenes at 1:30 today and you're going to be called to the stand at that time." He spoke rapidly.

"All right, we can make it if we hurry." I hung up, notified the record room clerks and the three of us dashed downtown to the courtroom, again loaded with medical records.

On the stand, I answered Collins' questions easily enough. With almost a flourish, Collins identified me as the patient's physician, something everyone already knew. Andrews was strangely quiet but wrote with a pencil on a legal pad as fast as he could.

I testified that my patient indeed had pulmonary tuberculosis, not silicosis, and I described how the diagnosis had been made. I named the causative organism and how it had been found in the material from the patient's lungs.

Abruptly, Collins digressed from his line of questioning. I was uneasy—he had not told me of any change of tactics.

"Doctor," he asked, "have you ever seen the counsel for the plaintiff prior to seeing him here in this courtroom?"

"Yes."

"Where?"

"In my office." I was abrupt.

"Where is your office?"

"At Herman Kiefer Hospital."

"Why was he there, Doctor?"

"He said he was there to discuss my patient."

"Did he ask you to testify that your patient had silicosis?"

"Yes."

There was a sudden flurry of motion and sound from Andrews' position at the long table. He leaped from his chair, nearly knocking it over backwards. The court watched in surprise, as he snapped his pencil in two and rushed toward me. Trapped in the witness chair, I could only wonder what theatrics were coming. Up came his arm, and the fist began to shake. My god, I thought incredulously, he's aiming it at me!

"That is a lie," he shouted. The fist was now under my nose.

Like his pencil, something in me snapped. I forgot where I was and why I was there. Rearing back, I planted my foot in his midriff and pushed. He staggered backwards. Now free to move, I leaped to my feet, drew back and delivered one cracking punch to the side of his jaw.

This changed his course of direction. He flew against the judge's bench and landed in a heap.

Horrified at what my reflexes had done, I stood uncertainly while the baliff helped him up. My hand hurt and my wrist, when I glanced down at it, appeared to be starting to swell. Fleetingly, I thought about broken bones. A plaster cast would play hell with the surgery I was supposed to be doing.

Judge O'Brien's gavel came down and in the uproar, his voice was all but drowned out.

"The baliffs will clear the court! Members of the jury, you are excused!"

He turned an impassive face to the two attorneys.

"Both counsels will please come with me to my chambers."

After the judge and the attorneys and the jury exited, the others in the courtroom, including other witnesses, burst into a circus of sound and motion. The three of us from Herman Kiefer made our way to the corridor, followed by most of the others in the courtroom. All were milling about the corridor.

An hour went by. I was greatly concerned. The court had every right to find me in contempt and Andrews could probably charge me with assault and battery.

A well-dressed man came up to me and said, "That man deserved what you did to him, but you may be in trouble. If so, we will certainly defend you and I will speak to Mr. Collins about it." He was a Chrysler official who had been sitting in court all the time and I didn't know it.

Finally, court reconvened. We all rose at the baliff's "Hear ye, hear ye! This court is now in session."

Judge O'Brien appeared from the paneled doorway at the back of the bench, his face creased in displeasure. From my seat in the courtroom, I stared. Were the corners of the judge's mouth twitching? I couldn't tell from a distance and I was too worried to consider the possibility for long. He could even impose a jail sentence on me. I wished heartily I never had heard of my tuberculosis patient and his nasty lawyer.

The judge directed me back to the witness chair and the jury was recalled. The record room women, still clutching the precious files, were trying to suppress their desire to laugh aloud. They shivered and their eyes watered with the effort to contain themselves.

Judge O'Brien gaveled the court to order. "This could and possibly should be a mistrial," he said to the counsel and jury. "These parties, however, and the government, have already gone to considerable expense over a period of nine days. We will, therefore, proceed."

He turned to the jury.

"You are to disregard what counsel Andrews said to the witness and what the witness did."

At this, the record women's faces screwed up and they ducked their heads. I wondered how long they were going to be able to contain themselves.

The judge leaned back in his chair.

"You may proceed, Mr. Collins."

* * * *

On the witness stand again, Collins asked me a few more simple questions regarding the diagnosis of silicosis and ended his direct examination.

"Your witness, Mr. Andrews," Judge O'Brien said.

"No questions, your honor."

"Mr. Collins."

"No further questions, your honor."

I was excused from the stand. Collins stated the defense had finished—Andrews said they had no more witnesses.

Judge O'Brien read brief instructions to the jury, then excused them for deliberations.

Attorney Collins touched my arm.

"Doctor, while we're in recess, will you come with me?"

"Of course," I signaled the record room clerks and they hurried over, the files cradled in their arms. Their faces were not quite composed. We had not used a single additional item in the trial!

We stood uneasily in the little room.

"Mr. Collins," I asked. "why did you rest your case so abruptly? I thought you said Dr. Gardener would be here to testify tomorrow." Dr. Leroy Gardener was a famed silicosis expert from the Sarnac Lake Laboratory and one of my former teachers. I had been looking forward to seeing him again.

"After your act, we don't need Dr. Gardener," Collins said. "I wired him not to come and I'll write him later with an explanation.

"I'd rather you didn't," I said pointedly.

Not knowing whether the jury would be out an hour or a week, my record room assistants and I left the federal building. I was glum. "Ladies," I said, groping for words, "Please don't report my fiasco . . ."

Unable to restrain themselves any longer, the women burst into laughter. They giggled in the car all the way back to the hospital and were still twittering when I dropped them off. The hospital staff, incredibly, had heard the story before I even drove into the physician's parking lot. I was met by a barrage of grinning colleagues. One of them handed me a message to call Mr. Collins at his office.

I dialed the number, feeling like there were egg beaters turning in my stomach.

"Dr. Stringer," Collins was exuberant, "The jury returned a verdict in our favor. You may have saved Chrysler more than a million dollars."

"Nice work, Mr. Collins. But, I don't think I'll ever be the same again." I hung up. The only positive thing from this horrible episode was that my hand and wrist were not injured.

About two weeks after the trial, I received a letter from Judge O'Brien apologizing for Attorney Andrews' behavior in the judge's court. There was no reference to my decking the man.

Walter Chrysler, founder and then chairman of the board of Chrysler, wrote me a letter of appreciation along with an autographed copy of his recent biography. I loaned the book to one of the Chrysler engineers and never got it back.

CHAPTER 11

WHERE SHOULD
I PRACTICE?

Chest surgery was just becoming a recognized surgical specialty in the early 1930's. At that time, a man didn't start practicing thoracic surgery just because he was a surgeon. I used the pronoun "he" definitively, for there were no women chest surgeons. Women were not often admitted to medical school, probably because they were discouraged from applying. There were, however, two women in my medical classes, and in all of my years of practicing thoracic surgery, I never knew of a female chest surgeon.

But back to my struggles in those early years. Where a young doctor began practicing depended greatly on his finding contacts with influential medical men.

I bumbled about during my last months of residency training in Detroit and eventually reduced my choices of a location to either Detroit or the Hawaiian Islands. My friend, Dr. Bruce Douglas, Medical Director of Herman Kiefer, had gone to Hawaii at that government's invitation to survey their enormous tuberculosis problem. He came back, warmly enthusiastic at the possibilities of a rewarding career there—both professionally and financially.

"How Hawaii got all their money is really intriguing, Chris."

We were in his office where I had come at his request.

"TransPacific Shipping grew fast during the 1930's," Bruce said, "and shipping companies made Honolulu a port of call. This was great for the seamen, except that large numbers of the sailors contracted venereal disease and . . ."

"Now, Bruce," I interrupted smiling, "my expertise lies a little further up anatomically and I hardly . . ."

He held up both hands, grinning at me.

"Now just hold on—it's true the shipping companies planned to stop putting in at Honolulu because of the venereal disease problem. But one company came up with the idea that each of them should offer to pay to the islands $200 per docking if the government earmarked the money to start and maintain a public health program for disease control."

I began to see what he was getting at.

"Their objective, naturally, was to eradicate venereal disease. A good, workable program was set up and within a few years, venereal infection decreased markedly, with the result that money had begun to accumulate. The agreement was quite broadly written, and did not limit the use of the funds specifically."

"And that's where you came in," I said. "Someone saw the TB rate was as high as VD had been and asked you to do the survey."

"Yes," he said modestly. "They've begun construction of good facilities, but there's not a chest surgeon in Hawaii."

My mind raced. This could be a fine opportunity.

"How much time would a surgeon have to spend in the operating room?" I asked.

"Three days a week, I would guess," he said. "The rest of the time you could use for private practice."

I probably looked as though I was about to say yes, so he threw in the punch line.

"They even offered to provide a native Hawaiian girl to serve you punch and fan you when you're down on the beach," he laughed. Coming from Bruce, a proper Quaker, I was surprised he even passed that message along.

"I'll talk it over with Ruth," I said. But visions of Hawaiian punch were beginning to dance in my head.

Ruth was apprehensive about the Islands' school system. Our first born was less than a year old but we wanted the best education for Christopher Junior, whom we called Jim.

"It's too good an offer to let pass," I pressed, and Ruth capitulated. We sold what little furniture we had in our Detroit apartment and prepared to exist in limbo until we closed our affairs there. Ruth went back to Iowa with our baby to wait until I was settled. I moved into the hospital for the few weeks remaining of my residency.

From Ruth's journal:

"Chris had packed one formula bottle in my bag without my knowing it and the rest of the bottles and paraphernalia were in a separate bag. Wouldn't you know after our train left and Chris went back to his borrowed car, there was the special bag. I missed it, of course, and remember thinking 'Chris will get it to us,' and wasn't even worried. Then I had a wire on the train telling me where the emergency bottle of formula was in my bag and that the special bag (refrigerated) would catch up with me in Chicago.

I was being met by the Webers, college friends of Chris, and would spend the day with them, then take a night train to Carroll, Iowa. We went to their place, more friends of Chris' came by to view the baby and later Verne Weber took us back to Chicago to pick up the bag. We had the Oak Park departure time, not Chicago, and barely made connections. I got on the train with the baby, not knowing if Verne had been able to get any of the bags on. He did—threw them on the platform of the last car and they were brought to us!!"

Ruth was still marking time in Iowa; I was living out of a suitcase at the hospital when suddenly, another choice came bouncing out of Lansing. Again, by the way of Bruce Douglas. The Ingham Sanatorium there was offering me the directorship. It was a tuberculosis hospital.

"Bruce—Ruth and I have decided to take the Hawaii offer. I'm afraid they're too late."

"Well, just doing my job. I'll tell them. My regards to Ruth and the baby."

That, of course, was not the last of it. The board of control at the Ingham Sanatorium, which was to become the Chest Hospital, kept sweetening their offer until it became part-time. This would allow me to develop a private practice in chest surgery, and I would have complete access to the hospital facilities and an office in the hospital for my private practice plus the availability of staff.

Ruth liked the idea—probably she wasn't thrilled with the thought of south sea beaches anyway. She urged me to reconsider. It certainly would be less strain to move 80 miles instead of 5,000.

As if those two choices weren't enough to keep me agitated, my mentor-teacher and friend, Dr. Pat O'Brien, and, of course, my chief, while I was still working as a last-year resident at Herman Kiefer Hospital, had been keeping himself informed of my job-seeking efforts. I knew that. I knew, too, he wanted me to stay in Detroit with him and Dr. Bill Tuttle and Dr. Claude Day. Dr. Day had preceded me in the Kiefer residency program two years before and had become a member of the permanent staff and a partner with Dr. O'Brien and Dr. Tuttle. Dr. Paul Chapman was co-resident with me but later became interested in administration and in time became the tuberculosis controller for Detroit. Dr. Day and Dr. Chapman were single at the time and we enjoyed having them as dinner guests at our small apartment. Pat gave me the next day off to go to Lansing to negotiate with the hospital board. But before I was able to get away from his gregarious Irish charm, I compromised with Pat. I would accept the Lansing position for three years, do what I had in mind to improve the hospital and establish a chest surgical facility, then return to Detroit and join O'Brien's thoracic surgery group.

* * * *

Ruth wrote, in part, in her journal:

"The Lansing situation looked inviting and Chris took it, promising to return in three years . . . that we didn't do . . . Lansing was in our blood by then . . . Chris' practice did well!"

71

When we made the decision to come to Lansing, there were many things to do beside complete my residency. I owe much to my friend and fellow resident, Paul Chapman, who loaned me his Ford to make the necessary trips to Lansing during the negotiations. Having personal transportation smoothed the transition from Detroit to Lansing.

In addition to winding up my work as resident at Herman Kiefer during the last six weeks in May and June, 1938, I drove to Lansing each weekend to get started on some of the backlog and to do pneumothorax refills on the patients who required this. I worked seven days a week, but was happy with the start of my own surgical career.

* * * *

When I moved to Lansing (actually there wasn't much to move—just my clothes, books and papers), I lived at the Roosevelt Hotel—long since converted to a state office building. I was exceedingly busy but I also had to find a place for my family to live. Ruth and baby Jim waited in Iowa.

Borrowing on my life insurance, I brought a new DeSoto on the advice of a Chrysler engineer—(yes, the same friend who borrowed my autographed book). I was inordinately proud of that car and it served me well.

My first three months in Lansing I spent practically all of my time at the hospital. I was either in front of the lighted viewing boxes reading x-rays from a stack a foot and an half high, or searching for records, most of them covered with dust, and some which didn't exist.

One time I stayed up until 4 in the morning using the dictaphone to catch up on all of these back records. The next morning when a typist picked up the fragile, old-fashioned cylinders, they slipped out of her grasp and fell to the floor, where they shattered into a thousand pieces. I redictated all the records, feeling like a martyr.

I had left my housing problem with a real estate agent by the name of Butts. He was doing his utmost to help me find a house I could afford to buy and was not having an easy time.

One morning he phoned me at the hospital.

"Dr. Stringer—would you be interested in renting my home, furnished? Mrs. Butts wants to go to Florida right away. I could make the rent within your means and you may have it as long as you like."

My head whirled! What incredible luck. Oh, wouldn't Ruth love this.

"Yes, I'd like to rent it," I said trying for matter-of-factness. I was in a dither of happy anticipation when I phoned Ruth and she said they'd take the next train out.

It was three in the morning when Ruth and little Jim, who was now nine months old, came in on the overnight train. The Grand Trunk Railroad had the civilized practice of dropping the pullman off on a siding and letting the passengers sleep until a reasonable hour.

I was awake before dawn, and at the station, hopping from one foot to the other when 7 a.m. came, and I felt I could wake my family. I found their pullman and we had one joyful reunion. I got to dress little Jim.

In my borrowed-money car, I drove them to our new rented home. Carrying Jim, I took Ruth's arm as we went up the steps. Inside, I handed the baby to the young woman standing by. Her name was Doris and she wore a little apron and cap. Ruth's eyes were wide with excitement and I was immensely proud, even though luck had brought us here. We sat down then, to a delicious breakfast Doris had waiting for us.

Ruth still says, "I never had it so good!" Each day we enjoyed the elegantly furnished house, the exquisite china, the silver, the fancy coffee maker and the Coca-Cola machine. There was even a young man who had been paid in advance to wash and take care of our car. We stayed there for two years. When we bought our first home, Doris went with us.

* * * *

It is said that the first hospital buildings at Ingham were built in an apple orchard, but when I came in 1938, the apple trees had disappeared, except for two scrubs on the corner of Washington and Greenlawn.

One of the original frame buildings, Dakin Cottage, was

still standing. When this structure was built, outside bed rest was still in vogue and the practice of rolling patients and beds to outside porches was considered essential.

Dr. Oscar Broegel was the first medical director for the Ingham Sanatorium. It later attained national stature as the Ingham Chest Hospital and subsequently converted to a general hospital known as the Ingham Medical Hospital or Center. For a time, there was a proclivity to call anything having to do with the practice of medicine from solo physician's offices to great teaching hospitals, a "center". Actually, the so-called Ingham Medical Center is one of four general hospitals in Lansing.

Oscar, a general practitioner in Lansing, served on a part-time basis. There was no medication and no surgery for tuberculosis during those years. The patients were kept in bed and exposed to fresh air and given cough mixtures containing codeine.

Since the heavy iron beds were rolled out onto the "cure porches" twice each day with much sighing and grunting by the nurses who had to do this donkey work, Dr. Broegel conceived the idea of building railroad tracks into the floor of the rooms and porches, and placing the iron wheels of the beds on the tracks. He had metal workers flange the inner edge of the bed wheels like those of a railroad car to keep them on track, and they were installed when Dakin was built.

CHAPTER 12

SOLDERING
IRON SURGERY

My first troublesome case, after I came to Lansing to practice chest surgery, appeared to be such a "no win" situation, I almost sped home to tell Ruth not to unpack things in our recently rented house.

In those years, Lansing hospitals had a rule requiring any new surgeon in town to be observed at work for one year before being allowed to operate without supervision. This was an excellent safeguard, but I came into the Lansing medical world alone in my chest surgery skills. In all humility, no one else in the area was trained in thoracic surgery and qualified to oversee my work.

The chiefs of staff, after considerable haggling, informed me that one of the senior general surgeons would observe all my work. The surgeon they assigned me was, naturally, the very last one I would have chosen. He was a strutting, pompous egotist. I am sure I wasn't alone in my feelings about him.

"Ruth, he'll drive me batty," I complained one evening at home.

"Well, honey, you trained under Pat O'Brien," she reminded me. "You should be able to handle any situation of that sort."

****

The patient was already in Sparrow Hospital seriously ill and had been referred to me by Dr. Oliver McGillicuddy. I did a thorough examination. She was a young woman from a well-known Lansing family. She had aspirated a peanut and it had lodged in the left lower lobe bronchus. Another doctor had managed to remove only parts of the nut; a lung abscess resulted.

I did a bronchoscopy and suctioned out as many peanut particles from the area as I could, but segments of the nut had disintegrated and I couldn't identify the pieces. I'd seen many cases where patients aspirated peanuts and an abscess formed but they often coughed so much that the abscess drained adequately and major surgery was unnecessary.

This young woman wasn't so fortunate—her temperature had risen to 105 1/2. Since this was before the advent of antimicrobial therapy, which would have permitted cutting away a section of the abscessed lung under an antibiotic umbrella, we would have to use standard treatment of the era—a hot iron cautery straight into the abscess cavity to provide drainage.

The "surgical tool" was an ordinary electric soldering iron about an inch square and pointed on the far end.

It was brutal surgery but it was all we had.

The patient's abscess had to be drained. She was a very poor risk, but the infection was progressing rapidly and it would certainly be fatal, if we didn't take action.

We prepared the patient and brought her to the operating room late in the afternoon surgery schedule. (This was because infected cases easily contaminated the surgical area. Being the last operation of the day meant there was more time to work at sterilizing the operating room before surgery began the next morning.)

I had fluoroscoped the chest and marked the location of the abscess with indelible ink on the skin of her chest wall.

A lot of anxious thoughts went through my head while the nurses painted her left chest with iodine and alcohol. (This type of skin preparation is no longer used.) They draped the chest with sterile white towels and an overlaid drape sheet.

I took a few deep breaths and began. Directly over the ink spot, I cut through the skin and subsutaneous tissue and began cauterizing the small bleeding vessels. On down to the fourth rib, I cut through the periosteum and resected it from the rib. I then removed a four inch segment of the rib and incised the underlying periosteum. The piece of rib was placed on the Mayo table. (The nurse would take the speciman to pathology where it would be studied and eventually incinerated.) This exposed the membrane which lines the inner surface of the thorax.

It was a critical point in the operation. In a moment I would know if the pleura were normal—that is, the lung would be moving in the space beneath the parietal layer. If there was movement, I knew I'd have to pack the wound with gauze and leave it open for three or four days. This allowed the pleural surfaces to stick together and avoided collapsing the lung, when the abscess was opened. Then the patient would be brought back and the operation continued. Surprisingly, this wasn't as horrible or as painful for the patient as one would expect.

In this patient, however, I saw no movement of the underlying lung. The inflamed pleural surfaces had already adhered to each other. I could go ahead and finish—a relief for me for I did not relish having to anticipate the terrible burning for another several days. Better for the patient too; her fever might go out of control before we could get to the surgery.

I brought up and sutured the intercostal muscles above and below the rib bed and up to the skin—this made a funnel-like depression leading down to the drainage site I proposed to form. The anesthesiologist knew not to use inflammable gases since we were going to use an electrically-heated iron to drain the abscess.

Then came the risky stage.

My assistant, John Wellman, tensed; the nurses became very quiet. I paused briefly to gather strength. I needed the best of my surgical skills and luck to save this woman. Even then, that might not be enough. At this crucial point, the fluoroscopic location of the abscess might be off as much as one to two inches (yes, x-rays were iffy in those days) and if I didn't find the pocket of infection with the first probe, I'd have to probe generally until I located the abscess and cauterize and thus lose that much more lung.

"Is the iron hot?"

"Yes, sir."

"Hand it to me, please."

I grasped the handle of the soldering iron which was wrapped in a sterile towel, and slowly brought it toward the surgical incision. Every eye in the operating room was on the tip of that white hot iron. I sensed that other personnel had entered to watch the procedure, but I blocked everything out—all except the incision beneath my hand—the prepared channel which waited for that awful tool that might or might not strike the abscess at the first attempt. I thrust the glowing soldering iron into the lung. The terrible smell of burning flesh floated up. The hot iron cauterized enroute and I plunged on slowly.

There was a sudden gush as the iron struck the core of the infection and the foul-smelling pus welled up into the wound. John Wellman and the anesthesiologist breathed "Wow" at the same time.

My hyperactive and overly-critical assigned observer made a strangled sound and left. Others told me later he was weaving unsteadily as he lunged out the swinging doors.

I pulled out the soldering iron, cleaned the abscess cavity with suction and packed it with gauze. I applied a heavy dressing, leaving the surgical wound open wide, and the nurses wheeled the patient back to her room. That first night her temperature dropped dramatically and it was nearly normal the fourth day.

I saw the patient regularly, of course, and watched as the incision filled in, but left an ugly scar. Later, I removed the scar surgically and restored the chest wall. At this writing she has remained well and is still living, and her traumatic surgery can be seen in only a fine, white line.

I wonder what my assigned-surgeon-observer would have said if I'd missed finding that abscess with the hot probe. I didn't see him again after that piece of surgery, at least not for a long time. And when I did meet him, he was to become my patient. But that is another story.

CHAPTER 13

BOTTLES AND BULLETS

On December 23, 1938, soon after I had started to work in Lansing, Mr. Pat Van Wagoner, Michigan State Highway Commissioner (later Governor of Michigan), called me for help. One of his highway contractors had been shot in the chest by a disgruntled employee.

"His doctor says he's in critical condition," Van Wagoner said. "But I want to do everything possible for him. I can send a state car and driver, if you'll go up there."

"Let me see what I can do," I said and hung up. I walked to the window of my office. It was snowing so hard I couldn't see 50 feet away.

I called to my secretary, "Get Dr. McCoy in Alpena on the phone."

Dr. McCoy expressed the opinion that it was indeed a hopeless situation, but he too wanted me there. There might be a small chance to save him if I went; certainly there were no other chest surgeons anywhere near Alpena.

I allowed myself to be persuaded. I hurried to surgery to prepare a pack of instruments—the little hospital wouldn't have specialized chest tools.

The phone rang again as I was putting the last instruments in the two bags I would take with me. It was Van Wagoner again.

"I've talked to my people up there," he said. "It looks too serious to take the time to drive. I've arranged for a state plane and pilot."

"But visibility . . ." I began. I felt I should point out that it wasn't a sensible thing to do.

"Walter Carr will be flying you," he broke in. "And he is a crack pilot. It's a bi-plane with fiber wings and very stable. You'll be safer than on the ground driving."

Neither possibility appealed to me.

"OK—send the car to my home," I said. I checked my instruments once more and drove home, the snow swirling madly toward the car's headlights.

Ruth was more worried than annoyed with me.

"Chris, it's dangerous for you to be going out at all—let alone flying in this storm and besides, tomorrow is Christmas Eve. When the driver comes, just tell him you can't do it. Dr. McCoy doesn't think the man has a chance anyway."

"I said I'd go, honey. I'll do what I can, leave instructions and I'll be back before you even miss me."

The doorbell rang—I kissed her and hurried through the storm.

At the Lansing Airport, Walter Carr waited, the engine warmed and running. I climbed in, introduced myself and Walter taxied into the wind. We took off, due north. The plane had no instruments so we could not climb above the snow clouds—had we tried, we surely would have gotten lost. So we flew contact under the clouds, the flakes so numerous we barely saw the trees, whose tops we were skimming over.

We landed on what was called an air "field". It was a field all right. There were no runways and the field had at least a foot of snow. A jeep sprang to life from somewhere out of the darkness and whirled out to meet us.

* * * *

My patient was a 65-year-old man in deep shock. He had one bullet in the left lung and from what I could determine,

81

another in the heart wall. The heart size in the x-rays appeared enormous, about the size of a basketball, due to the blood in the pericardium. Worse yet, I could detect no pulse even though he was being transfused.

I quickly withdrew part of the blood from the heart sac, knowing that this was a dangerous tactic. It was dangerous because it was probably serving as a tamponade and preventing further bleeding. But it was about to stop the heart. The seconds ticked by.

"His pulse has returned."

Dr. McCoy gave me a faint smile, as if he weren't permitting himself to hope too much.

The patient suddenly began to cough up blood from the lung wound. I used a bronchoscope with some difficulty and then did a tracheostomy, a small opening in the wind pipe through which I inserted a metal tube. As I was proceeding with the work that would either help him or not help him, Dr. McCoy filled me in on the victim's history.

"He is a severe diabetic," he said, "and an alcoholic with equally severe liver damage."

There was no blood bank in those days, and the man needed to be replenished for the great amount he had lost. So I had fashioned a pump and some tubes and whatever else I could find into a mechanism which took the blood from the pericardial space and pumped it back into an arm vein.

The tracheostomy seemed to be helping so I tried to sleep for an hour the following night in a room adjoining the patient's. I lay there wondering if the contraption I had rigged up was going to be effective.

I looked at my watch when I awoke. I'd been in the hospital two nights and a day and it was now near morning of the second day.

The man's a wreck, I thought. I doubt if he'll live long enough to pursue any more alcoholic pleasure.

I washed up, put on my jacket and shoes and went into the room where the family was gathered, waiting, around his bed. I described what I had done for the patient and why. I also said that I felt his outlook was hopeless, that I had done all I could and was returning to Lansing.

"Dr. McCoy will call me if I can be of any further help," I said.

Outside, it was still snowing and bitterly cold. The roads were two lane, slippery and lonely. It was Christmas Day and as we crawled southward, the driver of the state car and I commiserated with each other. I was able to rest a bit, and when I walked up the steps to my own home at 4 that afternoon I was ecstatic. Ruth and my son, then 15 months old, met me at the door, and their smiles were beautiful. The house was ablaze with evidence of Christmas—a spectacular tree with carefully wrapped gifts piled beneath. Jim was gleefully jumping up and down. I wasn't sure whether his glee was because Dad was home or because it was Christmas.

*   *   *   *

Three months later, my 65-year-old diabetic, alcoholic, liver-damaged patient, with one bullet yet in his lung and another imbedded in the heart wall, showed up at the Chest Hospital in Lansing. (Dr. McCoy had previously called me about removing the bullets and I had refused to do so.) He had been to the Mayo Clinic, the Cleveland Clinic, the University of Michigan Hospital and Ford Hospital trying to persuade someone to remove the bullets. No one, naturally, would touch the case.

"How do I look, Doc?"

He thrived for ten more years with his bullets and his bottles. I never lived the case down. I also learned never to tell a patient's family that the patient was going to die.

CHAPTER 14

CONNED INTO GOING TO THE UPPER PENINSULA

The metallic voice of the hospital's public address system attacked the silence of the east halls. I paused. Not my name. I took a deep breath and headed for the doctor's lounge, two of the surgical residents following. If I could hide in there a few minutes, prop up my aching legs and have a cup of coffee, I should be able to make surgical rounds in better spirits. I'd been a full day in the operating room and right then I had seen all the sick lungs I wanted to see this summer day in 1940.

I wasn't fast enough. There was a small click and my name began to reverberate about the ivory-painted walls. "Call your office," the female voice ordered. God is probably a woman, I mused. Who else directs a medical man's life more completely than that clear, no-nonsense voice coming from somewhere up there.

Looking longingly at the coffee pot, I picked up the phone.

"It's Dr. Newitt," my secretary, Elvi Trethewey said. "He says he has a little problem." I asked her to find out if my assistant could take care of it.

"I tried that and Dr. Newitt said definitely not."

I could not know then that Dr. Newitt's "little problem" was to change the course of my professional life.

* * * *

We clapped each other on the back and sat down.

"What brings you here, Art?" I tried to be cheerful and not worry about the patients I should have been seeing.

"Well, Chris, I've got just a couple of things in mind that aren't right, but that I think we can do something about." His dark eyes squinted with concern. Art was tall, gangly, and mustached. Soft-spoken, slow to anger and fearlessly frank, he had been like the brother I never had.

"You're doing a great job here at Ingham Chest Hospital, Chris," he said. "The past two years since you took over this old tuberculosis hospital from a one-man operation to what it is now, is phenomenal."

I smiled my thanks, wishing he would get on with it.

"You've got expertise, and you're a good teacher—judging from what I hear about the new residency training program."

"Enough, enough." I waved him quiet. "What's the trouble, Art?"

Relieved to be done with the preliminaries, he jumped into the cold-water reality of epidemiology. Art was an M.D., the tuberculosis control officer of the Michigan Department of Health.

"There's too much tuberculosis and mortality from tuberculosis in the Upper Peninsula," he explained, running a hand through his dark hair. "There's no, and I mean NO standardized or even effective chest surgery up there. And the area is so poor most cases are going untreated. Someone has to do something."

"I can see you've given this considerable thought," I said, "What do you propose?"

"Well, now." He hitched his chair closer to my desk. "Briefly, I want you to initiate and develop a chest surgical program for the Upper Peninsula. You could start at Houghton. Right now . . ." he looked at me a short moment, then plunged in.

". . .right now, there's no money to pay you, for your time or that of your assistants, and you'd have to provide your own transportation, gratis."

I stared at him. So much for his little problem.

85

He was leaning back in his chair, more at ease. He knew I believed him. And knowing me as well as he did, he probably could hear the gears whirring and meshing in my head.

"You know how I feel about better standardization of surgery for tuberculosis," I said slowly. "You also know I'm ignorant of everything about the Upper Peninsula of Michigan, except what you just told me and that it must be a thousand miles away . . ."

But I learned. Within four months of that hot July day when Art came to me for a "few minutes", my adventures began. I never learned how many other chest surgeons had been offered this golden opportunity before me.

* * * *

The next eight weeks was programmed madness. Art Newitt and members of his staff spent a lot of time in my office. Yet I had to continue to improve the surgical program which I directed in the Ingham Chest Hospital, carry my weight in the operating room, keep an eye on the fledging chest surgeons in residency, and most important, see my own post-operative patients every day. The only way I could put more hours in the day was to sleep less. Ruth complained mildly but I assured her that it was a temporary thing.

It seemed to me the place to start digging into the Upper Peninsula's tuberculosis problem was with the originator—the Michigan Department of Health. That Department, I told Art, should conduct a detailed medical audit of tuberculosis treatment everywhere in the state, not just our Northern Peninsula. He looked sheepish.

"As a matter of fact, there isn't any money for that either," he said.

I threw up my hands.

"But we can finagle," Art said quickly. "Let's just toss this around a bit."

So we brainstormed. One idea came out of my presidency of the Michigan Thoracic Society and being a member of the Board of the Michigan Tuberculosis and Respiratory Disease Association. I bombarded leading members with phone calls. We contrived to get Art scheduled to present the total picture to the Thoracic Society.

Art was admirable. With his silver tongue and a lot of leg work by both of us, the Michigan Thoracic Society agreed to a man that such an audit should be done. They further agreed that the Michigan Tuberculosis Association, now the Michigan Lung Association, should be asked to finance the study. The Board of the Michigan Tuberculosis Association was in session just down the hall from our Thoracic meeting. As I look back now, it seems incredible that the funds were appropriated within hours after that. We were ready to roll.

* * * *

The problem for the medical audit team was that we had no idea what we were going to find once we did start rolling. For the first time in medical history, a group of medical doctors were agreeing to a survey and a medical audit of their own work to be financed by the Association of which they were all members.

When I explained what a monstrous job it probably would be, Ruth said, "Well, this is something that you've felt should be done, so go and do it. The boys and I will get along all right."

I knew whom I wanted to be on the team, and I was lucky that each accepted the challenge: Dr. John Barnwell, Professor of Medicine and Chief of the Tuberculosis Service at the University of Michigan; Dr. Bruce Douglas, Detroit's Tuberculosis Controller; and Dr. Roger Hanna, Director of Jackson County Tuberculosis Hospital. John Barnwell agreed to be chairman.

"Art, my friend," I said, "guess who is going to act as observer on this renowned team? YOU!"

He grinned. "I anticipated this. I'll have one of my associates go along, too."

After endless planning meetings, we came up with an itinerary, and a data form on which each team member would tabulate information covering his initial observation about each patient. At the bottom of the page was the zinger. The team member wrote his independent opinion of whether or not the case had been properly diagnosed, and if correct treatment were being carried out.

Once the survey was completed, we had agreed to follow certain steps. One: The team would review its findings in each separate case, and submit a confidential report to the medical director of the sanitorium. Two: There were to be criticisms ONLY in those cases where all team members concurred that the case should have been treated differently.

The third was a built-in restraint I was rather proud of. We demanded records of all patients discharged from the hospitals during the preceding three months and we reviewed these in exactly the same way. This forestalled the possibility of doctors quickly discharging certain patients whose treatment might be questionable and of interest to the survey team.

We were ready. It was 1940, the middle of November. We had chosen four hospitals in the Upper Peninsula to begin the first phase, and Art was chomping at the bit.

"Gawd! What are you going to do?" he asked, when I told him on the night before the team was to go north that John Barnwell had phoned me saying Bruce Douglas had been appointed Commissioner of Health for Detroit. This meant he would be unable to go with the survey team.

"Relax," I said, "there's no time to indoctrinate someone else. I'll substitute until Bruce can get back."

The next morning I began what was to be a twenty-five year relationship with the Upper Peninsula. Much of the time I wasn't comfortable but it was always interesting. And there were times when it was exciting and downright dangerous.

* * * *

We traveled out of Lansing with Dr. Thaddius Koppa, Dr. Newitt's associate, driving. The weather was yet mild, and

I had dressed accordingly. In any case, there had been no time for me to consider more adequate clothing since I didn't know I would have to go with the committee until late that night before. My colleagues, however, not having been raised in Louisiana like I was, were layered with woolens and came clumping to the car in big black galoshes. They knew that Mother Nature does not consider the upper portion of Michigan as being related to the lower; she just lumps the Upper Peninsula under "Arctic", with a reminder to herself to "start sending snow no later than October 30th".

We began our trip on the opening day of Michigan deer hunting season, and soon were wedged in a line of autos at the Straits of Mackinac. We seemed to be the only humans not wearing red wool outfits and carrying rifles. We cooled our heels, literally. The traffic was backed up for six miles from the ferry docks. We waited for 12 hours until our turn came to drive into the innards of the huge ferry boat. Forty minutes of socializing in the ship's midsection and we inched our way off the boat into the white expanse of the Upper Peninsula. Moments later, we were stuck in the snow. Since I was so thinly clad, my job was to sit behind the wheel while the other four pushed.

"Stringer," they huffed, piling back into the car, "maybe you're not so stupid, after all."

Our first stop was at Powers, the Pinecrest Sanatorium. Dr. John Towey had been medical director and administrator of Pinecrest since its opening in 1922. He spent his entire professional life in developing and operating the hospital until it ceased as a tuberculosis facility in 1961.

They were ready for us. As we had requested, Dr. Towey and his staff had prepared a resume of each case; the folders were piled neatly on a table in the conference room. Representative x-rays were already selected. All other x-rays, John Towey told us, were available if requested. We settled ourselves and "Big John" (a nickname he had all his life) stepped behind the conference table, reached under and came out with a 45 pistol in each hand, cocked and aimed at us!

"Gentlemen," he said, leering at our shocked faces, "I know you're going to be in complete agreement with our decisions!" Understandably, it was another five minutes before we rallied from his practical joke. Big John put the representative x-rays on the viewing boxes and the survey proceeded. I soon noticed that he had positioned himself in such a way that he partially blocked our vision of certain films. Maybe he didn't want us to study these too long. We counteracted this maneuver by meandering around the table and planting ourselves in front of the questionable x-rays. Big John laughed and backed off.

Following the day's work (it was to take several full days), we would adjourn to Big John's camp. Towey's handy man, Jewel, made it his business to get to know all the doctors. Jewel, a short, stocky, agreeable Finn, always had all kinds of toothsome foods and hearty drinks waiting for us. He was a man of many skills, but we all thought cooking was his greatest talent. His broiled steaks were the size of a roast and were so tender they hardly needed chewing.

"You know," Art said to nobody in particular as he slouched comfortably in front of the fireplace, "we could be snowed in here, twenty miles from town in the pine woods . . ."

I finished the thought for him ". . . unable to get out for days, and when we did get back to work on the survey, we might have a tendency to hurry things along, thereby getting out of Big John's hair that much sooner."

Big John roused from his Lawson chair and feigned outrage. "Knowing me the way you do, how could you dream of such a thing?"

The plain truth was, he well could be that devious. That weekend, some of Big John's friends had joined us in camp. On Sunday morning, he, along with all the other Catholics, had driven off in the only two cars to attend early mass. Since we had eaten all the provisions on Saturday, and Jewel didn't show up, we were stranded. At sundown, John Barnwell and I talked it over.

"I think we should head for town," I said. "Will you hoof it with me?"

"Better than dying of hunger cooped up here," he said. One arm was already into his coat.

We began trudging down the narrow wilderness road. The forest lay green-black on either side and the sky was starless. The air was so cold my nose stuck together inside when I inhaled. The only sound was our footsteps, mine still without overshoes. We'd given up conversation after the first five miles.

Half way to town, we saw auto lights coming from the opposite direction.

Dr. Barnwell and I jumped for the snowbank. It was Big John and he was driving like mad. The car slid to a stop, the driver's window rolled down and the apologies began.

"I just got busy," Big John said, "and forgot about everything else."

"Anyone who would leave his friends in camp to die of hunger, thirst, and hypothermia is not to be trusted," I said warming my hands under the dashboard. "I doubt if I could ever be induced to come to this camp again."

I did, of course, return there many times in the next three decades.

* * * *

Our next stop was Morgan Heights Hospital in Marquette. It had been the first county-owned and operated tuberculosis hospital in Michigan. It opened in 1911 and had had a succession of medical directors until Dr. James Acocks took over in 1947.

We stayed at the Northland Hotel in downtown Marquette. One evening, after a day of grinding investigative work, I left the other team members at the bar and went to bed. An hour later, a tapping awakened me. I stumbled to the door, opened it and the apparition there wanted to know if I had sent for her. I was not so drugged with sleep that I didn't hear my friends laughing down the hall.

"I think you have made a mistake. The room you want is where you see those gentlemen." I gave her a little bow and closed the door.

The following evening we met Dr. D. R. MacIntyre, a close friend of John Barnwell. MacIntyre generously hosted the entire team to dinner at the Mather Inn in Ispheming. But it was Sunday, and alcoholic spirits weren't sold anywhere in town. We were tired and dry, all the more so when we knew there were no spirits. Poor MacIntyre had to suffer through an evening of constant good-natured criticism for living in a town which would permit such barbarism. That same evening, we journeyed on to Houghton, where we had reservations at the Douglas House.

Houghton, Michigan, had been a wealthy copper mining center but now most of the buildings were drab and unkempt. A few businesses managed to survive, but with a welfare load of 95 percent of the population during the depression, little money was being spent anywhere in the Upper Peninsula.

The twin towns of Houghton and Hancock were built on hills—sloping to a canal separating the two. A rickety old bridge connected the cities; flooring was wood planks topped by a rusting iron superstructure. Nothing new anywhere.

It took several concerted attempts to park the car on the snow-and-ice-covered inclined street, near the entrance to Douglas House, and when we finally got the back end of the car to stop slipping downhill, we were all grumpy. The possibility of another dry meal was uppermost in at least some of our minds.

We skated across the sidewalk, gingerly making our way inside to the lobby. The night clerk was gaunt, completely bald, dourly silent and so tall that I wondered if he were standing on a platform.

Even John Barnwell had to look up. The clerk peered, counted us off and hesitating only a moment, ducked under the counter. The five of us looked at each other and shrugged. After Big John's antics, we were getting used to bizarre behavior. The clerk handed a bottle to Barnwell and one to me. We later learned that Dr. MacIntyre had gotten busy on the phone, called a friend in Houghton whom he knew would have a couple of bottles of scotch at home. MacIntyre also made delivery arrangements, complete with a description of the five of us and directions to make the presentation before we registered.

With the good whiskey to sustain us, and an excellent meal in the Douglas House dining room, we didn't get around to registering until almost 2 a.m. The ancient hotel had plenty of rooms available, so we decided to take single rooms for a good rest in order that we would be alert for work the next morning.

The clerk asked if we minded that the rooms had connecting baths. We were agreeable; the world looked much rosier than when we had been trying to park the car a few hours ago. Bath-sharing with a team mate would be no problem. We discovered, though, that what the clerk meant was that the bathrooms were connected with those of other hotel guests. Art came through the bathroom to what he assumed was the room of another team member. The occupant was in bed. Art spanked him on the rump and was astonished to discover he was trespassing in the quarters of another guest. But the really astonishing part of the little drama was the guest's identity. He turned out to be Art's own son in town on a business trip. He did not even know his son was in the hotel, or, for that matter, in Houghton.

After two days of survey at the Copper County Sanatorium, I took the wheel again. Hardly a chimney smoked; the desolation made it seem even colder on this north country road to Ironwood. Two feet of new, slick snow hampered our progress as we traveled northwest by fits and starts. I would cling to the steering wheel and try to keep the speed fast enough to propel us through the ever-deepening snow. Too much acceleration would fishtail us in our tracks, too little speed and we were stuck. Either way, we were immobile, whereupon the other four would have mild fits, clamber out, and push. With luck, I could start up again while the other four ran like crazy to catch up. Then came the tricky part . . . jumping into the moving car. By the time we reached Ironwood, they were exhausted, but as a finely coordinated quartet of pushers and leapers, they had no equal.

The hospital here was unremarkable, as was the stay in a relic of a hotel. Our visit to Hurley, Wisconsin, just across the border from town, was not. Hurley was reputed to be the toughest town in the United States. It had prospered through the timber era and had been doing well in the mining era until the depression hit.

"No survey would be complete without its social inquiries," I said. Thus, after work and nightfall, we surveyed a three-block neon lighted saloon and bawdy house district of Hurley. We agreed when we started out that the five of us would not become separated in one of these places. Every opening on the street for the three blocks was the door to a saloon and house of prostitution. Each new arrival was met at the door by a bevy of prostitutes in evening gowns. We would struggle through the mob up to the long bar and order a short beer and leave. As scientific observers our objective was to survey the entire street, counting places of business as we went from one to the next. There were seventy. Most of them had dining areas where it was said excellent food was served.

John Barnwell said he diagnosed more cases of tuberculosis among the prostitutes than he had in the hospital.

Returning home we stopped at my house in Lansing for dinner and told Ruth we had been in seventy whore houses in one night. She said, "You are bragging."

When I started making regular trips to Ironwood to do the surgery at Grand View Hospital, I took Ruth along on one of the trips. We were guests in Dr. Lajacono's home and I had asked him to make reservations for the four of us for dinner at one of the "joints" in Hurley.

As we went in the prostitutes were much in evidence but Ruth, still naive, thought they were other guests or entertainers. We were given a nice table in the middle of the dining area, had a drink and ordered our dinner. While we were waiting and watching the traffic I motioned one of the girls to come over to our table. She was an attractive girl, well dressed and talked openly about her business of the night. Ruth was convinced. The food was excellent but I don't think Ruth really enjoyed it. Later when we were back at Lajacono's, she said, "Don't you ever do that to me again." However, she can't say she has never been in a whorehouse.

*   *   *   *

Once home in Lansing, we spent hours as a team again, going over the collected data. We composed reports to medical directors of the hospitals. They were necessarily critical, but criticisms were limited to those cases in which all three members agreed that the patient should have been treated by a better method.

The weeks we spent in Northern Michigan answered the original question of Art Newitt. Yes, there was a tragic lack of standardized and effective chest surgery, particularly in regard to tuberculosis. Three months later I had my first surgical conference at Houghton.

CHAPTER 15

THE DECISION TO STAY IN LANSING

Near the end of my third year in Lansing, it became more and more apparent that Ruth and I had formed ties with colleagues and friends that we didn't want to break. We'd also been blessed with another son, John. Because of the children, we had delved into the Lansing educational system and found it suitable. We were settled and completely satisfied.

Professionally, however, I needed to do much more to attain significant recognition for my hospital. Most certainly, we had to add to the available beds. We needed to build a surgical wing and a proper nurses' residence.

The county board had definite negative feelings about the availability of funds for these needs. I didn't give up. I went to meetings, made myself apparent and pleaded for the chance to ask for a millage increase.

The board shrugged their consent to place a hospital millage on the upcoming ballot. Ross Hilliard, the long-time county clerk, aided my cause in a left-handed way.

"It will be all right to put it to a vote—won't pass anyway."

But it did pass and I felt committed to remain and see the project through to completion.

With a mass of guilt lying heavy on my heart, not to

mention fear, I gathered courage and told Pat O'Brien I could not honor my commitment to leave Lansing and join his surgical team in Detroit.

As I anticipated, he exploded. He bellowed that I was an ingrate, I had broken my promise. I had led him on. I admitted to his accusations, although I didn't believe I was quite that bad, I still had to do what I felt was right. Someday, I promised, I would make it up to him.

* * * *

The time came for me to mend some fences. It had been more than a year since I had broken the news to Pat O'Brien that I would not be returning to Detroit and even though I felt Pat could have been more understanding, I still wished I hadn't made the promise in the first place.

At this point in our lives, I had become president of the Michigan Tuberculosis Hospital Association, and Pat had been chairman of the State Sanatorium Commission for many years. It certainly seemed that the two groups should meet and discuss their mutual interests and problems.

With some trepidation, I phoned Pat with this suggestion. He was wonderful, and I sensed that he was as happy to renew the friendship as I was. He came to Lansing and spent three hours discussing plans with me at the Chest Hospital. We had lunch there, finalized the data and when we shook hands upon parting, we felt we had made progress in many areas.

Meeting time came for the two organizations; Pat presided and all went well, especially certain proposals for important legislation.

I had made myself comfortable in the well-appointed meeting room of the Olds Hotel, when the bellman tiptoed to my side and whispered that there was a Dr. Leon in the hall. Dr. Leon, he said, thought he was to attend the meeting.

I left the room and went to the hall. Dr. Leon came toward me, smiling shyly. He had a slightly rumpled, old world look about him.

"I am a member of the Michigan Sanatorium Commission," he said. His English was poor and I had to ask him to repeat himself.

"Dr. Leon," I said, "will you wait here a moment? I'll be right back."

I had to interrupt the meeting to speak with Pat. He said there wasn't anyone by that name on the commission.

Back in the hall, I tried to speak slowly and explain to the man that he must be in the wrong place. He became, suddenly, greatly agitated, and began to pull crumpled papers from his coat pockets. I looked them over and could not see that any of them had anything to do with the Sanatorium Commission.

"These papers aren't . . . " I started to say. Suddenly he attacked me with a blow to the head. I never knew what Dr. Leon thought I said. He swung wildly and got in a couple good licks before I realized I should defend myself.

Ted Werle heard the commotion and stuck his head out a door at the far end of the meeting room. I saw his incredulous expression before he turned and yelled at the conferees inside.

"That man has attacked Chris!"

Everyone began streaming into the hall, but by that time Leon was hanging over a chair holding his head and yelling. I only hit the lunatic once and I really didn't think I had hit him that hard. We still couldn't understand him. I felt awful. How had I ever gotten into such a mess! Why hadn't I just left the room instead of returning his blow? Cursing my reflexes inwardly, I let my friends hustle me back into the conference room. Bruce Anderson, the hotel manager, appeared with two more bellmen and escorted Leon out of the hotel. That, however, was not the end of Dr. Leon.

Pat O'Brien phoned me the following week. I was operating and it was probably four hours before I got back to him.

"I'll bet you're tired, Chris, but I'm afraid I must tell you this. That fellow Leon is a recent Governor's appointee to the Sanatorium Commission! Apparently it was engineered by some small ethnic group in Detroit. I hadn't been notified of his appointment. Besides that, the man is totally uninformed—I checked.

"He has retained a lawyer," Pat continued, "who happens to be a state senator and they plan to sue you for bodily harm, assault and battery and embarrassment. But listen . . . he doesn't know you and so far neither he nor his lawyer can identify you. In fact, the only two Leon can identify are Bruce Anderson and me.

"Now," he said warming to the intrigue, "I have talked with Bruce and we will tell the truth—that we didn't see the ruckus. But that is all. If somehow Leon finds out who you are, you could still probably beat him in court because he attacked you. But it would be a nasty mess and I know you don't have time to fool with it. So stay cool. Don't discuss the incident with anyone."

After that, Pat phoned me two or three times a week at home with information on the legal proceedings. They finally brought suit against Pat, asking for damages because he refused to identify me. Leon didn't know that Pat had mistakenly told me Leon wasn't on the Commission.

Finally, when Pat called one evening, his demeanor was reserved. That was out of character.

"Are you sitting down, Chris?"

"No," I said, "is it that bad?"

"Well, sit down. Leon is dead!"

I was stupified! What had I done? In trying to defend myself, had I killed the poor man? My stomach churned at the horrible turn of events, and my mouth became so dry I couldn't speak.

"You can relax, Chris. He died peacefully of a coronary. I went to the autopsy and I have a copy of the death certificate right here in my pocket!"

Unseeing, I sat down. Pat talked a few more minutes and hung up. I said a small prayer for Leon—and one for myself.

CHAPTER 16

BLOODY COMPLICATIONS

One of the awful things about pleural adhesions was that patients often were not aware that they had them. After I came to the Chest Hospital in Lansing, I became personally responsible for several cases of closed pneumonolysis. It was with a feeling of apprehension, if not downright dread, that I scheduled such a case, young Rose Stone, for closed surgical cutting of dense adhesions. At least, I reminded myself, I've got a good operating room staff.

Rose was being treated by pneumothorax, and dense adhesions were preventing an effective collapse of the involved lung. She obviously needed a closed pneumonolysis.

The patient remains conscious during such surgery and a local anesthetic is used. When I had the thoracoscope in place, I could see dense adhesions, especially when I placed the light in back of the adhesions and trans-illuminated them. I saw, with a sinking heart, that the adhesions were very short. That gave me little safe space to work between the lung and the chest wall for the adhesions extended into the area of a large artery. However, they appeared to trans-illuminate fairly well and the subclavian artery did not appear to be pulled into the adhesions.

I was making good cutting progress, when there was a terrifying swish and rush of blood over the entire surgical area. It obscured the operating field and rapidly filled the whole pleural space. I had cut into the subclavian artery!

The patient cried out, "Dr. Stringer!" and lost consciousness. A hundred thoughts darted through my head—all of them dreadful in outcome. How could the artery have moved into the surgical field without my being aware of it!

"Drop out!" I cried to my second assistant. "Start artificial respiration with the anesthetic machine!"

"Get blood—never mind crossmatching." I was shouting. The surgical supervisor ran the six steps to the hospital blood bank (the only one in Lansing at that time) and in less than a minute she had the blood hooked up and being pumped into the vein.

In the meantime, I had called for a surgical tray. Anticipating me, the first assistant had ripped off the drape sheets, exposing a larger area of chest for major surgery.

My staff's marvelous teamwork fanned the small fire of hope in my heart. I held out my hand to Christine Howe, the surgical nurse, pushing back memories of two deaths, when the surgeon I assisted was unable to control the hemorrhage.

Christine slapped a large scalpel onto my hand and I cut through the chest wall in two strokes. There was little bleeding here, for blood pressure was too low. Without bothering to use a rib spreading retractor, I thrust my hand into the wound. Blood gushed against my fingers like water from a garden hose. A deathly stillness had come over the room, making the shhhhhh sound of escaping blood seem louder. Which artery was cut? The great force suggested the subclavian, but it could be any of a half-dozen others. I was close to the subclavian so I would have to take a chance—if I were wrong the woman would bleed to death. She wasn't far from it—I had perhaps seconds of time. I probed with my left index finger and thumb. There it was! I compressed the vessel and the awful rush of blood ceased. My heart leaped with hope, then fell back. I could be wrong. Maybe the patient had expired and there wasn't any more blood pressure. I thrust away the thought and replaced it with a prayer. An assistant had put the Fieuchetto retractor in place and was spreading the ribs. With an aspirator that Christine made ready, she sucked the blood from the pleural space. I exposed the artery using a long surgical scissor and a tiny sponge on a long hemostate. I WAS LITERALLY HOLDING THIS WOMAN'S LIFE IN MY HAND, as I saw that this was, indeed, the torn artery! I clamped it, above and below the tear.

With both hands free, I was ready to go ahead with repair. The new blood being pumped in had given the patient a detectable pressure.

I cleaned the surgical field and it was apparent at once what had happened. The cautery knife had completely severed the adhesions, thus freeing the artery from the traction which had been pulling it down. The artery had been drawn down into the operating field, into the path of the knife.

I repressed a feeling of elation. We weren't out of the woods yet.

I began repair. Christine again thought ahead and had a long needle forceps waiting before I even reached out.

So far all went well. The next move was to get the clamps off the artery. If my sutures held, the patient had a chance. If they didn't . . . desperately I was trying to sort out all the alternatives, if the suture line didn't hang tight. None of them promising and all were dangerous.

I took the clamps off; there was no more bleeding!

"The sutures are holding." My assistant's eyes glowed above his mask.

"Start pressure and re-expand the lung," I said to the anesthesiologist.

I hardly dared to hope. Yet she was alive, and in a few minutes was doing her own breathing.

We closed the chest as swiftly as we dared while the patient continued to receive unmatched blood. Some last wrap-up touches . . . and the whole surgical team followed the cart back to the patient's room.

"Stanley," I said to my assistant, "go talk with the parents."

"What shall I tell them?" His face was a picture of dismay.

"Tell them the truth—and that I'll see them as soon as I can."

"What!" He stood, rooted.

"Go!" I was tired, unsettled and short of patience. I hurried after the team, who were now moving down the hall like a swarm of drones around the queen bee.

Half an hour later Dr. Stanley returned.

"What did the parents say?" I asked. They had every right to have strong feelings about the accident. I could handle any recriminations they might have, I thought. Seeing this young woman alive is my strength.

"They are upset, naturally." Stanley was still anxious.

"I'll stay with the patient a bit longer and get with the parents then," I said. "Thanks, Stanley."

Within the hour the patient's condition improved.

In the waiting room the father spoke.

"Well, Doctor, we understand just how crucial time was in that operating room. We're glad our daughter was being operated on by a surgeon who knew how to get into the chest quick and do what had to be done!"

What wonderful people!

In a week their daughter was fully recovered from surgery. Later, she married and raised a family. I saw her recently and she appears to be in good health.

I was fortunate. The high-caliber surgical team support was at the root of my success in cases like this one. I was well repaid for the time I spent training operating room personnel and insisting that equipment and supplies be on deck for the remotest emergencies.

CHAPTER 17

PEMBINE—
A CONFERENCE FRONTIER

Within a couple of short years, word had traveled throughout the medical world that the Michigan Tuberculosis Hospital survey team, (the one that Art Newitt had conned me into starting, and ultimately contributed to the eradication of tuberculosis in Michigan's Upper Peninsula) had inaugurated a plan which should be shared.

By June of 1942, the Michigan and Wisconsin Thoracic Societies had completed plans for a joint meeting. John Towey instigated, then tenderly nurtured, the arrangements that ended up at the Four Seasons Club near Pembine, Wisconsin,

The original idea was to have one tuberculosis hospital director from each state prepare and present for the critical evaluation of the other conferees, the records of the first fifty patients dealt with in his hospital during the preceding year. The director was required to "show and tell" these cases chronologically and to exhibit serial x-rays, hospital chart summaries and have complete records available.

That meant that each of the nervous presenters stood before a critical audience for a full day, attempting to defend his decisions. The committee stipulated that no favorable remarks be made to the presenter—only criticism of case management would be allowed. If nothing was apparent to criticize about the case being presented, then the presiding committeeman or sometimes one of the conferees called out, NEXT CASE! The penalty, should a conferee absent-mindedly praise the handling of a case, was that such a conferee wouldn't be invited again.

We named this type of meeting the "Consecutive Case Conference" and there was a great deal of informal discussion, that first joint meeting with Wisconsin, about the frontiers entered by the early Michigan Survey Team. We saw, when the survey results were tabulated, a pitiful discrepancy of treatment between the states and an equal disparity between the very hospitals within the states. It was worse than we had suspected.

For example, Wisconsin doctors generally refused to do phrenic nerve surgery for minimal tuberculosis. In Michigan, conversely, it was a routine operation, especially in the Detroit area, all for the same disease and for the same amount of disease.

Detroit's king of phrenic nerve surgery in the 30's and 40's was crusty Dr. E. J. O'Brien, Chief of Surgery, Herman Kiefer Hospital. It was claimed that Pat O'Brien met each newly admitted, minimal case of pulmonary tuberculosis at the front door of the hospital, scalpel in hand, ready to do phrenic surgery on the spot! At one regular staff conference during my surgical residency at Herman Kiefer, the following dialog took place between Dr. O'Brien and a new medical resident, a young man named Newman, who had the unenviable chore of presenting his first patient to the surgical staff.

"What, in your opinion, Dr. Newman," asked Pat O'Brien, "is the diagnosis?"

"Minimal tuberculosis, in the right upper pulmonary lobe, sir."

Dr. O'Brien nodded, "That is right. And what do you recommend in the way of treatment?"

"Phrenic nerve surgery."

"Why?" A routine question.

"Because she hasn't had one."

In the big conference room of the Four Season's Club at

Pembine, the Consecutive Case Meeting progressed. Masculine voices boomed in heated discussion (and argument) about the relative merits of phrenic nerve surgery. (This meant the interruption by crushing of the phrenic nerve on the involved side. The phrenic nerve has its origin from the 3rd, 4th, and 5th cervical nerve roots. It serves as the motor nerve for the diaphragm and its paralysis causes the diaphragm on that side to stop moving and become fixed in an elevated position, thus producing partial rest for that lung.) Some medical men, particularly the Wisconsin participants, questioned the effectiveness of this procedure.

My own good friend, Dr. Stewart Willis, Medical Director of Mayberry Sanatorium for the City of Detroit, began to urge me every time we met, to do a blind study on the value of phrenic nerve surgery for minimal tuberculosis. He had strong doubts about its value—rank heresy in Michigan and particularly in Detroit.

"But, Stu," I said, "you're talking to the wrong man. Why don't you go to the Detroit surgeons?"

"You know very well, Chris, that Pat O'Brien would never admit the procedure might possibly be ineffective."

Yes, I did indeed know that.

"I know you have repeatedly told me that to deny phrenic surgery to a group of patients in order to compare them with the operated group is unfair and risky for the unoperated group but I have also heard you say that the greatest hazard is to risk nothing."

Stu knew he had struck my Achilles heel; trapped me with my own words.

Finally for a year, I did a study in my own hospital. Every other case of minimal pulmonary tuberculosis admitted had phrenic nerve surgery. The other, of course, did not. Both groups were at bed rest. The study terminated after 100 cases. I reviewed these hundred patients blindly at one, two and three years intervals and entered the results by case before looking at the records to find out which ones had phrenic surgery and which ones had not. Four years after the first joint Pembine Conference, in 1946, I tabulated the results of the study. There was very little difference in the improvement of the two groups. If anything, the unoperated group faired slightly better.

Later, and with mixed feelings, I presented these findings to the members of the Mississippi Valley Thoracic Society at the annual meeting in Milwaukee. Dr. Ivan Feinger from Minneapolis remarked, "Chris must be very humble to conduct such a study as this in Michigan of all places, and present the results in an open meeting."

Big John Towey guffawed.

"Humble, hell. It takes *courage* with Pat O'Brien sitting here."

It appears that this study and report signaled the doom of phrenic nerve surgery for the treatment of tuberculosis. Thousands of patients had been operated but there was no looking back. I had ventured out of a comfortable, accepted procedure from within my peer group, and the frontier, although more easily conquered than some I attempted, was hard on my nerves.

We looked forward—those of us who promoted the Pembine Conference—to retaining the consecutive case formula, but necessarily came up with variations. A later innovation was for chest surgeons to take turns presenting "Ten Cases I Wish I had Never Seen"—one surgeon from each state presenting each year. The Michigan men thought that since it was my idea, I should be the Michigan presenter the first year. One of the patients in my group was referred by Dr. James Acocks of Marquette. He called me:

"I have a man here in the hospital," he said, "and he's got two abnormalities. I'd like you to see him and help me decide if either or both of them should be operated." From the concern in his voice I knew he had a problem.

"What are these abnormalities, Jim?"

"Well, one is in the upper lobe of the right lung and the other is the pylorus of the stomach—they are both possibly cancer."

At the next surgical conference at Morgan Heights, I examined the patient, his x-rays, and the file of four previous gastro-intestinal examinations during the year. I thought an abdominal operation should be done first since this was the least hazardous of the two surgical procedures. M. D. Bennett of Marquette, a general surgeon, opened the patient's stomach and found, to his amazement, a whole dill pickle stuck at the pylorus. It was much larger than the x-ray density had indicated. When the patient awoke, he heard the good news.

"But I never swallowed a whole pickle," the patient said firmly.

"But it shows up in the x-ray taken several weeks ago—while you were hospitalized, and the food department has never served pickles that size," the doctor demurred. The patient was a heavy drinker and, of course, the pickle must have been swallowed when he was in his cups.

"I'm glad it's not cancer," the patient said, grumpily.

I subsequently did a thoracotomy and resected the cancer-containing right upper pulmonary lobe.

* * * *

Another of the "Wish I'd Never Seen" cases involved a terrifying diagnostic and treatment problem. The man eventually turned out to have a disease I'd never seen before; in fact, the malady had never been reported in Michigan.

The patient had a history of apnea and asthma, and Dr. James Acocks (yes, my good buddy did it to me again) reported there was probably some emphysema present. The record said that he had had a coronary occlusion. He was coughing up blood. A partial obstruction of the left lower lobe bronchus prevented us from getting a bronchoscope past it. The stuff he coughed up contained cells strongly suspicious of malignancy.

"I suspect a cavity in the left lower lobe, Chris," Jimmy told me by phone. "I don't believe he can tolerate removal of the left lung—maybe you could just resect the left lower lobe."

"Thanks a lot, Jimmy!"

I thought about his chancy case. The patient was deteriorating fast—he didn't look as if he would survive. I ordered blood transfusions, conferred numerous times with Dr. Acocks and, with a feeling of dread, I operated.

I felt even worse when I exposed the left lung. It was completely encased with thick, fibrous scar tissue—the result of some kind of unknown previous inflamatory disease. Tediously I peeled this tissue away and exposed the root of the lung. I found numerous lymph nodes up to two centimeters in diameter, mercilessly compressing the bronchus and blood vessels. It is ordinarily more hazardous to remove these than to take out the lung, but since the patient was in such bad shape and the referring physician had cautioned against pneumonectomy, I just prayed a little harder and dissected the purplish-gray enlarged lymph node from around the arteries and veins and bronchi of the lung root. The lung drew in air and fully expanded for the first time since I had seen the patient.

He survived. I think everyone involved in the case, and particularly the patient, was surprised. I felt especially curious about the diagnosis of the peel from the lung and the enlarged lymph nodes, something new to me. The patient had been operated at Sparrow Hospital in Lansing and when the Sparrow pathologist, after dilly-dallying for three weeks, hadn't come up with a diagnosis or even a report, I sent the "mystery material" from my surgery to Dr. E. S. Beneke, head of the Department of Mycology at Michigan State University. Dr. Beneke speedily established that it was geotrichosis. Geotrichosis is a fungus infection of any tissue, possibly inhaled from a barn yard, and was the first recorded case in Michigan.

That provided another new experience for me, and a new chance for the patient, who recovered satisfactorily and went back to selling shoes in Marquette, breathing with both lungs.

* * * *

Other interesting ideas came from the Pembine conference. Participants decided to invite Minnesota to join them. They also decided to limit the "guests" to sixty, and change the meeting time to the first weekend after Labor Day. Since it was invitational, the committee allotted the conferees on a population basis. Fifteen from Minnesota, fifteen from Wisconsin, twenty from Michigan. The remaining ten participants came from the country at large. The committee consisted of three members, one each from Michigan, Minnesota, and Wisconsin, and no one except the state chairman knew who served on the invitational committee.

The Four Seasons Club, with its sprawling, brown painted complex of buildings, still operates from an island in the Menominee River near Pembine, Wisconsin. The island connects with mainland Wisconsin by a rusting plank-floored bridge. During the warm months it's a private club, but for the designated three days each year it is reserved for the Pembine Conference.

Dr. Tad Koppa and Dr. John Barnwell, working in different areas, organized these "Pembine-Type" conferences throughout the United States. I monitored personally, the initiation of Pembine-type conferences in Ohio, Indiana, Kentucky, Missouri, and Nebraska, glad to be asked to serve at these meetings. It meant an opportunity to extend the consecutive case concept.

CHAPTER 18

UPPER PENINSULA AND ELVI

Significantly, the high death rate from tuberculosis in the Northern Peninsula of Michigan in 1940 at 51 per 100,000 of population could not be blamed on crowded or ghetto conditions. Urban jamming spreads disease in highly industrialized cities like Detroit, Grand Rapids, and Flint. Because of this, I expected to see a much higher mortality rate than the 32.8 per 100,000 reported for the Southern Peninsula. Out of the Michigan Survey Team findings came a chest surgery program which I shall describe further.

The Northern Peninsula, we discovered, having been a center of immigration from many countries, had grown into a sprawling tuberculosis-laden semi-wilderness. This disease became the people's major health problem for decades to follow.

Ted Werle reported in the medical Journal, *Hygenia,* in 1942 that the death rate from tuberculosis in Finland was 200 per 100,000/year. Many Northern Peninsula migrants were Finnish, especially in the Keewenaw Peninsula. The mortality figures seemed to say that Finns, at least, were four times more likely to remain free of tuberculosis after migration to the Northern Peninsula than if they had stayed in Finland.

In April of 1942, I had my first surgical conference in the Upper Peninsula at the Copper Country Sanatorium. During the next decade, we extended surgical schedules and surgical conferences to include hospitals in Marquette, Ironwood, and Powers and to an equal number of hospitals in the Lower Peninsula.

Briefly, the program called for a review of the medical records of all potential surgical cases. If a patient needed relatively minor surgery, it was done at the home hospital. Major surgery patients went to my primary base, the Chest Hospital in Lansing.

The program rocked along; we revised, deleted, added here and there. A custom developed in which the hospital director consulted with the post-operative patients to follow-up their speed of recovery, general health, etc. If indicated, the medical director requested the post-operative patient to come back in when I made my next surgical visit to that hospital.

The preceding year I had operated on a young, attractive Finnish lady referred to the Chest Hospital by Dr. Smith, Medical Director of the Copper Country Sanatorium. Elvi Seppala Trethewey was a petite, brown haired, vivacious girl, married to a Cornish man, Robert Trethewey (called "Toots"), who was employed in the copper mines in the Houghton area.

I was glad to hear that Elvi had recovered nicely and returned to her job in charge of the Secretary of State's Motor Vehicle Division Branch Office in Houghton.

She had been quite ill when I operated on her and was confined to the Chest Hospital for several weeks before being transferred back to her home hospital.

Even while very ill and going through several stages of major surgery, this bright, cheerful lady always seemed to be motivated to do things for other people—patients or staff or whoever needed help. Everyone in the hospital got to know her. I later learned that "Toots" was also a kind, generous man.

"How are things in Lansing?" she asked, when I saw her for a post-operative check-up.

I glanced up in surprise. She seemed genuinely interested.

"The hospital personnel shortage is so acute I have to write part of my reports in long hand."

A few weeks later Elvi appeared at my office in the Chest Hospital in Lansing.

"I have two weeks vacation," she smiled. "And I can type. How would you like a grateful office worker for free?"

I could hardly believe her generosity. But she meant it and before the two weeks ended Elvi became my secretary and never returned to Houghton. Her husband found work with Olds Motor Division in Lansing. That was forty years ago and she is still my personal and business secretary. Dear Elvi has been a steady, dependable part of my professional life.

Years later I had a heart problem requiring rest so we packed to leave for Florida. "Toots" called the house. Ruth answered. He said, "Just be sure Doc doesn't worry about a thing. I will come out to your house each day to check if there is anything else I can do."

Promptly after Elvi came to my office, she reorganized it, changed the filing system and transferred certain items to the hospital business manager, who should have handled them in the first place.

On one of my birthdays, she had prepared Finnish pasties, which she knew I loved, and asked Olive Henderson, the dietician, to bake a cake and arrange a surprise feast for the senior staff in my small private dining room. The only trouble was that I didn't show! I was at St. Lawrence operating.

If patients' families from the Northern Peninsula were short of funds, as most of them were, Elvi would take them home without my knowing it, and provide board and lodging. She was my eyes and ears in the hospital milieu but never gossiped. All the doctors in the area got to know Elvi on a first name basis and I discovered that some had tried to entice her away. I am flattered that over a period of so many years she never even considered a change.

Elvi Seppala Trethewey soon knew all the members of my

family well, remembered all special days and saw to it that I remembered. If she found that I hadn't time to shop for some event, she did it for me.

Even now, she takes care of my bank account and Ruth's household account. If Ruth needs more money for some special reason, she doesn't bother me; she calls Elvi and the transfer is made. She looks after all the receipts and disbursements and prepares the income tax returns. At 70 years old her incredible memory still functions flawlessly. Above all else, Elvi is a good family friend.

* * * *

Early on, in the World War II years, the staff of the chest surgery program often consisted of me alone.

I felt beholden to carry as much load as I could in the absence of my colleagues, now in military service. If I were out of bed at 3:30 a.m. and took off in a little single engine plane an hour later, I could be 600 miles north in the Upper Peninsula hospital by 9:00 a.m. A wonderful alternative to train travel through Chicago and 3 other states, to get from one Michigan peninsula to another! I would operate in as many hospitals as needed and be home by 10:00 p.m. the night of the last work day.

There was one hitch—Michigan weather. Thanks to the great bodies of fresh water, which keep our state humidified on three sides, the climate is fickle.

If the flight were socked in on a designated morning, it disrupted people badly on the other end of the line. Patients tended to go into psychological trauma when their operation was cancelled. The doctors and nurses felt the pressure too.

Dr. Smith, "Smitty", in Houghton, decided that if I were bent on flying, I should do so the night before the scheduled surgery and conference, or, in case of bad weather, I should simply drive up that night. But it's not so simple to drive 600 miles alone, and at night, after having worked a ten hour day. Occasionally, I felt sorry for myself.

114

One time, I had been scheduled for Sunday surgery at the Houghton Hospital. Smitty met me at the airport Saturday and I spent the night with them. When I walked into the lobby early that Sunday morning, the director of nurses hurried up to me. She looked distracted.

"Doctor, the surgical nurse who is supposed to work with you today is ill."

"Isn't there someone else who can fill in?"

"No ... this is Sunday, you know, and we're already short-staffed here."

We all stood around uncertainly. A few others on the staff,hearing of our plight through the healthy hospital grapevine, ventured a suggestion here and there. Someone mentioned Helen Smith, Smitty's wife.

"Well, she might," Smitty said. "I can call and ask."

"She'll be right over," Smitty said. I headed for the operating room. In a short time, small, dark-haired Helen arrived, raring to go. Her quick hands and cheerfulness brightened the whole scene. In moments she had arranged all the needed equipment in the surgical area, scrubbed and announced that everything was in order.

I looked around this small wing to the old white frame building, a new addition to this little hospital. It held the operating room, the x-ray room and Smitty's office (which he shared along with his assistant when he was lucky enough to have one). This same office also served as a conference room and the x-ray viewing room. Not exactly luxurious, but very few facilities in the Upper Peninsula were even adequate in those days.

"Helen," I said, "most of the cases are bronchoscopies. Ordinarily they would be prepped in a separate room."

"Since we don't have one here, we will do the preparation in the hall outside the operating room," her husband said. "I'll prepare them there ... the patient will be sedated and their throats anesthetized with a 5 percent solution of cocaine."

"Will you assist us too?" Helen looked confidently at her husband.

115

"Yes, I'll bring each one in and hold their heads while Chris does the surgery."

We began. The patients were wheeled in on a cart and slipped onto the operating table on their backs. Smitty carefully pulled the patient down to the end of the table, so his or her head hung off. Then, cradling the head with his right arm, he reached around with his right hand to put the bite block between the patient's teeth holding the head back with his left hand. With the head back at the correct angle, I could slip the bronchoscope down the throat as Smitty continued to support the head.

Helen assisted with the instruments, and she was a crackerjack—as if she had never retired.

Sixteen operations later, we were through. Helen went through the door with a spring in her step.

"I'll go home and get supper," she said.

"Let me take the three of us to dinner, Helen," I said. "You must be tired too."

"No, you will be more relaxed at home," she said. "See you there."

Smitty and I looked at each other. We felt exhausted and she was still bouncy.

"Let's hold the surgical conferences now so we know how many new cases you'll have when you come back next month." Smitty said.

We dragged ourselves into Smitty's office conference room and began review of a stack of x-rays and charts.

We finished about eight that evening, and Smitty drove us to his home in Hancock, across the Portage Canal from Houghton. Almost dizzy with fatigue, I followed Smitty into the house through the back door. Helen bustled around the kitchen with the two Smith girls, Dot and Mary, helping. Wonderful smells floated out.

Afterward, I revived. "Helen, you're one of a kind! How can I ever thank you for all you did today?"

She laughed. "What did you expect?"

I certainly wished I had her pep and endurance.

I flew back early the next morning for surgery in my own hospital at 8 a.m., but I didn't set any speed records that day. Katherine Purdy, the director of Nursing, came in while I was scrubbing.

"You'll burn yourself out," she said. Her bright eyes expressed concern. Kay, slim and lovely as a movie star, with long red hair, was an excellent nurse and an even better administrator. I sought her advice about many things. She worked a lot of overtime, too.

"Look who's talking," I chided.

"Never mind me—you're running too tight a schedule, Doctor. You can't keep it up."

She was to remind me of this many years later.

* * * *

Making the 1200 to 1400 mile round trip up to and back from the Northern Peninsula was my biggest concern in the early days of providing chest surgery for this geographically segregated and impoverished area. I had a feisty Wolverine by the tail. Train and plane did their best under capricious conditions, but my anxiety level would rocket, when, for instance, the train was eight hours late.

When everything clicked properly into place on these trips I would climb aboard the Milwaukee railroad's Copper Country Limited in Chicago. I felt blessed. Eight hours to relax, eat, and sleep. Sometimes several of my colleagues were aboard and I had the extra joy of informal sociability.

In the 40's, an "all-Michigan" passenger train left from Calumet in the U. P. It rolled down through Hancock, Houghton, L'Anse, Marquette, St. Ignace, Mackinaw City, Saginaw, and all cross roads in between. Twenty-four hours after departing Calumet, it arrived in Detroit.

Sometimes, it was an exercise in self-discipline to board one of those railroad cars. They must have been old at the turn of the century. It had no sleeping or dining cars and not a crumb of food for sale. By asking around, passengers could usually find out at which station it paused long enough for them to leap off and scurry about like mice in a pantry, in search of edibles. I rode this train, the Duluth and South Shore Limited, only once and that once only because my family was at a cottage on Lake Mitchell near Cadillac. It would be nice to get off at Mackinaw on the way south, and have Ruth drive from Cadillac to get me. I longed to be with my family in our vacation cabin.

I phoned Ruth, who made plans to drive to Mackinaw City to pick me up. She was, as usual, right on time, but I wasn't, that sweltering July day.

Extremely uncomfortable, I sat plastered by perspiration to the tattered seat of the decrepit day coach. The upholstery was completely gone from the arm rests of the seats. They were of bare sheet metal and those arm rests closest to the windows were heated by the glass's intensification of sun rays to a point well past human comfort.

The windows themselves could not be opened. Even worse, several ladies had small children in the car, and carried their noon meal in box lunches. If it hadn't been so beastly hot, I'd have felt some envy at their forethought. As it was, I loosened my clothing, tried to stretch out and relax. I had just closed my eyes when the vomiting began.

I think every child in the coach upchucked, if not from motion sickness and heat, then to get as much attention as the others. The stench was awful.

We crawled east and south, and at the Straits of Mackinac, the entire train carefully was pushed onto the car ferry. By now, four and a half hours late, the train was met by a fresh steam engine at the other side of the water. There, I left the other passengers, imprisoned by their need to travel, and stepped out into the cool, sweet night air. I drew my first deep breath since mid-afternoon. I was wretchedly tired, but so was poor Ruth. She had been waiting in her car for five hours, not a little concerned about the family she had left back at the cottage. It was a toss-up as to who was the most out-of-sorts.

* * * *

One early spring day, in Marquette, I had just finished operating for Jimmy Acocks. I was surprised to see, while I

118

was dressing, that at least a foot of new snow covered the ground. It was June!

"I'll drive you half way to Houghton," Jimmy said. "I have phoned Smitty and he'll drive half way to meet us."

"Fine," I said, "I hope the snow lets up. I'd hate to get stuck and have to reschedule the Houghton surgery. I'm behind as it is."

"Never fear—I'll take John with me for company on the way back."

It sounded like a good idea to take the little fellow. He was about three years old and would no doubt love being with his daddy. So we swung by Jimmy's house on the hospital grounds and picked up Johnny Acocks. He was an active, talkative, healthy child and kept up a constant chatter. Jimmy tried to converse with me but couldn't override Johnny's rapid-fire talk. He held his hand out and worked his fingers up and down to imitate Johnny's chatter.

The snowfall abated slightly but the wind blew hard and grew colder. Jimmy clung to the steering wheel as we twisted and slid. Little John and I clung to each other.

We'd gone only three miles or so from the hospital when the car eased into some heavy snow and stuck.

"Well," Jimmy said, "I guess here is where we walk."

"This is where you walk. I don't have galoshes. John and I will stay while you go for help."

Jimmy agreed that it was better not to take the youngster out so he heaved from the car and started back towards the hospital. We waited for more than an hour—I could have worn out my cuff looking at my wrist watch, not to mention the ignition of the car, which I snapped on and off to provide some heat.

Little John grew more and more anxious and fretful about his daddy. Finally we saw a tremendous snow plow coming from the direction in which Jimmy had disappeared.

"Don't worry," I told him, "we will ask the driver of that plow to push us out of the snow bank."

To our surprise, the plow stopped abreast of our car. It looked two stories tall. All we could see were huge black tires and a glint of bright orange metal. I lowered the car window and we craned our necks. Out of the cab of this monstrous machine climbed Jimmy Acocks!

"I found it abandoned in a snow bank about a mile back," he grinned. "The keys were in it, so I started it up, rocked it a while and got unstuck."

"My God, Jimmy," I marveled, "is there no end to your talents?"

"Never mind," he said, "just shut the window and steer while I get the car out."

Jimmy plowed away as much snow as he could and somehow maneuvered that big plow behind us. In minutes we were back on the road. Jimmy left the snow plow better off than he found it, and returned to us and his car. We crept back to Marquette and finally reached by phone, a cold, worried Smitty. He had driven his half of the journey, waited, and at length turned back to Houghton. He hooted when I recounted our adventure.

* * * *

The experience with the snow plow didn't alarm me as much as the time I was stuck in my own car by a roadside. A snow plow zoomed by at full speed, showering sparks as it hit patches of concrete under the thick new snow. Without slowing a fraction, it thundered past, completely covering the car. Bewildered, I sat frozen in the sudden darkness. I was buried! There wasn't time to panic. I unlatched the door locks and swung around in the front seat. Placing my feet firmly against the door, I pushed. Nothing happened. I kicked and kicked some more. The loosely packed snow gave way, little by little, and eventually I crawled to freedom.

* * * *

The airport at Ironwood in the northern peninsula was an open field, graded but without hard-surfaced runways and not long enough for heavily loaded aircraft.

Accompanied by Wally Badgley, an orthopedic surgeon, we once took off from this field for Lansing. We were slow getting off the ground and when we reached the end of the field and looked down, the telephone wires looked to be only inches beneath us. Wally actually lifted his feet off the floor.

We flew as the crow, across Northern Michigan and Wisconsin, directly over Lake Michigan. We were both needed at our own hospitals in Lansing, so we hurried. It wasn't a very smart thing to do. Our single engine conked out over the big lake. I think our hearts stopped when that motor sputtered and died. It caught on again but we had a glimpse of the everlasting over that gray-blue water.

Still in the air by ten that evening, we were three hours late and distinctly on edge. I was busy and didn't notice my partner thoughtlessly flicking the navigation light off and on. Below, the Mt. Pleasant Air Control Tower perceived it as a distress signal and reported a small plane in difficulty in the air.

We weren't aware of that, of course, and we certainly weren't thinking ahead enough to realize that a distraught board of trustees member from the Chest Hospital was pacing the corridors of the small Lansing airport, waiting to pick us up. (Andrew Langenbacker was a new and exceedingly conscientious member of the hospital board). As time passed, he became more and more nervous. By the time airport officials relayed to him the message about a small plane being in trouble north of Lansing, he seemed about to collapse.

When we did land, poor Andy went to pieces. He was ashen and trembling.

"What happened?" he croaked. "I've been watching for you from the tower for hours!"

"I must call Ruth," he said after we explained. "I felt I should warn her that we thought the plane in trouble was yours, so I told her right away when the radio report came in."

"Andy, sit down and relax," I said, putting a hand on his shoulder. "I'll call her."

"Oh," Ruth said when she heard my voice. "I wasn't worried. This has happened so many times before and you haven't been hurt yet."

Shaking my head a little, I went back to my two friends.

"I don't think I can handle the driving," Andrew said apologetically.

We trundled Andy into the car and I drove him home. I dropped Wally off at his house and went home, leaving Andy's car in the driveway. By morning, he'd have his composure again and figure out a way to get his car back.

* * * *

As our work progressed the State of Michigan provided air transportation in emergencies since the treatment of tuberculosis was supposed to be publicly funded. Walter Carr, employed by the state, flew me in these emergencies. He was a skilled flier and I enjoyed the trips. We had some great chats and I learned a lot of what I know about flying from him.

Sometimes I garnered unsolicited publicity when the state flew me. During a railroad strike such an emergency occurred and the Lansing State Journal headlined a front page article "Surgeon Soars Out of Capitol City Airport on Errand of Mercy". Ted Werle, Executive Director of the Michigan Lung Association called Elvi and wanted to know who my Public Relations man was.

Certainly Michigan was not alone in its fight against tuberculosis. Everywhere in the United States, the battle continued. No area, however, was more obstinate than Michigan's northern peninsula. It took the combined and massive effort of public health departments, tuberculosis associations, tuberculosis hospitals, physicians and surgeons to beat the disease.

The program worked well and the area experienced a rapid decline in tuberculosis morbidity and mortality. In 1954 the death rate in the Upper Peninsula was less than in the Lower Peninsula.

Many years elapsed between Dr. Newitt's challenge which precipitated the northern peninsula project, and the victory we won over tuberculosis.

In retrospect, the plain hard work, surgery, administration, residency training of chest surgeons, controversy with appropriating agencies and uninformed and unsympathetic hospitals boards—all were worth the winnings.

Sometimes the long, weary days and nights of travel almost drained my will to continue the fight. Then I would think about those living who otherwise would be dead without surgery, or I'd get a proper night's sleep, and would be ready to go again.

Those Upper Michigan days were certainly among the most rewarding experiences of my professional life.

* * * *

Pinecrest Sanatorium at Powers in the Upper Peninsula always had a heavy schedule. John Towey and I would work through the mornings seeing patients, examining x-rays, and dictating consultation reports. Then we'd wash up and have a light lunch at the hospital cafeteria. Afternoons we'd operate, if necessary, well into the evening, then continue dictating surgical reports.

Often it would be nine or ten p.m. before we left the hospital for the Towey home on the hospital grounds. John's wife, Rega, would wait up with a frosty pitcher of dry manhattans for us on the cocktail table of their comfortable living room.

Rega would prepare a steak and salad and over dinner we'd catch up on what had happened in both of our families since my last visit the month before.

Directly after the meal, we all retired. I had to be early on the road for another day, much the same as the preceding day. I dashed around then, hopped into bed and tried to fall asleep before John did. His bedroom was next to mine and his snoring shook the walls.

Excruciatingly early, he'd be at my door bellowing, "Daylight in the swamp!"

* * * *

I once had to make a special flight to the Upper Peninsula, Morgan Heights, using a small single engine Cessna plane and a pilot.

I might have been unfamiliar with this particular kind of plane, but the pilot seemed to be unfamiliar with everything connected with flying. It was also his first time in the Upper Peninsula.

The Marquette area has two airports—one at Sawyer Airforce Base and a much smaller county field. The county airport was ten miles nearer to the hospital.

Somehow, the pilot figured that out.

"We'll go on to the county field," he said as we looked down on Sawyer Air Field. That seemed reasonable to me.

By the time we reached the field, it was closed in with fog. Lacking instruments to land, the pilot turned the plane back toward the other airport. The fog played no favorites. It was there, too, by the time we had backtracked.

"Well, back to the county airport," the pilot said, "maybe it has lifted since we left."

I was disgruntled but I wasn't exactly in control. For that matter, neither of us were, for the fog had socked in the entire area.

The pilot hunkered about in the seat beside me checking the few instruments the plane afforded.

"The fuel's getting low," he said. His voice cracked. "I don't know whether we're over land or over Lake Superior."

I glanced at him quickly. He was in a panic. "Take it easy," I said, peering at the compass and speculating on the ethics of taking over a captain's command, even in a two-seater.

Common sense won and the pilot passed the steering mechanism over. We flew and flew, the gas gauge pointing nearer and nearer to "empty".

I was beginning to feel panicky myself. I had maintained a high altitude in order to rise above the fog but it wasn't much help. We could see nothing but a thick blanket of clouds below us.

Gradually, the cloud layers thinned and we flew into a beautiful, rosy sunset. I took the plane down to what appeared to be about 3,000 feet but the altimeter didn't move! I didn't have time to worry about its nonfunction. Forested wilderness spread out below but I could see a railroad track. It ran north and south, so I descended a bit more and followed the railroad track south.

I sneaked another quick look at the pilot. He was slumped passively in his seat. I got the feeling he could hardly believe he wasn't headed for a cold, watery grave. Below and ahead I spotted buildings. And beyond them there appeared a landing strip, apparently on the edge of town.

I leaned back and relinquished the controls.

"You know more about this thing than I do. Land it!"

With some difficulty, the pilot roused himself and took over. His hands trembled but he put us down safely.

I did then recognize the town, even in the twilight. It was Escanaba. We taxied up to the shack that was optimistically labeled "terminal".

"What do you want me to do now?" the pilot asked me as I gathered up my luggage.

"I don't care what you do," I sighed. "I know I won't be going back with you."

I got a cab to the hotel in Escanaba and called Dr. Jimmy Acocks. He was still waiting for me at the county airport.

"OK, Chris. Get a good night's sleep. I'll pick you up in the morning about 8."

I thanked him and hung up. I needed rest, for sure.

* * * *

Jimmy Acocks alleges I have made similar calls to him from everywhere in the Upper Peninsula.

"As soon as I hear 'Jimmeee' I know who it is," he grumbled. "And furthermore, I know that he is stranded again."

* * * *

Houghton didn't even have a real field, let alone one which was paved or even graded. We had to land on the dark stampings from the copper mines. This stuff, called stamp sand, had been dumped along Portage Canal.

Stamp sand dumps are smooth and firm. The driver of the pick-up car from the Houghton Hospital would wheel across the solidly packed waste to where ever we landed. It was reasonably safe to land there when it was snow covered and, primitive as it was, there was no worry about power and telephone wires.

Other winter landing areas were a risk—we would just have to take a chance on the ground being level underneath the snow and hope it would support a small plane. We would take off on a return trip naturally, the same way.

* * * *

By the early 1930's all recognized tuberculosis hospitals were staffed and equipped to carry out a pneumothorax treatment program. Once the air pressure is built up in the patient's chest, it has to be maintained. Usually, this meant a weekly "fix", since the body has a natural tendency to absorb the air. These weekly "refills" had to be continued after the patient went home.

When patients traveled or were away from home at refill time, a responsible physician could make arrangements for them to receive their air refills at designated places across the country.

One day John Towey observed a patient drive up to his Upper Peninsula Hospital in a limousine. The lady appeared to be wealthy, accompanied by a chauffeur and a female companion who doted on her. Apparently they were touring in luxury. The lady's doctor in New York had arranged for her to refill at Dr. Towey's Pinecrest Sanatorium.

After John had proceeded with the refill, Mrs. Lotsamoney asked how much she owed.

"Our charge is $5.00," John said.

Mrs. Lotsamoney wrote a check and handed it to him.

"I'm curious," John said. "You've had pneumothorax refills in many places. What does it usually cost you?"

"Doctor," she said, "I've never paid less than $25.00 before. If you will give me that check, I'll write another more appropriate for this service."

"No, thank you," John said thoughtfully. "But I am learning fast."

Not long after, a young man came to Pinecrest under somewhat similar circumstances. He needed a refill and also appeared prosperous. He, too, had a chauffeur and a female companion.

When Dr. Towey finished the refill, and the young man asked for the amount of the charge, John, remembering Mrs. Lotsamoney, thought quickly.

"Just pay me whatever you are accustomed to paying."

The young man wrote him a check for $5.00.

* * * *

At home in Lansing the clock's alarm clamored in the winter morning darkness. I heard it distantly, like church bells pealing over a countryside lying deep in snow. I was paralyzed with fatigue—for that previous day and most of this night, I had either been operating on patients, making rounds, working on records, or en route to a staff meeting. I drifted off again. A few precious moments later Ruth tugged at my blankets.

"Chris! You're not going to have time for breakfast. You're due at the hospital in twenty minutes."

I was too tired to groan. Staggering around the bedroom, I

somehow dressed and found myself outdoors. The frigid, pre-dawn air jolted me awake.

"Hessie," I said to my car when it took its time about starting, "you're not any colder, hungrier or tireder than I am."

I drove carefully down the familiar streets to the hospital, wishing I could rob some sleep from my neighbors who lay behind darkened windows.

At the hospital, all was frantic. Too many patients; not enough personnel. I pushed myself.

"Dr. Stringer," my secretary reminded me, . . . "You'd better leave for Houghton and now."

I glanced at my watch, tossed her a chart and headed for the door. I would just have time to speed by car to Battle Creek and catch the train that went on to Chicago to connect with the one to Houghton. Not exactly the shortest way between two points, but it was that or drive the whole way alone.

I missed lunch but consoled my complaining digestion system with the thought of a good meal on the diner of the Chicago to Houghton train. I visualized myself getting in my berth and SLEEPING the rest of the journey northward.

Life has seldom been crueler to me. Some fool railway official had taken off the club dining car. There wasn't even a stale sandwhich to bribe from a porter.

I tried to sleep, but my stomach complained so loudly and at such length that I just rolled around for the next 14 hours.

It was 9 a.m. when I stepped off the train at that bleak, grimy railroad station to greet Dr. Smith, the Medical Director of the Hospital. I was glassy-eyed and all but inert in spite of the 20 below zero weather. Smitty hustled me around the Houghton stationhouse to his car. Lord knows how long he had waited there.

"A late train puts us pretty far behind, Chris. What do you say we go straight to the hospital? We can wait until noon for a bite."

I came alive suddenly. Over this I had some control.

"No," I said stiffly. I wanted to roar. "I haven't eaten since day before yesterday. I'm sure Helen will make me some breakfast."

"Of course," Smitty said, eyeing me guardedly and shifting gears. We careened toward the Smith home.

* * * *

"Collapse." When a surgeon used this single word, he was talking about one of several surgical procedures that were often used in the days before antibiotics.

It was an apt word, for that is what the surgery did— partially collapse the involved lung.

I was making rounds with Smitty at the Copper Country Sanatorium in Houghton, when we came to the bedside of a recent admission.

"The studies are not all completed here," Smitty explained.

I looked down at the fellow. He was dark-haired, black eyed; an Italian laborer, I figured. His eyes sought ours— frightened but trusting. He seemed to be straining to understand what Smitty was telling me about his condition.

Smitty went into detail describing the patient's disease, particularly the x-ray findings. Making some entries on the Italian's chart, Smitty turned to leave.

"What I got, Doc?" the patient burst out, half rising from his pillow.

Smitty paused, and thinking the man had asked "What I gotta have?" he answered, "Collapse, I suppose."

The patient fell back, his dark face a picture of woe. "What, Doc, I got that too?"

CHAPTER 19

STORM CLOUDS OVER
THE UPPER PENINSULA

Somehow, I developed a reputation for bringing stormy weather with me to the U.P. Dr. William Gladstone, who practices general medicine in Norway, Michigan, near Iron Mountain, knew this.

I met him when I found myself spending several days a month in the Northern Peninsula. On one of my early trips, I had checked into The Lewis, Iron Mountain's one hotel, an ancient three-story building painted white. There were no functioning locks on the old room doors, and the walls were so thin you could hear normal conversation in the next room. My room furnishings were just as ancient. There was an old iron bed frame with a felt mattress on open steel springs. The one window looked out on the tarred roof of an adjacent building.

Iron Mountain had been an iron mining town but more recently the sustaining industry was a Ford Motor factory that made the wooden bodies for station wagons and other Ford parts. With the advent of steel automobile bodies this had also faded and one of the Ford buildings was being used for the making of charcoal.

Bill Gladstone heard I was in town. (He must have informants everywhere because he knew all as soon as it happened.)

I had unpacked and was about to step into my pajamas when my hotel room door burst open. Bill stood there grinning, and filling the doorway with his hulk.

"Chris, what in hell are you doing staying in this relic of a place? Get dressed—you're coming home with me."

"I just checked in! Besides, you don't need a last minute guest in your home."

"Come on," he said ignoring the fact I was wearing nothing but my underwear. I grabbed the clothes I had just taken off before he could throw them into my suitcase.

"Good timing. You're quick in places besides the operating room," he said. He threw the last of my clothes into my bag and snapped it shut as I shrugged into my suit jacket.

I checked out at the hotel desk and the clerk didn't raise an eyebrow. People in Iron Mountain and Norway were used to Bill Gladstone taking charge.

Thereafter, whenever I came to Iron Mountain, I never tried to stay anywhere else, for the Gladstone home and hospitality was better than the finest hotel. Greater yet was their friendship.

Bill and Jean Gladstone called immediately in August, 1962, when our son, Jim, was killed in a mountain climbing accident. They urged me to bring my family and join them at their cottage on a lake in the wilds of the Northern Peninsula. We appreciated the chance to share our grief.

With our twin sons, 12 years of age, (John, 22, who was a senior in advertising writing at Michigan State couldn't get away) we drove up to the Gladstone home in Norway and from there, to their cottage in Bill's van. We eventually arrived at the cabin. Bill owned all the land around the lake, and there wasn't another building in sight. The forest came right down to Gladstone Lake, except for a clearing in front. The substantial cottage and furnishings provided comfortable bedrooms for all of us.

Once settled in, we learned that Bill and Jean had farmed out their three little daughters with friends so they could spend the entire week with just us. How wonderful it felt to let out our grief and terrible sense of loss to these generous, understanding souls! Ruth, the twins, and I will forever remember this kindness.

* * * *

I grew to love the land of the Northern Peninsula, and the people, too. With Elvi's encouragement, I returned there often to vacation. She and her husband generously gave us invitations to use their cabin in the Upper Peninsula.

"Dr. Stringer . . . you and Mrs. Stringer need to get away, and alone," she said. "Why don't you take some time off? You can stay at our cottage on Keewenaw Bay."

What Elvi said made sense, as it always did, so we arranged for our children's care and started north on a bright, hot day in July of 1963. But as we crossed the Mackinaw Bridge, sure enough, it began raining in hard, driving sheets and continued as we drove northwest to Marquette.

There we passed the Marquette State Maximum Security Prison, dreary and forboding against the heavy dark skies. The old iron mining town, built among the steep hills, seemed sunk in the doldrums since pelletizing iron ore for more economical transportation had not been developed.

"Morgan Heights is right on the way," I told Ruth. "See— there's the hospital. I'd like to run in and say hello to Jim Acocks."

I eased the car in and under the porte cochere, where I could climb out of the car without getting drenched.

"You don't mind if I stay put?" Ruth asked, pulling her sweater closer about her shoulders.

"No, I'll just be a minute."

I passed the reception desk on the way to Dr. Acock's office. One of the reception clerks called to me.

"We were just talking about you, Dr. Stringer, and decided that you must be up here. You always bring storms like this."

The weather cleared during the two weeks at Elvi's cottage. Ruth and I did nothing more than those things necessary to survive and we laughed a lot. Elvi was right. I needed that respite.

* * * *

Some weeks later, during a surgical trip to the north country, I again visited Bill and Jean Gladstone. They had recently built an elegant but comfortable home in the forests outside of Norway, Michigan. Jean had put on a delicious dinner, as usual, and afterward, we relaxed in the living room. I intended to retire early because the next day's schedule was tight.

The youngest Gladstone daughter, Kathy, was about two years old. She curled up beside me on the davenport and went to sleep. For me, it was a special time . . . my children were boys and I particularly enjoyed the little Gladstone girls.

A storm raged outside our peaceful scene. Bill chuckled, saying it was the first bad weather since I had been there on a previous trip. Thunder boomed, the wind jerked tree branches in all directions and lightning slashed through the blackness. An especially loud thunderbolt crash woke little Kathy. I put an arm around her.

"Do you hear water running?" I asked Bill and Jean. "It sounds like it's coming from the basement." We listened. Bill dashed to the basement door and looked down.

"Hey! It's filling up with water!"

Clattering down the stairs, he waded through the flood and shut off the main valve. Jean and I, with Kathy hanging on behind, hurried down the hall and hovered anxiously at the basement doorway.

I was about to ask Jean if there was an adequate drain down there when I smelled a fearsome, acrid odor.

"Jean," I said carefully, "Don't panic, but I think I smell smoke."

She lifted her head and sniffed. "I do too! Where's it coming from?"

We followed our noses to the wall of the house next to the garage. I opened the hall door, leading to the garage. The

133

ceiling was ablaze! I slammed it shut. Jean was already running to the phone.

"There's no dial tone!" she yelled. "Oh Bill! Bill! What shall we do?!" Her husband had come upstairs, wet to the knees, just in time to see the flames.

We stood, terrified, knowing that behind the back door the fire licked and spread toward the main rooms of the Gladstone's picture-book home. I thought of all the things we might have to do; more precisely, a dozen unfinished thoughts flitted in and out of my head. Over my shoulder I could see the three Gladstone girls in their nightgowns, huddled together out of the way of us scurrying adults.

"Get the cars out!" Bill cried and pushed past me. "Chris, you take one and I take the other." The double garage doors were open, the keys, thankfully in the ignition and we reverse jetted out of the flaming building. Bill spun his sedan around and kept on driving for the Norway Fire Fighters.

I parked the car a safe distance off and sprinted back to the kitchen. I asked Jean if she had any pails and she produced two large buckets from somewhere. She filled them in the laundry tubs, one after another and I dashed water up to the garage ceiling nearest the house. I'm not sure how much this helped. Volunteer firefighters arrived quickly and were surprisingly efficient.

No one was hurt; the house sat, smokey but intact, in its woodlands. Feeling very lucky, we inspected the premises later, and discovered that lightning had struck a tree near the house. The bolt, unbelievably, had traversed the ground to the place where electrical wiring entered the house. In doing so, it dug a straight, symmetrical trench about a foot deep and a foot wide, struck the doghouse enroute (blowing the thick concrete floor to bits) but remarkedly did not injure the two dogs.

After the fire was drowned and the excitement had died down, Bill faced me squarely, deadpan.

"All right, Stringer," he said, "that's enough out of you."

My reputation for bringing bad weather to the Upper Peninsula was greatly enhanced by this storm and its con-

134

sequences. But not all storms were caused by the elements. Not long afterward, Dr. Gladstone, phoned from his hospital and said he needed help with a man who had been brought in from the woods. The patient, he said, was gravely wounded and probably would not weather this storm.

"They brought him in a few minutes ago . . . shot with a deer rifle through the chest. The bullet passed through the right lung and came out the back. He's bleeding profusely and coughing quantities of blood. Can you get up here quickly?"

"I can do as much from here, Bill. Now listen. Did the bullet exit near the spine? Is there any evidence of paralysis?"

"No, he's thrashing around, moving his legs."

"Is the right lung collapsed?"

"I'm not sure, Chris. There are audible breath sounds and a lot of gurgling. I haven't even done an x-ray because I don't want to move him any more than I have to."

"Good thinking. What position is he in?"

"We have him on his back with heavy dressings front and back."

"O.K. But Bill, I can't get up there in time to do your patient any good."

I thought ahead, my mind straining to imagine the scene in the little hospital in Norway.

"Move him to his right side and keep him there. This will aid in controlling bleeding and hopefully keep blood from spilling into the undamaged left lung. I know you'll transfuse, but make it massive. Introduce an intratracheal catheter and aspirate the tracheobronchial tree continuously as long as there is gurgling."

"Yes—I'll monitor the lungs carefully." I could sense some of the strain leaving his voice.

"Do the usual things for shock—keep his blood pressure at about 100-110, no higher. Cut down the transfusions if it does rise."

"If he were in the Chest Hospital," I went on, "I probably would operate just to control the bleeding—but since he's not here and you're not a chest surgeon, you'll be doing the best thing possible under the circumstances."

"I'll get right on it. And, Chris, thanks."

The receiver slammed and I wondered about Bill and his wounded man. I couldn't know it then, but in later years, chest surgeons started treatment of most gun shot wounds exactly as I had told Bill—and left surgery as a very last option.

Early evening came and Bill phoned to report that he was unable to aspirate the tracheobronchial tree sufficiently to keep it dry.

"You'll have to do a tracheostomy, then," I said.

"I believe I can, but I don't like to."

"I understand. Listen carefully. Make a small low incision directly over the trachea, transverse and not more than one inch. This will limit the anatomy you will be dealing with. I believe you have a set of Stringer neck retractors, so use them. Cut a small section of the fifth tracheal ring, about ¼ inch, instead of inserting the tube through the interspace between the cartilages.

Turn the cut segment of the tracheal ring up and insert a number 8 tracheostomy tube. Tell the nurses to be sure to aspirate the bronchi through the tracheostomy, as long as there is anything to aspirate, whether or not there is gurgling."

Bill thanked me hurriedly and hung up. When I hadn't heard from him by 8 the next morning, I phoned him.

"I believe we've won," Bill's usual low-key manner was gone. He sounded elated. "He doesn't appear to be bleeding now. The chest is quiet and the blood pressure had stabilized."

"You did good work, Bill," I said. "Congratulations—you've made my day, too."

In about 10 days, Dr. Gladstone discharged his patient. When friends of the patient drove him south to his home in Detroit, Bill asked them to stop in Lansing and have me check the patient over. I was happy to do it, although as it turned out I never told Bill what transpired during the "check up".

When I examined the recovered man, I saw that he had an excellent result and was lucky to have been under the care of a physician of Dr. Gladstone's caliber. Although his chances for recovery had been slim, Bill had pulled the man through.

This unappreciative patient didn't think so. He complained of a little numbness along the right rib margins. He also wondered if the scars on his chest from the bullet entrance and exit were larger than they needed to be. "I think I should talk to my lawyer," he said.

I can't remember ever previously getting angry at a patient, but this ungrateful scoundrel sent my blood pressure sky high.

"Look, you! If you had been brought to me in the shape you were in I probably would have operated on you and there's a good chance you'd be dead." I was really getting hot under my starched collar. "You should be forever grateful you had a conscientious and skilled physician taking care of you. Now get out of here. If you want to sue someone, sue the person who shot you!"

CHAPTER 20

MANAGEMENT HEADACHES

George Stucky, Medical Director of Ingham Sanatorium, had been a tuberculosis patient himself at Saranac Lake before he recovered and assumed the responsibilities of the Ingham Sanatorium as the first full-time medical director. He was a frank, honest, capable man. He had answered my question as to why he had resigned as medical director at Ingham very simply. "Because there were too many dishes to wash." He was saying that he no longer wanted to handle the stress of the mountainous piles of details.

To me administration was a great challenge—a frontier waiting to be tapped. I felt a little like the tough mountain men who went into unexplored territories, carrying all they owned on their backs. Within them lay their real assets—a determined, adventurous spirit and knowledge of survival; from without—rugged good health and physical endurance.

Without hesitating, I had accepted the responsibility. Like the frontiersmen, I possessed very little, materially, to enter the new territory; but I believed I was a well-trained, competent surgeon. I figured the various departments of the hospital pretty much ran themselves. I could solve the dirty dish-type of problem and get on with overseeing the practice of good medicine and surgery—and especially the preparation of a program of training chest surgeons.

I discovered instantly that a frontier is not what you make it. It is already there; it's harsh and demanding and extends no favors. For awhile it seemed like I had done only one thing right—I had set, as a condition of my acceptance, the privilege of full authority to employ and organize a staff in such a way as to relieve me of managerial details.

My board of trustees came made-to-order. There were five men. (This was 1938, and women did not have the smallest chance of being appointed, even if one had had the courage to apply.) Two of the board members were physicians. The remaining three were businessmen—one of whom had been treasurer of Michigan State College and one who had been Ingham County's clerk. Vacancies occurred, of course, along the way, and I treated the issue of appointments seriously.

At times, I had to advise a new member of the board that if we should weaken and employ a friend or relative, or direct purchases to a member's favorite business, these requests might just go against the aspirant. The device worked. A small victory over the politics of a new territory.

The hospital, in time, gained stature in the local and state medical community and received some national recognition. This was a result of much planning and plain hard work. As a result, a few poorly qualified politically ambitious men, coveting prestige, aggressively sought access to the board of trustees. The County Board of Supervisors controlled these appointments and sometimes voted in men of such low ethical caliber that in defense I became an amateur detective. Occasionally, when my "research" turned up a weak and/or questionable character, I could head him off by finding a strong effective businessman or physician to accept this volunteer job, then redouble my efforts and try to convince the County Board of Supervisors to see it my way. I had varying successes here but I never gave up.

* * * *

Within a week after I arrived, I saw that I was going to have to use the power I'd asked for in choosing my own

139

staff. While studying hospital records, I found no job description for the assistant superintendent, a woman whose desk was across the hall from my office. After glancing up a few times to see her working on her fingernails, I checked again. Still no duties described anywhere for an assistant.

I was also concerned about the performance of the superintendent of nurses. I knew in the past several days the "super" had made an honest attempt to carry out my orders. But the idea of change seemed to render her ineffective. She appeared nervous, fluttery, and commanded no respect from her nurses.

Feeling like the villian in a Dicken's novel, I talked to each of the two ladies on the same day. I said, to the lady who was called assistant superintendent, as delicately as I knew how, "There is nothing for you to do. Your title is assistant superintendent but there is no one called superintendent of the hospital, so whom do you assist?"

"I haven't been feeling well lately, Dr. Stringer," she said quickly. "You'll have my resignation today."

I nodded and mumbled something about official forms and walked to the superintendent of nurse's office.

"The work is more than you can handle," I said, hoping I sounded reasonable. "I believe you could do well on general floor duty and be rid of the administrative and employee problems."

"That would be a demotion," she said. "I don't want that, Dr. Stringer."

"But you obviously aren't happy and I'm not satisfied with the management of the nursing staff. I'm afraid you'll have to make a choice."

She glanced away from me and jammed her hands into the pockets of her white uniform. "Then I guess I'll have to resign."

"I hope you'll find what you want elsewhere," I said. I wasn't feeling very proud of myself.

* * * *

I could have saved my empathy. Within the hour, the president of the board of trustees was in my office protesting the changes. (Jacob Schepers and his wife, I discovered later, were frequent hosts of these two women at his cottage up north.)

I was surprised at his attitude. I had figured him, in the short term of our acquaintance, to be a quiet man who relished his small political conquests. He'd been president of the board for several years and, as I was beginning to find out, he was active in other facets of my job. He practically ran the hospital. So I guess I shouldn't have been surprised.

"I'll have to remind you," I told him, after he had asked for an accounting of my actions, "that the board agreed to abide by my selection of staff." I stared at this man who had been in power long before I came into the picture. Would he challenge me?

Without another word, he rose, nodded and left the room. I had the feeling he was vastly relieved to be off the hook. I heard nothing more from the two women.

Several months later the daughter of one of Jacob Scheper's fellow supervisors graduated from nurse's training.

Mr. Schepers was most polite when he asked me to hire her.

"Remember, Jake, that if we can find a place for her she'll be on a trial basis just like anyone else."

"Yes," he smiled, "I know."

Kay Purdy, the new director of nurses, did hire this young woman, Mary Wood, and she became one of the best nurses we ever had. When she later married and moved to Missouri, we hated to see her go.

Jacob Schepers resigned when the time came for the hospital's physical plant to be extensively enlarged and modernized.

I was unprepared for the letter and drove to his home in East Lansing to get a personal reply for his unexpected action. Jake and I had not always been in agreement but it was an amiable relationship. I didn't like the thought of losing his experience.

"You are going too fast for me," he said simply. "I can't handle that much change in such a short time."

I was greatly complimented and we remained good friends until his death.

* * * *

Well-trained, conscientious hospital business administrators, even now, are a rarity. In the 30's they had not entered my frontier. My perception of them, then, was that they had often been pre-medical students (male, of course) who had not been admitted to or hadn't graduated from medical school and had drifted into hospital management as a way of staying on the fringes of medicine. I had carefully and quietly tracked down and hired a no-nonsense director of nursing, a chief dietician, a chief engineer, a head of housekeeping, and a director of out-patient services. I saved the most crucial position for last—a business manager.

There weren't any hospital business managers in the Lansing area. When Cal Staley (I will call him) applied, I took a chance and hired him. He had been an accountant at the Oldsmobile Plant and although he wasn't specifically qualified to take over day-to-day hospital operation, he appeared to be capable of keeping financial books. I hoped to expose him to hospital management in some on-the-job training and eventually have him take over the non-medical operation of the hospital.

What a dreamer I was. The more I tried to give Cal these day-to-day operational responsibilities, the more he botched. And he did try hard. He tried so hard that he became progressively anxious and I had the uneasy hunch that often he was surprised by his own actions. Certainly he kept me in an agitated state—like an explorer who finds himself teamed up with a tenderfoot who's not sure how to use a compass.

Cal saved himself by managing to carry out my specific orders. I needed more than that—but with the market for business managers devoid of all good personnel, I resigned myself to a continued state of wariness.

When we were building the new and expanded surgical wing, I ordered a filing rack for blueprints to be placed in

142

Cal's office. Apparently, these prints terrified him. He avoided them and had to be coaxed into pulling a print from the file. So gingerly did he handle them, I half expected the prints to break into a blue flame.

Another administrative headache came in the person of one builder whom I shall call Jack. When we opened the construction bids, the hospital board felt duty bound to accept the lowest bid. What a mistake that was!

Jack started right out skimping on the labor and materials. At one point he tried to justify a long delay by accusing the hospital staff of not supplying the color information for decorating.

"Sir—we have had these specifications for several weeks," his own job foreman interrupted. Jack shrugged and wandered off.

I kept records, my staff kept records, and when Jack submitted his last statement for payment, we had compiled a list of about 50 items which were either not finished or improperly done according to the blueprints and specifications.

"We should not make final payment," I told the board of trustees, "until all is done properly. I would like to withhold $50,000 until the work is done correctly."

The board backed me up. Jack, however, didn't want to go any farther without more money. He called Andrew Langenbacker, a successful Lansing business man and president of the Duplex Truck Manufacturing Company, who had come on the Board two years previously and was by then president of the board.

"I don't believe you can get it until you have completed your work to Dr. Stringer's satisfaction," Andy told him.

Jack slammed down the receiver and high-tailed it to the hospital. He appeared in my office doorway, adamant, but I was also determined. We reviewed the plans and specifications, then toured the actual building from the basement to the top floor of the new wing.

We stepped into the elevator finally, for the trip back to the first floor. As it whined downward, Jack turned to me.

"The trouble with you, Stringer, is that you're a perfectionist."

"And the trouble with you, Jack, is that you're a damn crook."

The elevator stopped and the door opened. "Now, Jack," I said, "I don't want to see you until you've properly finished this job; then you can have the money you haven't earned yet."

He left and eventually finished the job.

* * * *

This episode happened near Christmas time, just before completion of the new units. During these exasperating final days, when Jack was still trying to avoid fulfilling his obligation, he sent a check to me marked "for patient's Christmas fund", and had it delivered on Christmas Day to my home, along with an elaborate silver coffee set.

I was incensed.

"Jim and John," I bellowed. My two oldest boys ran into the hall wearing their what's-the-matter-with-Dad look.

"Rewrap this stuff," I said. "Get the car out and take it to the return address."

Several years later I was chairman of a fund-raising committee to build an infirmary at the Mystic Lake YMCA camp. We sent out solicitation letters to hundreds of people using my signature stamp. Though I didn't know it, Jack's name was among those who received a plea for money. Jack wrote to the YMCA executive secretary, refusing to help, and said:

"I still have a check in my desk that Stringer returned to me."

* * * *

Food rationing during World War II must have driven a goodly number of providers close to mental breakdowns. There were periods I thought I was about to join their ranks. Since the Chest Hospital was public, it was not rationed, but it didn't seem right that so much of my energy should be drained to search out a minimun of red meat, which patients required.

I concluded that it was time for drastic forward action, and after a couple of restless nights I banged into my office, swept the morning's work aside and pulled out a sheet of typing paper. On it I drew a sketch; ideas flew from my pencil. I drew faster and faster, gleefully imagining the prime beefs being aged and packaged and made ready in good quantity for the hospital kitchen. An additional building, attached to the kitchen, emerged on the paper—it contained two walk-in freezers and an aging box—each 10 x 30 feet. There was a loading dock and a carving area.

I phoned Cal Staley and told him my new plan. We'd buy cattle on the hoof in the Lansing area and contract to have it butchered and quartered. We'd do the cutting, wrapping and storing in the new addition I was drawing up.

Cal was flabergasted. "How can we do that!" he exclaimed.

"Come on over and see," I said.

When he arrived, I showed him the hastily drawn lines, smiling a little proudly.

He stood there, just looking at the paper. It apparently intimidated him as much as the blueprints languishing in his office.

"Take it to our architect—tell him what it's supposed to be and that we want quick action," I said. "If he dilly-dallies, ask Ralph Hagermeyer (our contractor) to come directly to me and I'll deal personally with him."

Cal straightened up and followed orders. The following day Ralph materialized and Cal took him over to the kitchen building. Presently, they returned with my sketch. Ralph tapped the paper.

"This is all we need. When do you want it completed?"

"Directly," I said. "Can you give me a ballpark-cost figure?"

At my house that night, Ralph showed me some hastily drawn sketches and first-guess figures. The next day his crew moved supplies to the hospitals grounds to begin construction. In six weeks—a record, I believe during those war years—the building was done, cooling units installed, and a curing box ready for use. Ralph must certainly have had to borrow materials and labor from his other construction sites.

Gratified, I went with Cal and Ralph to inspect the final product. I thought it was sublime. We veered back toward the main building, and grinning, I turned to Cal. "Now go out and buy 20 head of beef and fill up the curing box. Start right now."

Cal stopped dead. He looked pained.

"How do I do that, Dr. Stringer?"

My delight evaporated.

"Go on back to your office," I said. "I'll call you in a few minutes." Yet, I didn't know anything about beef cattle. How could I expect him to?

Inside, at my desk, I phoned a contract butcher in East Lansing named Van Alstine. I didn't know him but I suspected he'd be knowledgeable. Van Alstine was able to give me names and addresses of four or five beef cattle feeders in the Lansing area. I picked up my coat and headed for Cal's office.

I hadn't warned any of the cattle feeders we were coming, and the first farmer was suspicious. He asked if we were from Detroit.

"No," I said. "We want to buy for our hospital and we are prohibited from paying a black market price. Will that make a difference to you?"

For an answer he led us to his feed lot. We all clambered to the top rail of the fence, sat, and looked over the beasts. "Those trucks over there," he indicated several vehicles going by on the road, "are Detroit buyers. They pay premium prices." He looked at me knowingly. But by the time we departed he had sold us ten of his prize steers. At the next two places we repeated the process—buying five steers from each.

Triumphant, we swung by Van Alstine's slaughterhouse and arranged with him to pick up the cattle, butcher, quarter and deliver them to our new loading dock.

Van Alstine completed everything the next day. By nightfall, we had 20 head of prime beef curing. I hired a meat cutter, part-time, for when the meat was aged properly and frozen. He then carved it into proper sections with an electric band saw, wrapped and identified each section and returned it to a freezer. That was the beginning of the freezers and aging box being put into constant use. Food service people loved me—they were preparing about 1,000 meals a day and now there would be no worry about meat in meal planning.

* * * *

"Good Grief!" Dr. Harold Miller, the secretary of the board of trustees sat at the mahogany table, holding the vouchers for the new construction and the meat to fill the boxes.

We glanced up, our eyes met and I grimaced. Neither of us said anything. We had all just had a superb steak lunch.

* * * *

Gradually, I was able to delegate most of the housekeeping responsibilities. Cal improved in his abilities but I always had to work around him. I used to wish desperately he would initiate action, any action.

Kay Purdy, director of nursing, married and moved away. Mrs. Nissel replaced her and when she retired, she recommended her assistant, Valerie Trapp. I hesitated. Valerie had kept a low profile and I hardly knew her. As a nurse, she was far too heavy and I wondered if she could take the physical stress the job entailed.

But Nissel hung on, bulldog-like, until I gave in and put Valerie on as director. She turned out to be a jewel.

Valerie was quietly competent, strict with her staff but very human. A widow, she ran the nursing department of

147

the entire hospital perfectly without me. Long tedious hours at work did not bother her. Without a husband to care for, she devoted her life to medicine. She also kept a close supervisory eye on the housekeeping department.

* * * *

The bright new wing opened, sparkling and blessedly cool as the humid Michigan summer's heat set in. We hummed along, operating on patient after patient. No more delays; we handled a greater surgical load with efficiency and safety. We were a happy surgical staff.

We had two weeks of pride and peace of mind before it happened; many incisions on recent surgical cases became infected! We had to open and drain these post-operative cases, and it was a painful drawn-out procedure for the patients, who should have been well into recovery. Daily, the staff had to monitor the continued occurrence of infections and change the dressings. It placed an enormous demand on the surgical staff.

One of the infected cases was the wife of a prominent Lansing internist. But she, as well as all the others, never complained. We told these patients of our shock at these unforeseen post-surgical consequences and that we were doing all possible to track down the source. The patients were wonderful. They could have sued the staff and the hospital—but they didn't. An attorney did approach one of the infected cases, and the patient, disgusted, sent him on his way.

That was a comfort but it didn't solve our mystery.

"It's got something to do with the cooling system," I said at the first hastily called staff meeting. "We all know we have never had an infection problem before."

"Dr. Stringer, that may be so," said one of the surgical residents, "but maybe your mind is set against the state health commissioner because of the specific regulations you had to follow in the construction of the new wing and . . ."

"That is true certainly," I interrupted.

"But some of those health department people out there are 50 years behind the times. However—the problem is on us now. Are there any ideas so we can start looking for the sources of these infections?"

There were several, and we moved to tighten up techniques wherever this could be done.

I still thought there had to be some connection with the cooling system. I talked to the architect and asked him to come to the hospital. He assured me when we met, that there was no way infecting organisms could be delivered to the operating rooms through the air conditioning system he had specified.

"Doctor, how could infection result if we are bringing in 100 percent outside air with a complete change once a minute?"

That remark finally got the truth through to me. Common sense told me that it is physically impossible to properly filter, cool and circulate 100 percent fresh uncontaminated air with a complete change in the operating rooms once a minute!

I called my friend, Don Cummings, the director of the State of Michigan Bureau of Laboratories, and told him that I was concerned about infecting organisms being brought into the operating room through the new air conditioning system.

"What you say makes sense to me," Don said. "But you know what the new Public Health code requires!"

"It is dangerous! The chances are that the people who devised the code have no concept of the impossibility of carrying out the provisions of the code and still deliver properly filtered and conditioned air. The commissioner simply does not understand this and also he does not understand the risks of high velocity air currents in surgical suites."

"Well, it sure sounds that way. What would you like me to do?"

"Send a couple of your people out here with culture material in Petri dishes and plant them through the duct system leading to the operating rooms. Also, place them fore and aft of the air conditioning system and at the outside air intake."

"I will bring them myself and be there this afternoon. I will also ask Irv Cope to come along. I know you will want him."

I certainly did! They arrived and plunged into the problem with gusto, crawling through the duct system with the hospital engineer to place the culture plates. They were marked for location and picked up the following day.

Dr. Cope, using a candle flame, found it would not stay lit over the operating table. A turbulence produced such a draft over the operating tables that it was like operating outdoors on a windy day.

Two days later, Don was back at the hospital, a very concerned man.

"Chris, this is awful. These culture plates are loaded with organisms capable of causing wound infections. The greatest concentration is at the intake where all your fresh air is coming in." (At the time, this didn't impress me as much as it should have, but I would recall it later.)

I sent for the Director of Nursing and told her our findings. I directed the hospital engineer, Harry Westwood, to shut down the air conditioning.

"Don't you think we should talk to the architect and arrange some sort of a corrective program before we discontinue the system?" Harry was seeing the problem, naturally, from engineer's eyes. "It will be easier to find defects if it is running."

"Harry, shut the air conditioning off NOW and lock the door to the control room."

We didn't use the operating rooms the following day but 48 hours later we operated without air conditioning.

We drew up and formalized an extensive remodeling plan for the brand new air conditioning system in our brand new surgical wing.

First, we got rid of the fiber filters and the filter housing on the air conditioner, and installed a huge self-cleaning electrostatic precipitator filter. Fiber glass prefilters were installed at the intake level and behind and in front of the electrostatic filter.

150

Second, we reduced the outside air intake to 40 percent with 60 percent recirculated. This provided for a complete air exchange every three minutes.

Third, we cut the velocity of air over the operating tables to the point where it wouldn't extinguish a candle on the operating table.

Having carried out these extensive alterations, we had a dry run over a weekend with culture plates in strategic places when we were not using the operating rooms.

To our dismay, we had overload problems with the electrostatic filter. We had to have the system rewired.

Then we set about the task of finding out why this expensive piece of equipment should break down. A representative from the American Air Filter Company of Louisville came to Lansing to help.

He noted that fairly large carbon particles were being drawn into the filter precipitating the electrical short. Where were they coming from?

With the factory representative and Don Cummings, we made a tour of the outside of the new building. About 100 feet south of the new wing, we paused and looked back. The incinerator stack was there in front of us. The construction engineer who worked with the architect had insisted that material placed in the incinerator would be promptly incinerated and all bacteria destroyed. I never did believe this. In fact, the draft through the stack propelled contaminated material out through the stack before incineration took place.

This didn't bother me so much, however, since it was well toward the back of the building and on the south, but when I looked up again, I saw the intake for the air conditioning system was NOT 20 FEET FROM THE INCINERATOR STACK! How could I have been so blind as to miss this! This thing had been placed in a position where it couldn't possibly do more harm.

The reason for the excessive growth of the bacteria on the culture plates in this location was obvious. Back in my office I couldn't locate the architect so I called the contractor. I could not have been more angry. He protested that he had finished the job.

"You will move the air intake to the other side of the building and do it promptly or this community is going to know just how much suffering you have caused and how much it has cost to correct your mistakes."

He moved it.

When this was done, we had another dry run. No organisms, no short outs. No failures of any kind.

We restarted the air conditioning on a Sunday and on Monday we were again working under comfortable conditions. Infections ceased.

We had won after being very close to losing. More importantly, all the patients who had become infected recovered.

I wrote a report evaluating our experiences and made it available to hospitals considering surgical air conditioning.

I felt like a pioneer in a territory where the animals, tiny as they were, had almost driven us out.

CHAPTER 21

ENDOSCOPY

A part of my chest surgery training, when I started practicing in Lansing, had been in using bronchoscopes and esophagoscopes.

It was then a new procedure. While I was in training, the examination, treatment, and removal of foreign bodies had just been perfected by an otolaryngologist, Cheveler Jackson of Philadelphia.

A bronchoscope is an odd-looking instrument—an invention which is slipped cautiously down the throat into the large bronchial tubes of the lung. It measures from 11 to 16 inches long, made of chrome-plated brass. The lumen of the tubes are from three to nine millimeters in diameter and mirrors are arranged within it. There is a lightbulb about the size of a grain of wheat in a recess on the far end. I had learned to use the attachments—forceps and cutting instruments—introduced through the channel of the scope to the bronchi that made the bronchoscope so valuable. I came to prefer the Broyles instruments because they have more and varied attachments, and a right angle and a retrograde lens system.

There was a real rhubarb in some of the medical centers about whether bronchoscopies and esophagoscopies should be done by chest surgeons or throat specialists. In Lansing, the only other doctor trained and equipped to do chest endoscopy was Dr. Oliver McGillicuddy, an otolaryngologist.

Since the procedure was quite spectacular, even dramatic, it received attention from the media. Often the story was accompanied by a picture of the patient and the doctor and the foreign body which had been removed. Sometimes the extracted object was a piece of toy, which had to be cut in pieces before it could be brought up. I was the only person in the area who owned a cutting instrument for this purpose, so I removed toy fragments from many children.

The peanut is the most dangerous foreign body, particularly in children where it might not be diagnosed early and removed. The peanut for all its wonderful nutritive quality, is deadly when it is sucked into the lung. It breaks down and produces an oil which is very irritating to the tissue of the bronchial walls. These walls swell, close the opening and collapse that section of the lung. Pneumonia and abscess results. Sometimes the chest has to be opened and the lung lobe removed. I often told Ruth if she left peanuts where one of our boys could get to them and aspirated one, I would bronchoscope her instead of the child!

Safety pins are tricky. They lodge nearly always in the bronchus, open, with the point up. They must be pulled out by impinging the point of the pin on the illiptical end of the instrument. The pin can then be removed by grasping the head with a forceps. Sometimes the pin can be closed with an instrument designed for this purpose, then safely removed. If this isn't possible, the point of the pin must be cut off and the two pieces removed separately.

For a short time in my career, Ruth and I enjoyed some precious days at a cottage near Cadillac, Michigan. Both of us were becoming exhausted—Ruth from the demands of the children at home and I from being so slow to learn how to say "no". It seemed at times I lived in the operating room.

During World War II we were fortunate to have for a friend, a grateful former patient, who was ever ready to help us make the most of those days at the cottage. He lived in Cadillac, and all I had to do to find the cabin opened, aired, and a fire burning in the fireplace, was to phone him and say when we were to arrive.

This particular weekend Mitchell Lake had never looked so inviting. We climbed out of the car, stretched, and trundled in with our luggage, enjoying the familiar, fresh, musky smell of the pines and sweet fern. Inside, a fire glowed. We let unpacking wait.

We had revelled in the quiet and peacefulness only a few minutes when we heard a police siren. Ruth and I looked at each other and froze. Before the patrol car's flashing light had invaded our little hideaway, I opened the door. A young state trooper jogged up the porch steps.

"Your hospital called," he said. "You're needed back in Lansing.'"

I thanked him and turned to Ruth. Her face was tight and she looked away from me.

"It may not be urgent, honey," I said hopefully. "But I'll throw the luggage back in the car just in case. We can drive to the police post and call the hospital from there."

We sped in silence to the square brick building outside of town and I hurried inside. The officer on duty dialed for me.

The case was indeed critical—a six year old boy had a nickel lodged in the trachea. He could hardly breathe and was cyanotic. The only other doctor who could have handled such a case had been called to military service. That left me with no choice and no time to waste.

"I have a patrol car available, if you'd like transportation," the captain on duty offered.

"I think I can make better time myself," I said. "I've got a state police courtesy card. Thanks anyway."

We careened out to Highway 27 South going half again as fast as when we had traveled the same route coming north. As the speedometer crept higher, Ruth saw we'd lost another small battle for rest and relaxation.

"It seems to me," she quipped, "you're going mighty fast to get some place to operate for a nickel."

Back in Lansing, I saw the little fellow was in grave

trouble. His parents and many brothers and sisters waited silently in the anteroom of the hospital. They were Mexican migrants, from the central Michigan produce fields.

We began by anesthetizing the child. With him in a propped up position, I eased a child's five millimeter bronchoscope between his vocal cords. There, just below the cords, almost horizontal and not quite blocking the airway, was the nickel.

I was able to rotate and grasp the coin with forceps, but I had to be extremely careful not to damage the vocal cords; for the bronchoscope, along with the forceps and coin, all had to be withdrawn at the same time, since the coin was too large to be brought up through the bronchoscope. I laid the apparatus, along with the deadly nickel, on the table.

Instantly, the child began to breathe well and the dark little face brightened.

I went directly to the waiting room and told the parents I had removed the coin and that their son would be fine. The room erupted in smiles and rapid Spanish. The father clutched my arm.

"What did you do with the nickel?"

I reached in my pocket and gave him a nickel. I was never to hear from the family again.

Fate, it seemed, was going to make good use of my lost vacation time. While I operated on the little Chicano, a nurse came in with a message from Dr. Mike Sharpe, who was working in a nearby operating room, that he needed me as soon as I was free.

That was an understatement. His patient, a woman having an emergency operation, had not had the indicated preparation. (This included fasting for twelve hours, which obviously hadn't been possible.) During the induction of the anesthesia, she regurgitated a recent meal and aspirated most of the undigested food into her lungs.

The anesthesiologist had brought up some of the material from the lung through an intratracheal tube, but he had no way of knowing if he had gotten all of it.

Dr. Sharpe filled me in on the the details as I prepared to

bronchoscope his patient. I used an eight millimeter bronchoscope and passed it between the vocal cords into the trachea of the unfortunate patient. I saw nothing there, but in the right and left main bronchi I saw several large pieces of undigested carrot, more than an inch long and completely obstructing the left lower lobe bronchus. With the forceps I was able to remove the carrot pieces, but I left the bronchoscope and light in place and inspected the entire bronchial tree. All was well; I withdrew the instrument.

"You can get on with your surgery, Mike," I said.

I left the hospital and drove home in the cool, quiet darkness. Ruth had preceded me to bed several hours before. I was exhausted. I had driven to Cadillac and back and done two cases since late afternoon. I ate a snack and fell into bed.

But not for long. Dr. Dan Carrothers phoned me from the Hayes-Green-Beach Hospital in Charlotte, Michigan.

In a fog of fatigue I heard Dan's voice saying something about a foreign object in a boy. Propping myself up in bed, I blinked and tried to orient myself. Yes, I was home and in my own room. But I had just done a little boy and a foreign object. Or did he say appendicitis?

"Dan, did you say you need a bronchoscopy? I thought I just heard appendicitis mentioned."

"Yes—I'm sorry, it is late, isn't it? Well, Chris, the boy is 12 years old, terribly undernourished; parents say he's been a feeding problem all his life. But I'm sure he has appendicitis. We took a flat plate of the abdomen, which included enough of the chest to show a round opaque object which appears to be in the trachea."

"Is there a history of aspiration of such a foreign body?"

"The parents say no."

"Did the boy have a shirt on or any article of clothing, or was there a sheet covering him that might have some article on it? Such an object could show opaque on the x-ray and would look like it were inside the boy's chest."

I paused, hoping that he'd say yes to one of the possibilities and I wouldn't have to stagger around and dress to drive the 20 miles to Charlotte. It was close to dawn.

"No," Dan said, "I'm sure the thing is in his chest. Don't you want to come over?"

"Not particularly," I said. "But I doubt the thing is in the boy's trachea. Get a lateral x-ray of the chest and if you are reasonably sure he has appendicitis, give him a general anesthetic, operate and I'll be there by the time you get through."

It was a tiresome, lonely drive in the summer darkness. When I arrived, the x-rays were ready. As I guessed, the object was not in the trachea but in the esophagus. This was dangerous—a foreign body can readily erode through the esophageal wall but is unlikely to break through the tracheal wall.

Also, removing the foreign body through an esophoscope can very well cause a surgical tear through the wall, which nearly always brings on an abscess.

My other option would be operate, expose the esophagus, incise it, remove the offending object and suture the wall of the esophagus back together.

I elected to look into the esophagus to see if the object were wedged into the wall and if so, back out and open through the chest.

The frail little boy was still unconscious with ether anesthesia, and its heavy, sweetish odor pervaded the operating room. As tired as I was, it wouldn't have taken much more to put me out.

I forced myself to move more deliberately. Introducing the esophagoscope into the lumen of the boy's esophagus, I pushed it slowly, about a third of the distance of the length of the esophagus. The lighted edge of the instrument came against something metallic. The far edge of this "something" appeared to be embedded in the wall, but the closer edge floated free. I grasped this edge between the jaws of my forceps and gently rocked it back and forth. This was a critical moment. I was working through a 12 inch-long tube in a field only seven millimeters wide—and part of that field was occupied by the forceps. In grasping the foreign body, I had to be extremely careful not to snare any part of the esophageal inner wall. If this episode of swallowing the

158

coin had been a recent accident, there would be no anxiety, since the object couldn't have had time to become embedded in the tissue. I did not have that safety.

I steadied my hands and delicately rocked the object again. Suddenly, it floated free and I inched the esophagoscope along with the foreign object up and out. I saw a coin, eroded and encrusted with secretions. It was a nickel!

There was no time for marveling. I had to reintroduce the esophagoscope and check to see if there was any damage to the esophagus from either the coin or my treatment.

It looked good in there—but if it hadn't, I would have had to open the chest and repair any damage.

The child's post-operative condition was fine. He was wheeled away to begin a new life of breathing and eating normally.

I turned to Dan, who was looking vastly relieved.

"Let's talk to the boy's parents," I said. "There's a bit of a mystery here."

"Good idea," he said, stripping off his surgical gloves and gown.

In the waiting room, we quizzed the happy parents. They were farm people and, after many questions, we got to the bottom. When the boy had been five or six years old, he had several coins in his mouth that he'd been playing with. The mother thought he had spat them all out when he choked. Later, however, he began to have periodic difficulty swallowing food. Other times, he could eat normally. Apparently, the coin had moved about in the esophagus. When it was on edge, food would bypass it. When it lay flat, it obstructed the passage of food.

The next morning Ruth teased.

"That was some weekend. Instead of a romantic interlude up north, you operate on three people for two nickels and a carrot."

I saw Dr. Carrothers six months later. He reported that the 70 pound boy had gained 40 pounds and now was normal.

"I drilled a hole in the nickel," Dan laughed. "I have it on my key chain."

Peanuts, pieces of toys, coins and many other items small enough to swallow or aspirate are foreign objects when they are found in the tracheobronchial tree and esophagus.

Certainly, one of the most difficult and often exasperating problems in endoscopy is the bronchoscopic removal of a straight sewing needle from the bronchial tree. It is also a potentially dangerous foreign body since the needle can and often does migrate into the lung. It is not safe there, like other foreign bodies such as bullets, which tend to anchor themselves, because the needle can continue to migrate.

Even when the needle is located and visualized in the bronchus, it is more difficult to grasp with foreign body forceps. Because of the absence of a head on the needle, it tends to slip out of the jaws of the forceps. A pin is less likely to migrate because it has a head and it can also be more easily grasped.

A call from Dr. Wall in Mt. Pleasant presented such a problem. He had a prominent, middle-aged Mt. Pleasant lady in his office who had come in that afternoon. She said she had been sewing and was wetting the end of the thread, preparatory to putting it through the eye of the needle when she coughed, inhaled deeply, and aspirated the needle into her windpipe.

X-rays at Community Hospital in Mt. Pleasant revealed the needle in the left lower lung field, which would mean it was out in the secondary bronchial area and very probably beyond the reach of a foreign body forceps. If this should be the case, and if the needle were in a location considered to be dangerous, major surgery to open the bronchus and remove the foreign body might be necessary.

I sometimes used an instrument with a magnet attached to the end to extract this type of foreign body. When this worked, it was spectacular, but if the foreign body had become impinged against the bronchial wall, as it is likely to do, the magnet does not work.

Dr. Wall asked if I could come to Mt. Pleasant to do the indicated bronchoscopy in the hope that the needle could be easily extracted. I couldn't get away that day. My own patients in Lansing required attention. Some of them were more seriously ill than the patient in Mt. Pleasant and the round trip to Mt. Pleasant and return to the Chest Hospital would be about 150 miles. This would require about three hours in addition to the time needed to do the surgery. If the patient needed something more than bronchoscopy, she would have to be transferred anyway.

I suggested that the lady be sedated and sent down by ambulance to avoid as much movement of the chest as possible and thus reduce the chances of migration. This was done and the patient arrived at the Chest Hospital by ambulance in about two hours.

Surgery had been alerted and all was ready for whatever we needed to do. After she was properly admitted, Dr. John Summers, the surgical resident, took a brief history. This revealed only one bit of additional information. The patient complained of intermittent sharp pain in the left lower chest. This didn't impress me too much. There are no sensory nerves in the inner bronchial wall but the needle could have traversed the bronchial wall. I told the resident to send the patient down to x-ray.

"Dr. Stringer, x-rays were sent down with the patient and they are good diagnostic films," he said. "The needle is there all right in the left lower lung field."

"I know, John, but we should find out if it has changed position during the trip from Mt. Pleasant."

Additional anterior-posterior and oblique films were obtained and I asked that the patient be kept in x-ray until the x-rays were processed and I could compare them with the Mt. Pleasant films.

The needle was there and it apparently had not moved. It was certainly well out in the lung field and the chances of removing it bronchoscopically were remote. This concerned me. How could the needle travel so fast? I was puzzled.

It must have seemed to Dr. Summers that I was procrastinating. After all, he had other work to do.

"Dr. Stringer," he said, "should we take the patient on up to surgery and get going?"

What he said made sense, of course.

"No, not yet, I want to fluoroscope her. Push the stretcher up back of the fluoroscopic screen."

"The x-rays . . ." Then he gave up, humoring the old man.

When the patient was positioned, sitting up behind the fluoroscopic screen and facing me, we waited for our eyes to adjust to the darkened room.

The view through the fluoroscope revealed the long sharp needle in the same position. I commented on this and the resident said, "Well, we really wouldn't expect it to move since the last x-ray was taken just a few minutes ago." I could sense that the resident (a real sharp physician) and the x-ray technician and the nurse and even the patient were all becoming a little testy with my hesitancy to do what had to be done.

I had already told the patient's husband and her daughter that bronchoscopy might be only the first step in removing the pesky needle.

While still fluoroscoping the patient, I wanted a little clearer visualization of the left lower lung field. The patient had rather large breasts overlying the lower lung. The fluoroscopy of the area was clear enough but nevertheless, I wanted the breast shadow out of the way, so while looking through the fluoroscope, I reached back of the screen and with my right hand lifted up the left breast.

The needle suddenly moved and fell out from beneath the breast onto the stretcher!

I asked for the lights, picked the needle off the cart and handed it to the nurse. "My gosh—," she marveled. "Magic surgery—and in the dark!"

Everyone just stood there with their mouths open until the resident said, "I'll be damned."

The nurse took my patient (almost my patient) to her room. She dressed and the family drove off laughing, with the needle in her handbag.

The needle had fallen out instead of in, and landed inside the lady's blouse and on down beneath the breast. The next time a female patient complained of lateral chest pain after supposedly aspirating a needle or anything else, I looked under the breast first.

I called Dr. Wall and related the story to him.

"Don't you dare tell that story in Mt. Pleasant," he pleaded.

CHAPTER 22

TELEPHONE OPERATION

"Chris—this is Bill Alexander in Iron Mountain. I have a patient with an intractable hiccup, which has persisted for four days. I tried everything I know with no response."

Oh, oh, I thought. Ten to one the patient was not young. Persistent hiccups in older persons sometimes results in exhaustion and even death.

"I've heard that diaphragm paralysis will often stop the hiccup," he continued. "Now, I talked with the family and we'd like you to fly up here. Bring whatever you think necessary. The family is well-to-do and can afford your fee. Maybe it'll make up for all the cases you've done for me and didn't get anything."

"Bill, there is no way I can leave Lansing now," I said regretfully. "I have a fully-booked surgical schedule the entire week and some of the cases are urgent. Do you want to send the patient down?"

"The lady is elderly."

I almost smiled as I congratulated myself on winning the unspoken bet. Bill's voice was professional but sympathetic as he went on.

"She is already exhausted and I just don't believe she could make the trip."

"Then I guess you will have to do the surgery yourself."

"Stop clowning, Chris."

"I'm serious. Can you get an extension phone into the operating room?"

I had an idea for Bill's problem. He might not want to try, but I could maybe intimidate him into cooperating.

"Yes, what are you trying to tell me?" He was wary.

"To get the patient ready," I said impatiently. The details tumbled out.

"Prep the left side of the neck—remember—the left. It will do no good to paralyze the right diaphragm."

I heard a sigh on the other side of the telephone. That Iron Mountain Hospital operating room had probably never seemed as uninviting to the eminent general surgeon Alexander.

"Get an Anson or Piersol anatomy text and open it to the neck section. Put the book on a stool beside you where you can refer to it while operating."

I went on to dictate a list of surgical instruments he would have to gather.

" . . . And you'll need Stringer retractors," I finished. "If you don't have these, I left a set at Pinecrest—send a courier out there for them."

"Who else should I have in attendance?"

"A physician or nurse assistant, a scrub nurse and an aide to hold the phone while I tell you how to do the operation."

"OK. I'll order the surgery set up."

"Good, I'll expect you to be ready in about an hour and a half. Call me then."

"All right, but Chris, I don't like it."

"Do you have a better suggestion?"

"No."

"Well then, I will have a telephone line open for your call."

* * * *

Two hours later a nurse who was to handle the phone called back and reported that Dr. Alexander was ready. But the only anatomy text they had was a Muller.

165

"Hold on, nurse, I have to locate a Muller."

The medical library was across the hall from my office. Good, the text was where it should be. I picked up the receiver.

I told her the page number. "Put it on the stool to Dr. Alexander's right. Now—hold the phone to his left ear and keep it there."

I closed my eyes and imagined the drama which was taking place 500 miles north in the little hospital. I spoke slowly.

"Bill, infiltrate the surgical area about a half an inch above the left clavicle . . . directly over the scalenus anticus muscle. This will be about midway along the clavicle. Now use a #11 blade and make an incision one and one-half inches long and one-half inch above the clavicle."

I studied the anatomy yet my eyes weren't seeing it. I saw the incision, the muscles, the blood of this brave little old lady, anesthesized only locally.

I tried to remember to direct Bill's moves slowly, recalling my own trepidation when I cut into new anatomy.

"Done," he grunted at each step, and I pushed on in what I hoped was a steady, supportive manner.

"Look, Chris, there is a hell of a lot of anatomy in that area of the neck."

"Yes, I know, but you are directing your attention to just one small area. That's the reason I limited your incision to an inch and a half so that you won't get lost in the morass of other anatomy. And remember, your patient is awake."

"Oh."

I continued talking him through the many procedures and he followed well. I could imagine the floating nurse wiping the perspiration from his face.

" . . . you are just lateral to the internal jugular vein now—but to be sure you're exactly where you should be, put your right index finger into the incision and onto the muscle. Ask the patient to raise her head slightly from the operating table. If you have your finger on the scalenus anticus, you can feel this msucle under tension as the patient raises her head."

"It seems to be the one," he said. "There is a large pulsating vessel in the lower part of the incision and another smaller artery crossing the mid-section of the muscle."

"The lower one is the subclavian and the smaller vessels crossing the belly of the muscle are the transverse cervical artery and vein." I went on to tell him how to retract these vessels and get them out of the way.

"I am looking. Yes! Yes! It starts a little higher than I thought it would."

We had now identified the phrenic nerve—the objective of the operation.

"Now, to be certain you have the phrenic nerve, press it lightly in the jaws of the hemostat. Ask the patient if this produces a pain in the back of the shoulder."

I could feel myself tensing; if Bill were off, even slightly, we were in trouble. Back-tracking and exploring the area could be dangerous.

I heard a rustling—voices muted in a brief exchange.

"Yes, she says it did hurt the back of the shoulder."

"You have the phrenic nerve. Now, inject this nerve with your one percent novocain. Have the floating nurse put the palm of her hand on the patient's left upper abdomen."

I waited a moment.

"Ready, Chris."

"All right. Now crush the nerve for two widths of the hemostat. The nurse should be able to feel the jump of the diaphragm through the abdominal wall."

Again I waited. This time the only sound I heard was Bill's slow exhalation.

"Done. Say, the patient isn't hiccupping any more." There was just a little pride in his voice.

"Well, you're the one who suggested a phrenic nerve interruption. Close the incision and I'll see you next month," I said.

CHAPTER 23

WALTER, GLADYS AND THE BLOOD BANK

The beginnings of Lansing's Blood Bank were so humble, I wonder now how long it would have taken to set up such a bank if it hadn't been for Walter Ammerman. Walter is a genuine hero and his story should be told.

The trouble was, as I began to write this chapter, I couldn't remember his name. And the more I grappled with my memory, the more it eluded me. I knew for sure that he had been a member of the Fraternal Order of Eagles. I grabbed the phone and called the Eagles Lodge.

Walter Ammerman answered the phone. After being out of touch for 36 years, I found him on the first try.

"You're the one I'm looking for! Yes—Walter," I exclaimed. "This is Chris Stringer."

"Dr. Stringer?" He was incredulous.

"Walter, there's a lot about the organization of the blood bank I don't know. I need details—can you help me?"

With my coauthor we met for lunch and he filled us in on much I'd not even been aware of. I had been busy using the donors, with appreciation, of course. But it had been Walter who conceived the idea of marshalling blood donors, typing their blood and cataloging the types for ready reference in times of need. So far as I know this was the first time in the U.S. or any where else that a walking live blood bank had been formally organized and implemented. At that time there was no way to store blood or fractionate the elements. Hospitals obtained blood from anybody willing to donate. Usually someone from within a patient's family or friends came forward.

Walter, as an active member of #1039 Fraternal Order of the Eagles in Lansing, had cast around and found a few blood donors within the lodge. He talked the organization into financing the cost of blood typing, and they necessarily used a private laboratory paid for by the Eagles. But the plan was loosely organized. Walter saw the immense potential and chafed at the bit when the hospitals would not keep records or follow-up on the donors he provided.

When Walter visited me at the Chest Hospital with his idea of cataloging blood types of volunteers, my ears perked up. Blood procurement was a terrible problem, particularly in emergent situations. This humble man's offer of himself, his lodge and his friends just might work. If it did, it would be a lifesaver for our patients, and a boon for me and other area surgeons.

During these early World War II years, blood had to be typed and crossmatched, and sometimes, the patient died before the right blood could be found.

"I am sure I can recruit the people you need as donors under ordinary cirumstances before emergencies arise," Walter said.

He sat before me, a medium-sized man, his brown hair stubbly in a crew cut. Behind his glasses, his deepset eyes were alive and observant.

"Then if you will have them typed and whatever else you must do before accepting them," he said, "—and if I can have these records, my wife, Gladys, and I will set up a cross file in our home."

I was impressed.

"Would you be readily available?" I asked. "People often need blood at odd times."

"We'll be on call 24 hours a day. You only have to call for the blood type and I will see that the donor gets to the hospital immediately. When I'm working, Gladys will handle the calls."

Walter was a supervisor on the production line at Motor Wheel Corporation.

"You've got something there, Mr. Ammerman," I said. "It's never been done before, but it's worth a try. I'll have to speak to my staff and the people at the other hospitals—and the lab. I'll get back to you."

I asked for a meeting with the administrators of the two general hospitals in Lansing and with Walter beside me we presented the idea. I had qualms, even though my inner feeling was that something really good was about to happen. But I'd been an administrator long enough to know there were sure to be pitfalls along the way. After all, Walter wasn't a medical person—he was just your man-on-the-street who recognized a critical need and wanted to help. And he had conviction and enthusiasm.

"I need the hospitals to give me a framework to build on," he said.

We met with Glen Fausey, Sparrow Hospital administrator, and Sister Mary Josephine, Administrator of St. Lawrence Hospital.

I briefly outlined the new concept, and brought up the problems inherent in such an undertaking.

"There is the matter of a hospital fee for administering the blood. What do you think, Walter, would be a fair charge for handling the transfusions?" I intentionally directed this question to Walter since I knew that my presenting it to one of the hospital administrators would precipitate an argument and endanger the proposal.

"I guess about $5.00 should cover it," Walter said.

Glen Fausey shook his head, "It can't be done."

Sister Mary Josephine smiled sweetly, "Yes, it can, gentlemen."

I thought I would have an argument but Fausey said nothing more.

"Well, Walter, you and I and Sister think it is possible. That's three to one. Now let's see if Don Cummings over at the Michigan State Laboratory will come in on this. If the project succeeds we will certainly need massive laboratory input.

Don came to my office at once and agreed that the lab could and would type all the prospective donors. Walter, speaking for himself and Gladys, who was to become a valued member of the blood team, took on the responsibility of persuading hundreds of people to report to the Chest Hospital.

There, my residents took a brief history, did a physical exam and ordered x-rays on these volunteers. At first I accepted only males between the ages 21 and 50, but when the women and others over 50 pointed out my silly prejudice, I included them.

Blood samples were drawn, labeled and sent to the lab. When the reports returned, these were attached to the history and physical exam data. The lab reports included only a Kahn test for V.D., a red blood cell count, and a hemoglobin and blood type.

Surprisingly, there were very few rejections. Some volunteers, assuming they were free of disease, learned they were not, and were referred to their own physicians for treatment.

Walter and Gladys Ammerman entered the drama at this point. The Chest Hospital made duplicate records of the volunteers and sent them a set. Walter then cataloged them by blood type, name, address, section of the city or environs, age, and sex. They maintained a "stable" of 1,800 people who were ready to give blood.

Walter was able to get the full cooperation of his employer, the Motor Wheel Corp., who transported the employees who were willing to give blood to the laboratory or to the Chest Hospital for typing. In time, as a result of Walter's pleading, other groups came into the program, including the Odd Fellows, Masons, V.F.W., and American Legion.

The Chest Hospital used these fine citizens as a source of blood for transfusions more than the other two hospitals, since our work was mostly major surgery and demanded more blood replacement. Often we called Walter's home in the middle of the night. Either Walter or Gladys would refer to their files and match our needs with the proper donor. They'd contact the donor, who sometimes had no immediate transportation. In these instances, one or both of the Ammermans would drive out and take the donor to the hospital, wait while the blood was being drawn, then deliver the donor back home.

During these times, I operated on a gun-shot patient with damage to the heart. We used 15 units of blood during surgery and two more the following day. The Ammermans and volunteers were busy people for an action-packed 18 hour period.

In 50 years of surgery, nothing has given me more reason to be proud than the work of Walter and Gladys Ammerman and their friends in the Fraternal Order of Eagles and the other groups and individuals they recruited.

Recognition or pay was never an issue with them. Because of these good people, many others lived out a full natural life who would have otherwise died.

Since the beginning, medical science, of course, progressed. We learned how to safely bank and later to fractionate blood. The Chest Hospital was the first hospital in the area to operate its own blood bank, and was highly successful.

In time, the American Red Cross contacted me for information about the flourishing program. An ad hoc committee of five invited the Red Cross to send a representative to meet with us. He came and saw the successful program.

Eventually, the Red Cross did come in and establish a regional blood bank. Walter and "The Eagles" were the main factors in keeping the program alive and extending its scope. They were greatly encouraged by Judge Robert W. Hansen, Grand Worthy President of the Eagles, who urged enlargement of the Walking Blood Bank, and later warmly supported the Stored Blood Bank.

Walter Ammerman and his friends in the Fraternal Order of Eagles have continued their interest and still recruit donors for the regional bank. Parades and conventions all over Michigan and the United States have proved to be first rate donor-getters.

In a recent discussion, Walter, now 82 years old and still active, told me his ambition was to have 100,000 units of blood per year contributed by donors to the Lansing bank.

I called Mr. Irvin Nichols, the Executive Director of the regional blood bank who reported that they had 106,000 units donated during the year ending in June 1983.

Nice going, Walter.

CHAPTER 24

ARMY

I sat, completely naked—except for a Stetson hat. The room was chilly. The concrete floor was cold and the benches felt like ice on my backside when we all had to shift to a new place in the waiting room.

The building had served as a barracks in World War I and had no furnishings except the benches. There was a pair of nailed-shut windows, too dirty to see through, and nothing to look at but each other and the dingy walls. I thought, vaguely, of a jail holding tank, but at least those inmates had the comfort of clothing.

"Hey, Stringer, are you afraid we're going to steal your hat?"

I looked over to this newly-made-acquaintance-in-misery. Around his grin he was a shivering mass of gooseflesh. I smiled back at him.

"It won't fit in the duffel bag with the rest of my clothes," I said, "and I'll be damned if I'll leave it lying around to get lost."

I was at Fort Custer in Battle Creek.

Our country was at War.

Two bus loads of us, all medical doctors, had been taken to Fort Custer for physical examinations. We were having a first taste of the Army and it was distinctly unpalatable.

We waited, hour upon hour, to be processed. Nothing

happened. No one in the recruiting office even came in to explain what we could expect.

At length, when I thought I would never be warm again, and fatigued and hungry enough to take a bite out of the thoughtless bastards inflicting this torture upon us, things started moving.

I drew a Captain Farsling. He gave me a physical examination, which would have flunked a first year medical student, and took an x-ray of my chest.

"Dr. Stringer, we can stop right here. I have to reject your application because you have pulmonary tuberculosis."

I stiffened with shock. Was it possible? I had taken particularly good care of myself to avoid picking up the infection, and had frequent x-ray checks in my hospital.

No, my common sense told me. The man was mad! For the first time since I entered the old fort I was warm.

"I would like to see the x-rays you based your diagnosis on, Captain," I said.

He started to refuse, then shrugged and led me to the x-ray room. He found my film and clicked it over the viewing light.

"That film is completely burned out," I protested. "No one could possibly make a diagnosis on the basis of this." When he started to argue, I almost shouted him down.

"I'm going to do two things. First—I'll get a quality x-ray of my lungs and secondly, I'll get someone to read it who knows how!"

I stomped out of the x-ray room with whatever dignity my nakedness and new Stetson could muster, and returned to the holding room to dress. It was pure luxury to be warm again.

Back home in Lansing my x-ray was entirely normal. I read it myself, but, of course, I needed another opinion. Old friend, Bruce Douglas, became my aide and abettor. He was then tuberculosis controller for the City of Detroit, Medical Director of Herman Kiefer Hospital and a member of the medical officer's recruitment board.

I phoned him and got mad all over again telling about the bungling.

"Sure, I'll read them. Come on down and bring the x-rays," he said. "I will also have the x-rays taken at Ft. Custer sent to me."

"I need to get an incorrect diagnosis off my record."

"I see your point, Chris. Could cause a lot of difficulty later on, especially in getting life insurance."

"Exactly—Bruce, Dr. Milton Shaw in Lansing, who has been in the reserves for many years, is anxious to get back into active service and he also has been rejected because of alleged tuberculosis by the same examining officer. May I bring him along?"

"Sure, but give me a couple of days to get the Ft. Custer x-rays."

I hung up and brooded. I hoped in all truth, to be accepted into the medical corp of either the Army or Navy for patriotic reasons, of course, but also so that I could slow down. The Chest Hospital was a killing schedule and there were times I got so little rest my staff complained that I was glassy-eyed. I felt worse than glassy-eyed. I was continually pressed with unfinished responsibilities. Ruth fussed that I was working too hard and I suspect I was irritable at times. However, as always, she continued to be supportive.

After three or four weeks, Dr. Douglas, in cooperation with Colonel Slevin, head of medical recruitment, was able to get the diagnosis of tuberculosis expunged from my record.

Milton Shaw wasn't so fortunate. The top brass had set up some pretty awkward guidelines. One of them was not to accept any applicant for military service who had calcification in his lungs greater than 5 m.m. in diameter. These calcifications are evidence of healed primary tuberculosis but have no clinical significance. Milt had such a calcification and no amount of pressure could get him into active service.

In the meantime, I was ordered to report to a base in Texas for infantry duty as a lieutenant on the basis of an old commission that I believed had expired. In fact, it had expired. The Texas brass didn't believe my story and it meant another tangle with the military and a trip to Washington, D.C.

With that foul-up successfully fielded, I was free to apply for a commission of the correct rank in the medical corp of the Army. The military had a policy of granting the next higher rank to officer candidates who were 1) a fellow of the American College of Surgeons, 2) a fellow of the American College of Physicians, 3) had completed a recognized residency program, 4) had administrative experience, 5) had teaching experience, and 6) had a college degree and an M.D. If all of the upgrades were honored, I would be eligible for Major General, yet I would have been in Texas, slogging around as an infantry second lieutenant if I hadn't protested their error.

So in August of 1942, I applied for commission as a colonel. (With my batting average, I'd have been foolish to ask for a general's commission.) In any case, the service didn't need high ranking officers.

So after I applied, I was ordered back to Ft. Custer for reexamination. Again, the bus to Battle Creek—again the same dank holding room. I thought, groaning to myself, I'll probably draw Farsling again. I did!

I stripped and stood around. Several groups of young inductees came through and were processed quickly. I sat, I walked around the room. Farsling let me cool my heels and everything else until almost 5:00.

He examined me, his face dark with displeasure. He obviously knew that I had overridden his previous findings and was chagrined and angry because his competence had been questioned. As he finished he practically tore the blood pressure cuff off my arm. "You'll never have a chance to do that again!" I could barely contain my anger.

He glared at me. "That is all. You will hear from us," he said with emphasis on "us" and turned away.

"Farsling." I said, "I don't know whether I'm in the Army or not, but if I am, I will outrank you by at least three grades and, you S.O.B., I hope I meet you somewhere."

I left him standing in the doorway shouting.

My staff at the Chest Hospital weren't happy at losing their chief, and I truly wanted to continue the chest surgery training program which I had initiated and guided. But the prospect of getting into a relaxing job at some base hospital had taken on a dream-like quality for me. Many of my colleagues, unburdened with the kind of ambitious teaching and surgical schedule I had carved out for myself, were enjoying regular hours, stressless schedules.

I discovered without surprise, that close colleagues and friends, including Governor Pat Van Waggoner, and Prentiss Brown, the United States Senator, had written letters to everyone in power saying I could better serve my country by continuing to direct the Chest Hospital in surgery and training programs. Quoting from one of these letters—"The Doctor really would like to get into the service if he could follow his personal desires but he is likewise aware of the necessity of his staying on his present job."

In the meantime, the Army's wheels had been rolling along and I received formal notification from the 6th Medical Corp in Chicago to report for commissioning in active military duty. Ordinarily the proposed rank would be stated in the order. It wasn't, but I had followed instructions and applied for a commission as full Colonel.

"Well, Ruth, at least we don't have to wonder any more. It's settled. I don't know what my rank will eventually be, but I will probably be in a base hospital in the United States or overseas. As long as I am in this country, there will be adequate quarters for you and the children with me, or you can stay here and I will get back as often as I can."

Ruth didn't like the disruption but there was some relief for both of us in the ending of uncertainty. The boys were seven and five and they were healthy and pliable, and Ruth was resourceful as usual. She decided to accompany me.

"Who will you leave in charge, Chris? And what about your surgical program?" Ruth asked. "Can you bring anyone in to teach?"

"No, I don't think so, but Ken Fenney worked for me during the summers as a medical student and has had a one-year internship and a one year residency. He is coming on staff. I expect you remember Ken. He is not in the best of health and he is physically disqualified for the military. I know he will do well and maybe I can get back occasionally. But the surgical training program will have to wait until the war is over."

"I'm really sorry for all this disruption, Chris, but a lot of our friends are experiencing the same war time chaos. Well, we've got a week, right?" Ruth said. "So we both better get busy!"

Four days later another wire came from the Chicago 6th Corp saying to disregard the letter of notification for commissioning.

Exasperated, Ruth said, "What now? Can't the military make up its mind? I am glad you will be home for a while longer but this uncertainty is not fair to either of us."

"Well, honey, there isn't anything we can do but go from day to day. With the war on, we're all going to be needed somewhere."

"Yes, and whatever happens, I am sure we're better off than the people in Europe."

For two long weeks we were in limbo. I allowed personal arrangements to molder, and sat tight. On the 14th day a letter arrived directly from the Secretary of War thanking me for the offer of my services but advising me that I had been declared essential in a civilian role. I stayed put.

Within a few weeks, I was appointed to the Advisory Council on Naval Affairs by Admiral E. P. Forestall, Secretary of the Navy. The council met regularly in Washington. Those trips were the extent of my military service during World War II.

CHAPTER 25

DOCTORS AS PATIENTS

Oliver McGillicuddy was very blond and tall—maybe six feet three inches. In later life the sun's effect on his facial skin was to wrinkle it deeply. I suspect some lines were laughter induced, for the man was an incurable practical joker. For example, I guess he got tired of listening to me brag about my perfectly kept lawn, and one night, before Ruth and I planned to entertain in our yard, he crept over and transplanted an enormous fully blooming dandelion right out in the middle of our yard in full view of the patio.

Oliver and I shared more than similar careers. We had formed a close personal relationship which survived until his death . . . and in spite of his Irish sense of humor. Oliver was not a thoracic surgeon; he was a nose and throat specialist. Strangely, though, the medical community chose to see us as competitors so far as endoscopy was concerned. We had some hearty laughs about this during the years when we were next-door neighbors. We had, in fact, built our house next to the McGillicuddy home at the urging of Oliver and his wife, Bernice.

We enjoyed wonderful, warm hours at day's end, when we relaxed at their house or ours, especially if the weather was good and we could be in our yards. We even served, occasionally, as each other's physicians.

There was a time when we saw an opportunity to enter a real estate venture together. With a little ingenuity, we found a minute here and there to plan. We called the company the Carina Corporation, for the carina is the site of the bifurcation of the trachea, which we both had to examine during bronchoscopy.

Legal work went forward well until a secretary in the lawyer's office, checking on the term, "carina" in a medical dictionary, discovered it also meant a part of the female genitalia. We honestly hadn't known this, but we took a lot of joshing from colleagues. We had specialized in the upper half of the anatomy so long we were short-sighted. But it was too late to change and Carina Corporation existed profitably for 15 years.

When my twin sons were five years old, Oliver removed their tonsils. Surgery was on a Friday. Looking back, we could have been smarter on that score because the Michigan State University and the University of Michigan football game occurred the following day.

Through the years, the McGillicuddys and Stringers had managed to finagle tickets for this particular football game. Our boys, Tom and Ted, lively, in spite of sore throats, would have been a worry to both of us had we left them at home, even though Ruth's valued helper, Bonnie, would have done very well with them. Ordinarily, tonsillectomies were discharged from the hospital the evening after surgery or the next morning.

Oliver suggested we leave the boys in the hospital until we returned from the game in Ann Arbor. This wouldn't have given us any cause for thought, or guilt as it were, except that Lansing hospitals were promoting early discharge. Someone could give us a hard time.

So, Oliver and I made a call on little Tom and Ted the morning of the game. They were playing in their hospital beds when we walked in with the nursing supervisor, and obviously were in no distress in spite of the recent surgery.

Oliver examined them; pronounced them fine.

Tom, in his kindergarden candor, said to the nurse, "We get to stay in the hospital an extra day so Mommy and Daddy can go to the football game."

Oliver and I looked everywhere but at the nurse.

"Shh-shh," we said. I hugged the boys and we hurried out.

Years later Oliver became seriously ill, spent some time in St. Lawrence Hospital and came home to recover.

Early one morning, hearing some unusual activity next door at McGillicuddy's we peered from our side window to see an ambulance team loading Oliver into the vehicle.

I soon learned that Oliver had been readmitted to the hospital. He was in the capable hands of another good friend, Dr. Theodore Bauer, an internist of prominence and skill. I wanted to stop in and see him but I certainly didn't want to give the impression to Theodore or Bernie that I was interferring with Oliver's treatment. I reasoned that if Dr. Bauer wanted me or needed me, he would call.

Two days later I stopped at St. Lawrence after church to check on some of my patients and was headed down the hall when I saw Dr. Bauer approaching from the opposite direction. He was distracted, noticeably upset. He looked up quickly and turned directly into my path.

"Chris, I have been trying to get you. We need you. I even called the church but you had just left. Mac is dying. Will you see him now."

I was shocked. I hadn't seen Oliver's wife, Bernie, in the past 48 hours, but I had assumed that someone would notify us if Oliver were in danger. He was as close a friend as anyone could have.

It couldn't be! He had been recovering so well. A sharp pain of alarm hit my stomach.

I wheeled around and accompanied Dr. Bauer to Oliver's room. Bernie McGillicuddy rose as we entered. Trim, brown haired, her face mirrored the shock of Oliver's sudden downward spiral. She held out her hand and I put my arm around her. I felt her small body tremble and when our eyes met, I saw complete trust. She was turning Oliver over to me. I was her hope.

Dr. Bauer was right; Oliver was critically ill—feverish, gasping for breath and cyanotic. I examined his chest. The breath sounds were markedly diminished, particularly on the left side, and his heart was racing.

The portable x-ray films Dr. Bauer had obtained were inconclusive. I examined him again and felt sure there was fluid around the lungs. It would explain the respiratory stridor. The pain had to be intense when he tried to take an adequate breath. My own chest ached for my old friend.

What kind of action should I take? Ideas sped through my head; I discarded most of them.

I straightened and met the agonized faces of Dr. Bauer and Bernie. I had just a glimmer of a plan of action.

"Do you know what the infecting organism is?" I asked.

Dr. Bauer inclined his head.

"Staphylococcus." He didn't need to elaborate. We both knew this organism could be resistant to any antibiotic we had, and it was.

"I have a suggestion," I said. "Shall we go out and talk for a bit?"

I led them away from the tortured sounds of Oliver's attempts to breathe and out of his hearing—no need to burden him with fears. There was a little closet across the hall from his room and the three of us—Dr. Bauer, Bernie and I crowded in.

"I have some hope that I can remove the fluid from around his lung and replace it with an air cushion," I said. "That should make his breathing easier." I turned to Bernie. "It's been 25 years since I used this treatment. I haven't had to because of the availability of antibiotics."

"But," I explained, "we've got essentially the same problem here that we had prior to antibiotics.

Bernie nodded.

Dr. Bauer asked, "After that, what?" He was aware that the procedure had to be followed by some kind of antimicrobial drug.

"First, I must tell you that removal of the fluid and installation of air might further reduce the lung available for breathing. Oliver could die then and there and . . ."

Dr. Bauer broke in. "Bernie, we have nothing else to offer. It's a losing battle not to do anything."

She brushed at quick tears but didn't hesitate. Pulling herself upright in the cramped antiseptic-smelling broom closet, she said, "Let's do it."

I was not nearly so confident. To treat any patient so critically ill is an emotional drain, but it becomes nearly unbearable when the patient is a close personal friend. It was a venture into the unknown. Since I had been drawn into it, my training told me to plot my course. Take one step at a time.

We returned to Oliver's room. Dr. Bauer and I conferred briefly. Moments later a surgical nurse wheeled in a cart containing the necessities for thoracentesis I had ordered. Most important were the ampules of a new drug that was untried in such cases as Oliver's. Called staphcillin, its manufacturers touted it as being effective against otherwise resistant staphlococci.

I would have to risk dripping the staphcillin intravenously in measured quantities. Giving it to him orally would be too slow, if he could even swallow.

I elevated Oliver's head; examined the chest again. There had to be fluid in the pleural space.

His small hospital room would necessarily be the operating room. He was too ill to move. With Oliver prepared, I steeled myself. Bernie left saying she would wait outside.

Dr. Robert McGillicuddy, Oliver's brother, had come into the room and moved quietly into the small circle. Having him there gave us a small lift. I continued as swiftly as I could. I anesthetized the chest wall with novocain, found the fluid with a #15 needle and drew out the plunger. I emptied the cloudy stuff in a basin, repeatedly using a threeway valve between the needle and syringe.

"I don't see how you knew exactly were that fluid was," Robert said.

I didn't have time to respond. With another clean, sterile syringe,I forced air into the newly vacated space around the lung. Then I injected a gram of the new drug into the pleural space.

From the side of the bed I waited for a change in his breathing.

Oliver's chest heaved. It was a deep breath and apparently without pain. The four of us, Theodore, Robert, the nurse and I, also took deep breaths—but none could have been more relieved than I was, except Oliver.

My work, though, was just starting. The lung disease was still there and would take sustained drug delivery by intravenous and intramuscular routes and all the supportive treatment Theodore and I could devise. I had to set up a continous drip in veins which had partially collapsed. The superficial veins obviously were so weakened that they would be further damaged by the irritation of the staphcillin. I needed, therefore, to use a larger and stronger vein. I made a small incision in the right anticubital area (this is in the front part of the arm at the level of the elbow) using local anesthesia. I found the bacilic vein along the medial side of the surgical incision and dissected it free. Then I incised the wall of the bacilic and threaded an intravenous catheter through this opening to the axillary vein deep in the axilla. The catheter was secured by two small sutures. I prayed a lot.

The only change that night was that he had more regular and less labored breathing. The following day I had to repeat the fluid removal and air installation around the lung, and make further adjustments in the intravenous drip of the drug.

I had stayed with Oliver all night—in fact, the four of us did—Dr. Bauer, and Bernie and Robert. The next 48 hours were "iffy"—Oliver was not improving as rapidly as we wanted. We clung to the hope that Oliver's will to live was as strong as ours was to have him survive. Another 12 hours elapsed; we took turns at his bedside, and Oliver slowly improved. He was still critical, but we now could let

185

down somewhat and get some rest. About midnight of the fifth day, I went home to sleep, leaving instructions that I was to be called at once, if there was any change for the worse.

The next morning when I checked him, I was greatly refreshed both in body and spirit. Oliver was awake and beginning to respond.

Oliver recovered completely and took up his busy practice. Soon after that he and Bernie came traipsing across our connecting back yards with a handsome table lamp. I had only recently opened an office in the new Medical Arts Building, and Helen Menzies, a friend of both families, had supervised the decorating of the rooms.

McGillicuddys—aware of this—had asked Helen's advice about something they might get for my new office. Accepting it, Ruth's face lit up at the heart-felt gift of thanks.

"I have just the place for it," she said, leading them to our living room. The lovingly-given lamp for my office still sits in our living room—a reminder of Oliver, who lived another 20 years after our traumatic experience.

During his retirement, he wrote an interesting autobiography. Quoting from that biography:

"I was very ill with pneumonia and empyema, an infection of the pleural cavity encasing the lungs. The test of my sputum indicated a staphlococcus infection, completely resistant to all antibiotics, except a new one that was just released. My life was saved by my friend, Dr. Chris Stringer, a thoracic surgeon, who tapped and drained the empyema and instilled this new drug, staphcillin into the lung cavity. They also gave me huge doses of the drug with frequent painful injections in the rump."

Actually, in addition to the injections in his "rump", Oliver was given staphcillin in large amounts by intravenous drip. And all he actually remembered about his deathly illness was the discomfort of the shots in his backside!

* * * *

I have had my share of grumpy, trying patients. My specialty, involving the treatment of serious, painful ailments, provided me with persons who had every right to complain.

Those I remember best, however, are those who suffered through the advancement of their disease or had serious injuries, and remained pleasant. It seemed a small miracle to me that these brave souls could accept the pain, seeing it as a temporary part of life and looking ahead to the time when they could be healed.

* * * *

I have a vast number of medical records covering the treatment of other M.D.s and their families. It seems to me that there was always at least one colleague in the hospital as a patient.

I believe the concept that doctors are difficult patients is a myth. I have operated dozens of doctors and members of their families and without exception they were grateful patients. Incidentally or not so incidentally they all recovered. The wife of a prominent internist was one of the massive infection cases resulting from the faulty air conditioning recorded in Chapter 17. Like the others she never once complained and neither did her husband.

There were a number of interns from the general hospitals in Lansing who developed tuberculosis while interning and were hospitalized at the Chest Hospital.

Dr. Thomas Barton was one of the patients with tuberculosis from the St. Lawrence Hospital intern group. St. Lawrence did not do routine x-rays for staff or new patient admissions.

Dr. Barton had an active minimal pulmonary tuberculosis which he had recently acquired. He recalled at least one autopsy at the hospital in which previously unsuspected far-advanced tuberculosis was found. The medical literature is replete with known cases of tuberculosis among student nurses and staff contracted while post-morten examinations were being carried out. These observers are likely to come into the autopsy room without being masked or gowned while the unsuspected tuberculous tissue is being sectioned with the large autopsy knife and tubercle bacilli are flying all over the place.

Dr. Barton did well and recovered.

But he was critical about the apparent lack of concern on the part of the hospital and particularly the pathologist, and so was I. He brought legal action against the hospital for damages and I was called to testify.

Unfortunately, Tom had an attorney who apparently had not prepared his case properly. Even though he called me as a witness (I believe by subpoena), he had not bothered to talk to me about the case before I took the witness stand in the courtroom. In fact, I had never seen him before.

After I was sworn, this lawyer asked me if I was sure that Dr. Barton had contracted tuberculosis as a result of his employment as an intern at St. Lawrence Hospital.

This was a leading question and should not have been allowed, but the attorney representing St. Lawrence was alert enough to realize that the question couldn't possibly be answered in the affirmative so he wisely didn't object.

I had to answer, "No", of course. I couldn't be sure. With that the poorly prepared lawyer yelled out, "Dr. Barton, you do not have a witness."

Had I answered such an ill-phrased question affirmatively, the attorney representing St. Lawrence could have made me look silly.

Tom lost the case.

The lawyer should have done his homework. If he had interviewed me before trial I could have coached him about what I could testify positively to and what I could not.

After he qualified me as an expert witness, his first question should have been whether or not the patient had tuberculosis. I would have testified in the affirmative. Then he could have asked me if, in my opinion, the patient could have contracted tuberculosis while assisting in doing an autopsy on a tuberculosis patient and I could answer that in the afirmative.

However, I could not say that to my certain knowledge he had contracted the disease in that way. Certainly I had not seen the organisms leaping out of the tuberculous lung on the autopsy table into Dr. Barton's lungs, although it is my opinion that this is exactly what happened.

Tom was disgruntled at me and I didn't like the outcome either, but he should have picked a more competent lawyer.

* * * *

This chapter would not be complete without further reference to a medical patient I'll call General Surgeon, who had been assigned to monitor my work when I first started practice in Lansing. (See Chapter 12.)

Doctor Bauer called saying the surgeon was his patient in St. Lawrence Hospital. He reported that General Surgeon was desperately ill and both he and the doctor patient wanted me to come.

I was able to get to St. Lawrence Hospital in about two hours. A review of the hospital record and examination of the patient revealed that he was indeed desperately ill with chronic obstructive pulmonary disease. His temperature was elevated and the pulse thready and rapid. He gasped for breath. In the x-ray I saw abnormal densities along the broncho-vascular pattern in both lungs. The symptoms had been progressive for about a month.

I considered bronchoscopy and discussed this possibility with his wife. She frantically asked me to do something—anything. This lady was already angry with two doctors who had tried to help but, of course, they didn't have a magic wand any more than I did.

General Surgeon also expected miracles; however, he was not as demanding as his wife. He knew of course, that no one could accomplish a cure in an hour or a day.

She expected an immediate cure, but of course I did remain patient; not to do so would only make matters worse.

The pulmonary secretions were examined for the causative organism and sensitivity studies were done on the recovered bacteria. I altered the antibiotics to suit the findings and then initiated postural drainage.

The patient's wife called me every morning at exactly 7:00 o'clock in spite of the fact that she knew I would be seeing her husband later that morning. Sometimes I hadn't had more than four hours sleep.

Finally, General Surgeon began to improve slowly and he did recover.

When he went home, his wife contacted Ruth and was very appreciative. She asked Ruth the name of the decorator we had used in our new home. Consequently, we received two beautiful table lamps which are still in our living room.

CHAPTER 26

OSTEOPATHS AND CHIRO-
PRACTORS AS PATIENTS

Doctors of medicine and osteopaths did not consult with each other in the 1950's. The differences in theory and practice were too great. Fellows of the College of Surgeons were even forbidden to consult with osteopaths. I was surprised, then, when the phone call came from a local osteopath.

"No, I'm sorry," I said when Dr. Local O. asked me to come to the osteopathic hospital to see his friend and patient, Doctor B., also an osteopath. "I would risk expulsion from the American College of Surgeons."

"I realize that, Dr. Stringer, but Doctor B. is certainly going to die unless something more is done. His temperature is 105 degrees and has been above 104 for four days."

"What do you think is wrong with him?"

"The entire right chest is opaque in the x-ray and he is coughing persistently. He's bringing up foul-smelling sputum."

"What have you done for him?"

"I am giving him massive doses of chloromycetin but it hasn't helped."

I was alarmed. Chloromycetin is a dangerous drug and may cause blood dyscrasia when given is large amounts. Usually it's reserved for treatment of typhoid or when other antibiotics are ineffective. I felt instant pity for the patient.

"If you want to transfer your patient to the Chest Hospital, we will do what we can. Whatever you do, discontinue the use of chloromycetin."

"All right—but can't you come and see Doctor B. here? He would rather stay in our hospital."

"You know I can't do that—besides, even if I did and active surgical treatment became necessary, you'd still have to transfer him. You're not equipped for chest surgery in your hospital."

He sighed and said he'd call back in a few minutes.

He was back on the telephone almost immediately.

"Dr. Stringer, my patient and his wife have agreed to his transfer. An ambulance is on the way—and Doctor B. will be there shortly."

I had just advised our admission desk when Dr. Local O. phoned again.

"Is it all right, Doctor, for me to help take care of my patient while he is in the Chest Hospital?"

"Now, you know I can't allow that."

"I just thought I would try."

* * * *

I ordered chest x-rays, blood chemistry, blood count and other routine admission procedures. I studied the resulting x-rays, then went to the patient, to examine his chest with the records of the resident physician's history and physical examination of Doctor B. in hand.

The patient was indeed acutely ill. His temperature remained at 104.5 degrees, he was flushed, his pulse was rapid, and he was gasping. I could barely detect breath sounds over the entire right chest. I made a provisional diagnosis—lung abscess involving all of the right lower lobe.

By this time, it was near 4 in the morning. The patient had had nothing by mouth since noon so I scheduled him for a bronchoscopy. I might effect adequate bronchial drainage of the lung abscess; with the addition of the proper antibiotic regime we could possibly avoid major surgery.

I was unsucessful in aspirating enough of the purulent material from the lobe but I sent a sample to the laboratory for culture and sensitivity studies. While we waited for the report, I started Doctor B. on a broad spectrum antibiotic—his records showed him to be allergic to penicillin and I hoped fervently that he would be able to tolerate what I was trying.

His temperature subsided somewhat but climbed up again. I didn't relish the idea of removing the lung lobe. The patient was very toxic and resection of a consolidated lobe can be a tricky surgical procedure. Usually adhesions to adjacent structure require the surgeon to work under the hard mass of the abscessed lobe, which obscures the operating field. Pus may exude through to the other bronchial branches. When this occurs, the anesthesiologist has difficulty aspirating the material, while at the same time maintaining adequate ventilation of the patient.

The night wore on—the patient became more feverish and feeble with each shallow breath. The minutes passed slowly and I became more anxious. A natural desire to help had gotten me in a tight squeeze. If I lost the patient, either way—by surgery or without surgery, there would be a howl.

Night thoughts tramped through my mind. "YOU SHOULD NOT HAVE OPERATED ON HIM! YOU SHOULD HAVE OPERATED ON HIM! YOU SHOULD HAVE LEFT HIM AT THE OSTEOPATHIC HOSPITAL!"

I shook myself a little and tried to put the thoughts aside. I called a meeting of my residents and staff and presented the case. Actually, I had pretty well decided that the only way to save Doctor B. was to operate. The staff agreed and I was a little surprised. They didn't always concur.

Partially relieved, I still felt heavy with responsibility as I explained the case to Doctor B.'s wife and son and they signed the permit for surgery.

The following morning, we operated. I cut through the chest wall and as we proceeded things began to look worse and worse. In his history, I had noted that the patient was a heavy drinker—admitting to 10 to 12 ounces a day. With regret, I saw that the patient's alcohol consumption, which had been above normal for years, was making it most difficult for the anesthesiologist.

When I got inside to the infected area, my assistants were unable to retract the greatly engorged lobe forward and out of the way so that I could get to the root of the lung. I had to approach the lung root by working beneath the abscessed lobe. It was risky, tedious, smelly work. The surgical team eased visibly in relief when I got the abscessed lobe out, into a container, and began the closing.

By evening, Doctor B.'s temperature had dropped to normal. Maybe I didn't have wings on my heels as I returned to the hospital to check my recently operated cases, but I felt plenty loose. I had gambled on odds that weren't good either way and won.

At 10 p.m., the hospital was always a whisper of activity. Nurses change shifts then, and my being on hand to talk to the oncoming night nurses helps set my mind at rest for the ensuing night.

Smiling to myself, I came to Doctor B.'s room. The door was closed. That was odd.

I turned the knob and walked into a scene so appalling I felt the hair rise on the back of my neck. My patient lay, his chest swathed heavily with bandages and his lower body exposed. Beside the bed stood Dr. Local O. vigorously giving the patient an osteopathic adjustment!

I was beside the bed in two bounds.

"Get away from that patient!" I shouted throwing the covers back over Doctor B. I turned, glaring, to face Dr. Local O. He had faded back when he heard my cry; a sheepish look replaced the one of intense concentration.

"He is doing fine," he said. "But he needs limbering up."

"This kind of foolishness could cause a ligature to slip off one of the major vessels and result in a fatal hemorrhage." Anger was replacing my fear.

"Now you get out of here," I shouted, "before I limber you up!"

He slunk out and I didn't hear from him again. Doctor B. recuperated well and returned to his practice.

* * * *

Dr. Robert McGillicuddy told Elvi to ask me to see a young girl at Sparrow Hospital. He had said the case wasn't urgent so I stopped at the hospital on the way home that evening.

The patient was a frail little 12 year old girl, the daughter of a local chiropractor. The parents were both there waiting for me and had been there all day. If I had known this I would have made an effort to get there sooner.

From the chart I learned that little Irene had been in and out of hospitals all her life. She was prone to upper respiratory infections and had a history of pneumonia three times during the past three years. She'd had a persistent cough during most of her life.

Physical examination of the little girl's chest revealed showers of moderately coarse rales gurgling and crackling over the lower half of the lungs.

I went to the x-ray department to review the many x-rays taken through the years. These really didn't help very much except to show evidence of peribronchial infiltration during the episodes of earlier pneumonia.

Back upstairs, I talked with the concerned parents. I told them I couldn't be sure about the diagnosis on the basis of the available information, but I wanted to do a bronchoscopy and have bronchographic x-rays taken. I mentioned the possibilities of congenital pulmonary cystic disease or bronchiectasis. These good people readily gave their permission and I was able to schedule the little girl for surgery the following morning.

I elected to try to do the bronchoscopy under local anesthesia in spite of the patient's age, because the bronchography would be easier if she were awake. I realized that if she couldn't tolerate the procedure under local, I would still have to use general anesthesia. There was no difficulty. Irene cooperated better than many adults.

The bronchography did indeed show evidence of cystic bronchiectasis, fortunately limited to the left lower lobe.

I reported the findings to the parents and wrote my recommendations on the chart for Dr. McGillicuddy to see when he made rounds later that morning.

When Dr. McGillicuddy saw the bronchographic x-rays and my report, he called me at the Chest Hospital. We were agreed that the left lower lung lobe should be resected surgically.

"Do you want to talk to the parents, Bob, if they are still there?"

"Yes, they are, and I will talk to them but I can tell you now, Chris, they will agree to whatever you advise. They are obviously pleased that you have become interested in following through and trying to do something for their daughter. They mentioned the amount of time you have already spent with them. They're very decent folks."

Frail little Irene was scheduled for left lower lobectomy three days later and she remained cheerful. There wasn't a tear or a complaint of any kind when she was brought from her room to surgery.

The pulmonary resection went smoothly, although the anesthesiologist was kept busy using suction to keep the tracheobronchial tree dry until the bronchus was sectioned and sutured. After that the bronchial tree remained dry on its own.

Post-operatively, Irene did very well. The remaining lung promptly expanded to fill the pleural space and she was discharged on the eighth post-operative day.

I saw her in the office two weeks later. She was smiling and the mother said she had no more cough. She was eating and sleeping better than she ever had.

About a year later Irene sent me a photo of herself. She had gained weight. Good health revealed a very pretty little girl.

CHAPTER 27

DEWEY

I became Dewey McDonald's friend when I took over as Medical Director of the Ingham Sanitorium in 1938. Dewey wanted to be sure that I continued the hospital policy of buying all of the dairy products from his dairy, Heatherwood, so he was congenial, cooperative, and generous. I liked him immensely, even if I hadn't been their frequent dinner guest. His wife, Grace, was a superb cook.

As my early Lansing days went by, competing dairies kept snapping at the heels of my hospital business manager wanting us to commit our purchases to them. They objected to Dewey's monopoly.

"Representatives from the other dairies are making me nervous," he complained. "They won't take no for an answer. What should I do?"

"What about this?" I offered. "I'll talk to Dewey and find out if he'll give up his butter order. Then we can give it to the competitor.

The business manager's face lit up.

"Spread it around. Good idea." He went off humming to himself, and smiling at his pun.

Dewey agreed to the compromise, so we notified the other dairy that we'd be glad to order the entire supply of butter from them.

The day before Christmas, our senior dietician, Olive

Henderson, quick-stepped into my office. She was wringing her hands—partly angry, partly distressed.

"The president of that other dairy phoned me and said they can't deliver any butter during the remainder of the holiday season or thereafter, unless we also buy all our milk from them."

I countered as best I could, promising to get back to her as soon as I phoned Dewey. This was his area of expertise, not mine.

Dewey's wrath knew no bounds. He boomed some short forceful words which I was sure anyone within 20 feet of the receiver could hear.

"Give me a few minutes," he growled. "I will call you back."

The phone rang 10 minutes later. It was Dewey's secretary. "Mr. McDonald said to tell you he'll be gone for four or five hours and will contact you as soon as he gets back."

I thanked her and hung up—more than a little bewildered. I wondered if Dewey really understood our dilemma. Butter was tightly rationed, in continuous short supply and hospitals were not allowed to use oleomargine. I was wishing I'd stayed with surgery and left management alone.

But I waited. With Dewey on my side I wasn't about to give in to blackmail. Toward evening, a triumphant Dewey appeared at the kitchen loading dock. He had two dairy trucks and drivers, and the three of them hopped out, ran around to the truck's large doors and began taking cartons of fresh butter to the hospital refrigerator. Everyone was bug-eyed when the news passed to the hospital workers.

It turned out that Dewey had marshalled the drivers, directed them to the sororities and fraternities at Michigan State College and garnisheed all the butter Heatherwood had previously delivered to them during the Christmas vacation.

Two hundred pounds of the precious golden brick went into hospital refrigerators that day and regularly thereafter. We ignored the other dairy people and they ignored us.

* * * *

198

Some months later, after enjoying another of Grace's exquisite dinners, she, Ruth, Dewey and I got to discussing our origins. I discovered Dewey was a native Iowan and further, that his home town was Cherokee, where I had lived and worked. I knew his parents and some of his brothers.

"Damn!" Dewey said. " I didn't have to spend all that money entertaining you."

Within three or four years, Dewey had some problems necessitating a stomach resection. He elected to have this surgery at Harper Hospital in Detroit where he knew one of the abdominal surgeons.

During the post-operative period, he was given large amounts of anti-coagulant drugs. I never knew exactly why.

A prothrombin time, to help determine the effect of the anti-coagulant, was ordered the day before his planned discharge. Before the prothrombin time was known, Dewey was discharged and Grace drove down to bring him home.

On the way home Dewey started to bleed from all the mucous membranes—and other areas—mouth, nose, under the skin, kidneys, bowel and probably other undetected places. The prothrombin time was obviously too low. This was apparent, but we didn't know how low until I called Harper Hospital the following morning and got the report. I admitted Dewey to Sparrow Hospital right after he got home. Obviously his problem was out of my field of practice and I needed help.

I called Dr. John Wellman, a well-qualified general surgeon in Lansing, and asked him to come to Sparrow to help. John was miffed because Dewey had gone out of town for his surgery, but he did come. He saw Dewey and was gruff with him and with Grace.

Out in the hall, I said. "Look, John, this patient is desperately ill and we need help, not conflict. Sure, it was a mistake to discharge him before the status of the prothrombin was known, but he is here now and it is our job to take care of him."

John left in a huff. I felt he really had not contributed anything.

I called my friend and internist, Dr. Theodore Bauer. While he was on the way to the hospital I recalled that the Bureau of Laboratories of the State Department of Health had been doing research on a preparation of Vitamin K to control such bleeding.

I called Dr. Donald Cummings at his home and told him the problem.

"What is the status of this Vitamin K preparation?" I asked.

"Well, we aren't sure but it looks pretty good."

"Don, I want the product quick. How do I get it?"

"I'll go to the lab and bring some to you at Sparrow. Now, Chris, this stuff is very thick and so far it appears that large quantities are required, so you will need 50 cc syringes with at least #15 intravenous needles. Have several of the large syringes because the viscosity of this product so far is such that it tends to cause the barrel of the syringes to stick. You should change to a fresh syringe each injection."

Characteristically, Don got the preparation to me in record time. We set up and I began injection of the heavy preparation.

Dewey had not lost consciousness. After two to three hours of treatment the bleeding slowed and by morning we were over the hump.

The Vitamin K preparation stimulates the production of pro-thrombin factor II in the liver. We didn't know then and we still do not know why.

Grace had been there all night, too, and Ruth had stayed with her.

Don Cummings and his laboratory were the heroes that night. Don must have felt great satisfaction knowing that his medical discovery had been so spectacularly successful. A frontier crossed for Dr. Cummings.

* * * *

Decades later, Grace McDonald phoned our home. It was evening. Ruth and I were entertaining some close neighbors.

"Chris, I have to talk to someone. Dewey is ill and won't see anyone about it. He's got severe pain in his right lower back and he is passing gross blood."

"That's out of my field, Grace, but I'll tell Free Harrold, He happens to be here."

Free came to the phone. "We'd better check on Dewey," he said, putting the receiver back on the hook. "It doesn't sound good."

Free and I left the party and hurried to the McDonald's home. Dewey was in poor condition. Dr. Harrold arranged for Dewey's admission to the hospital that evening.

The next morning, early, I assisted Free to remove a lower rib so we could get at the right kidney. The kidney was enlarged and malignant. We removed the tumor-containing kidney and Dewey did very well for a year.

He developed serious chest symptoms, which I diagnosed as being due to metastasis to the lung—that is, the malignant cells had transferred from the affected kidney or kidney area to the lung.

I did a thoracotomy and removed a solitary metastatic nodule from the lung. My good friend did well for two years and kept his word about coming in for an x-ray every three months.

Dewey's three month x-rays were taken on Thursday, so I went down to the x-ray department to interpret them as soon as I was notified. Ordinarily, I'd have left them until the next morning. But Ruth and I had something special planned, which included the McDonalds and I was concerned about Dewey.

THERE WAS ANOTHER METASTATIC NODULE IN THE LUNG! I could have wept. I had seen the terrifying deaths that ensued from the swift growth and deadly extension of these cancer cells. To do nothing would doom my friend to torture and an early death. To operate could prolong his life and improve the quality of the remaining shortened years.

I snapped off the viewing light and put away the x-ray films.

I drove home weary, sick at heart. Ruth was bubbling—we'd both been looking forward to taking three couples, including the McDonalds, to our club near Gaylord for a long weekend. I tried to hide my depression but the vision of that ominious lung mass kept flashing across my mind's eye. Some surgeons, not realizing the ghastly consequences, refuse to take the responsibility of operating such cases and the patient is doomed. These surgeons should move over and let someone else treat the patient. It is a doctor's bound duty, I believe, to prolong life as long as there is a chance of improving its quality.

Dewey had no chance for a cure, but he would die much sooner without surgery.

I dragged around the house getting in Ruth's way. Should I talk to Dewey and Grace immediately and cancel the long-anticipated trip up north? Or should I keep quiet and go ahead with the plans and report to them Sunday when we all returned? That way, only I would suffer.

Alone with the awful knowledge, I wrestled. Before the last garment and bit of equipment was packed, I had made a decision. Dewey deserved a vacation weekend without worry.

I didn't even tell Ruth. Before I left the hospital, though, I made arrangements by phone for surgery the following Monday morning. I had trouble sleeping that night.

The weekend was a huge success for everyone but me. Relaxed, sunburned, filled with good food, and good will, we drove home to Lansing Sunday evening. Dewey and Grace rode with us. I turned toward the hospital.

"Dewey," I said haltingly, "something has turned up. I read your x-rays before we left Friday," I paused. There was silence from the back seat. I could feel Ruth stiffen beside me.

I cleared my throat.

"There's another mass on the lung. I've already scheduled surgery for tomorrow morning."

In the silence, I parked the car.

We all climbed out and walked up the hospital steps. The summer night had taken on a chill. I opened the door and we filed inside, toward radiology.

* * * *

Dewey lived another two years and they were good ones. When he died in the spring of 1960, it was not from further cancer of the lung, but from metastasis to the skull and brain. All of the McDonald family came for Dewey's services. His many friends overflowed the funeral parlor. The family asked that Ruth and I be seated with them.

After the service, all the McDonalds gathered at our home. Harry, the Detroit brother, then Chairman of the Securities and Exchange Commission, played Ruth's Steinway and sang "Old Man River" with tears streaming down his face.

One of his sisters compiled a thorough and well-written family history. She wrote about Dewey:

"Through the years of his illness, Dewey found great comfort in the love and support of his good friend and doctor, Chris Stringer and his wife, Ruth."

Yes, I loved him. His death left a aching void in my life for a long time.

CHAPTER 28

TAKING RISKS

The man was 58 years old, a heavy smoker who coughed so severely and persistently I had difficulty passing the bronchoscope between the cords.

Through the right angle telescope I could see a protruding tumor mass, partially occluding the secondary divisions of the right upper lobe. I was disturbed. Its position prevented me from getting a biopsy which would indicate if it were cancer.

I withdrew the examining instrument and took bronchial washings for a cytological examination. They were strongly suggestive of malignancy. The tuberculin reaction was negative, which meant that the abnormality was probably not due to tuberculosis—although I couldn't rule out the possibility. The secretions he coughed up were examined and the cytology was strongly suspicious of cancer.

To add to the gloomy findings, we had no access to previous chest x-rays so I had no way of knowing if the tumor had been there for a long time and was, therefore, likely to be benign, or if it were fairly recent and probably malignant.

The only choice I had was to operate and remove a wedge from the tumor—rush it to pathology and wait for a report. If it were malignant, then I would remove the lobe or at worst, the lung.

The unusual aspect of this case was the man's appearance. He didn't look like a person with cancer. His color was good, he had not lost weight, and he had no familial history of cancer. It worried me that the lab reports were so strongly slanted toward malignancy.

I had no doubt, though, about emphysema. He had it; to what degree I wasn't sure. He could probably survive a lobe removal, but if I did indeed find cancer, I didn't believe he could tolerate an entire lung removal.

I talked to the patient; told him exactly what I knew. He agreed to surgery and he was flown from Iron Mountain to my hospital in Lansing.

Dr. Claude Burnett, a very competent surgical resident, did a pre-operative "work-up" on the Upper Peninsula native.

"I think his emphysema is more advanced than you first suspected," he said.

"Well, keep on it," I said. "I need all the data I can get on this fellow."

After three days of study and observation, I opened the chest. The tumor mass I had first seen in the Upper Peninsula x-rays was considerably larger than I expected. The lymph nodes around the vessels and the bronchus were definitely enlarged. I hadn't expected this either and it made me anxious.

Because of this, I cut a larger biopsy section than I normally would. Enlarged lymph nodes clung to the trachea so I removed these and sent both samples to pathology for frozen section.

The report came back; the tumor was malignant but the nodes were not. I was committed. The upper lung lobe would have to come out and hopefully this would be adequate.

I began surgery in earnest. Dr. Burnett had been right on target with his diagnosis—I found considerable pulmonary emphysema. I was sure the patient would not tolerate removal of the entire lung.

The right upper lobe is more difficult to resect than any other pulmonary resection, even when the lung root is

205

normal—and this one wasn't. Unlike most chest surgeons doing this operation, I prefer to retract the lung downward and expose the artery from above. Generally, that leaves the bronchus intact for traction without the danger of damaging the remaining blood vessels.

Another disquieting discovery—the tumor was so large and hard I couldn't pull the lobe down. This meant I had to work in back of and under the tumor-containing upper lobe. This also meant I had to deviate from my usual procedure and section the upper lobe bronchus first to gain access to the artery.

Tediously, I cut and sutured until I was down to the pulmonary arterial branches, still working under the tumor-containing lobe. During the long and tiring process of getting to the artery, my surgical nurse, Christine Howe, was Johnny-on-the-spot with the precise instruments I needed. This petite, dark-haired woman was not only attractive, but very bright. Given the chance, (which few women had in those days) she could have been a surgeon. She anticipated my every move during surgery. I was deep in the chest opening by then, ready to cut the artery. Christine slapped a short scissor into my hand.

"That is not what I need here," I said irritably. The surgery was going on longer and becoming riskier than I had planned and I didn't need my nurse letting down. Of course, I could have said—"A longer scissor, please."

"Use it," Christine snapped. "You know how."

The operating team tensed and I looked up, too astonished to be angry. Christine's eyes gleamed above her mask. Was she smiling? Or was she angry?

"O.K., Christine." I laughed, and used the short scissors. The team members chuckled.

We continued in an easier atmosphere. I finally got the awful lobe out, removed three more lymph nodes and closed up. This patient had been a much greater surgical risk than I had anticipated. I figured my surgery would improve the quality of his life for the possible three or four years that he might have left.

I brushed by Christine on my way out of the operating

room. "Nice work, Chief," she said.

The man recuperated and went to work in an automobile factory. He quit smoking and eventually retired to Florida. I heard from him a few years ago—on his 80th birthday!

* * * *

The preceding case is another gratifying example of the need to take risk IF SURGERY IS THE ONLY HOPE.

To the devil with statistics. I believe it is the duty of the surgeon to do whatever he can to save his patients, if it will improve their life quality and longevity.

I maintain that the critically ill patient who gets well is not interested in whether or not the surgeon has previously gambled and lost some severely ill patients who would not have had the smallest chance without surgery. Someone has said, to try where there is little hope, is to risk failure. Not to try guarantees it.

In one clinical pathological conference, the pathologist questioned my philosophy.

"Dr. Stringer, when do you give up?"

"Hell, I never do as long as there is a chance for my patient."

Another time, this same pathologist, whom I figured to be a lazy son-of-a-gun, wondered why I had ordered an autopsy on one of my patients. "I just want to know," I said with some heat, "why he didn't make it."

CHAPTER 29

SMALL AIRLINE WITH A BIG HEART

Nationwide Airlines (still limited only to Michigan), my surgical team and the Michigan Tuberculosis Association had a remarkably warm and successful relationship. Nationwide gave our patients nonstop, fast transportation between the Upper and Lower Peninsula.

I wasn't surprised, then, to be drawn into a dispute in 1952 when Wisconsin Central Airline petitioned the Civil Aeronautics Board to take over Nationwide's routes and the mail contract for the area. As a matter of fact, Wisconsin Central already had the mail contract but had failed to deliver the mail. Nationwide delivered! When I learned of the fiasco, I was upset. I knew a change-over could mean an undetermined number of piddling stops in Wisconsin for any flight between the peninsulas.

When Michigan's Attorney General Herbert Rushland, and Carl Stoll, President of the Chamber of Commerce of the Upper Peninsula, asked me to accompany them to Washington, D.C., for a civil aeronautics board hearing, I readily agreed, even though I had to spring for my own expenses. We were to testify in an attempt to retain Nationwide Airlines as an all-Michigan airline.

I arranged to meet Mr. Stoll and the Attorney General at Detroit's Willow Run Airport for a 7 a.m. flight. I left, without luggage, at 5 a.m. in the cold darkness and drove to Willow Run on ice-covered roads. I literally slid into a no-parking zone near American Airline's door, at the old airport, charged the first attendant I saw in uniform and threw the ignition keys.

"Just park it for the day and leave the keys at American's desk," I called as I ran for the gate.

Panting a little, I found my seat on the plane beside my two friendly witnesses.

"Can you support your allegation," Rushland asked, "that Wisconsin Central has had the mail franchise for Upper Michigan for several years and not provided service.?"

"It's all here." I tapped my briefcase.

* * * *

The Civil Aeronautics Board hearing room was huge, deeply carpeted and paneled with solid walnut to the ceiling. Chairs and benches, massive in leather and wood, dominated the scene.

Carl Stoll, without hesitating, found a chair and removed his coat, exposing broad red suspenders. He loosened his shirt collar, planted his hat further back on his head, leaned back in the elegant chair and opened a newspaper.

The referee, his associates, and other officials, expensively dressed in business suits, stared openly at this north woods native, who ignored them.

The hearing began. Representatives of each airline spoke first and things moved right along. I fervently hoped they'd continue to progress. I wanted to be home that night in my own bed.

The first witness called by Nationwide was the Attorney General of Michigan, Rushland. He did well, stating that although Wisconsin Central had had a reasonable time to establish service and carry the mail, it had not done so while Nationwide had. In fact, Nationwide progressively improved its service. He was quizzed concerning the character and volume of air traffic in and out of the Northern Peninsula and unfortunately he did not have the information. This seemed to me a big minus in our case.

Carl Stoll came to life. Now hatless, he leaned over the conference table, looking at his notes, and furiously scribbling others. He seemed to finish just as he was called. Hunching into his suit jacket, he ambled to the witness stand.

Rushland had parried the cross examination questions with considerable skill, as all had expected. But I could see the lawyers for the other airline shuffling papers and whispering excitedly, their mouths almost watering as they prepared to take on this lanky slouch from the country. As far as they knew, Stoll's only qualifications to testify were that somehow he was the current President of the Chamber of Commerce. I was very keen about this sequence, for it was likely I'd be the next witness.

Stoll was first queried by the attorneys representing Nationwide and as President of the Northern Peninsula Chamber of Commerce, stated his satisfaction with the services provided by Nationwide. The witness was then turned over to the opposition.

The first inquiry was apparently written by the conglomerate of all the attorneys representing Wisconsin Central Airlines and other airlines servicing the general area.

A young attorney, his white shirt so starched it appeared to prevent any lowering of his chin, posed the question.

"Mr. Stoll, will you tell the board what you know about the quantity and character of air traffic, and the potential for such traffic in and out of your city of Escanaba within the next decade, and the importance, if any, of directly tying this traffic to the Southern Peninsula, rather than permitting its normal flow through the communities of Northern Wisconsin, and on to Milwaukee or Chicago or to Lansing and Detroit?"

Mr. Stoll alleged that he did not understand the question, and asked the attorney to repeat the question. For some reason, when the question was read back, the word "normal" was left out.

Carl was silent a moment. He shifted, crossing his long legs. The opposing lawyers looked smug.

"Sir," Carl drawled, "when you refer to the flow of traffic through Northern Wisconsin, I thought you said 'normal flow'."

"That is exactly what I asked you," Starched Shirt said, "now will you answer the question?"

"Which one?"

By now the opposing lawyers were looking at each other and raising their eyebrows. I was beginning to guess what Carl was up to.

"The only one I have asked you," Starched Shirt said.

"Maybe I don't understand," Carl said, "but one time you asked me about flow of traffic through Northern Wisconsin, and the other time you asked me about normal flow of traffic, and it ain't normal for air traffic to have to go to several of your stops in Wisconsin before getting us to Lansing and Detroit within our own state."

I glanced quickly at the opposing counsel. They were leaning on the highly polished table gawking.

Carl continued to be a difficult adversary and it was with visible relief Attorney Starched Shirt finished with his cross examination. Actually, Carl was a well-informed man. He was President of his own company in Escanaba, a director of the bank and a civic leader.

As I suspected, I followed Carl on the witness stand. Lawyers for the opposing airline, having been unpleasantly surprised by the Northern Peninsula native's active savvy, got ready to hunt bear, with me as the bear. One or the other of them objected to every question put to me by Nationwide's counsel.

At length, the referee grew impatient.

"The hour is late," he said, "and I understand counsel agreed not to keep the doctor more than one day. I believe he may have additional information and opinions that would be helpful to the Aeronautics Board in making a decision. Therefore, I am going to allow his answers without further interruption except the opposing counsel may object for the record, and we will decide what questions and answers shall be deleted."

I was finally excused from the stand and by paying a cab driver an extra $5.00 to break all the traffic rules to get me to the airport in time, I just made it. I dashed to the waiting plane without bothering to check in at the counter. My ticket was in order and the helpful stewardess let me by. As I boarded the 60-place plane and sat between Carl Stoll and Attorney General Rushland, the stewardess said they had put on 59 meals so there wouldn't be any dinner for me. I told her I didn't care—I just wanted to go home. Carl heard this and projected himself into the dialog.

"Now why are you treating the doctor that way? Is it because he is small and bald-headed and was a little late? He is the only single man on the plane, and he told me he was going to marry the girl who brought him his dinner."

The stewardess laughed and brought my dinner first. I didn't know her name but talking with her after dinner I learned she was from Lansing and the daughter of Colonel Maitland, whom I knew had been promoted to the rank of Brigadier General the day before. She didn't know this and after I told her, we practically owned the airplane.

Nationwide lost the case. Their routes were absorbed along with the mail contract, and became North Central Airlines. (Now Republic Airlines) Our only gratification was that an important condition came along with the decision. It was that North Central would establish direct, non-stop flight between Lansing and Detroit in the lower part of the state to the Upper Peninsula.

Our small victory proved to be hollow, for North Central never abided by the condition and the flights still make several stops in Wisconsin. Frequently, it is necessary to change planes in Green Bay.

To be fair, North Central has expanded its services and improved its equipment, but something more important was lost. I often think longingly of the second-hand Lockheed planes Nationwide used originally. These dependable old birds made one round trip a day between the peninsulas and flew only on visual contact.

They were inadequately heated, and in very cold weather (half of the year up north), the co-pilot carefully wrapped each passenger in a wool blanket.

The chief pilot of this little Nationwide airline, like my other friends in the north, was certainly among the most accommodating folks on earth. The Whitefish story is a fine example.

*   *   *   *

In the 1940's, Lake Superior abounded with whitefish. Some of those warm-hearted people in the north wanted the patients at the Lansing Chest Hospital to enjoy fresh whitefish, as a gift. I made arrangements, primarily through Chief Pilot Cooley, for Nationwide to fly the Thursday whitefish catch from a Houghton fishery to Lansing. So skillfully did Olive Henderson and her cooks prepare the fish that both patients and staff eagerly awaited the Friday lunch.

One Friday afternoon, I boarded Nationwide's plane to go north. Pilot Cooley was on duty—a big personable man, who smiled a lot. (This contrasts sharply with the cool impersonal attitude of the pilots for most larger airlines.) Cooley loved his work and he knew his job. I often flew "shot-gun" with him in the cockpit when there weren't many passengers.

"Cooley," I said as I buckled my seatbelt. "What did you do with our fish yesterday? We had our mouths all set for it."

Pilot Cooley wagged his head.

"Doc," he said, "I flew over this town for an hour in the soup last night, trying to get your darn fish in here. I finally had to turn around and go back north cuz I couldn't find the airport in the fog."

CHAPTER 30

EMPHYSEMA

Essentially, we have conquered tuberculosis but Americans are thwarted by other problems. Emphysema, a slow insidious killer, has become rampant. The tragedy is that, unlike tuberculosis, which is caused by an organism, emphysema can usually be prevented by avoiding cigarettes and other dangerous inhalants.

The word emphysema derives from Greek, meaning "to inflate", precisely what happens to the air spaces in the lung of a person with emphysema. Unfortunately, these spaces are not meant to distend like an over-inflated balloon. They should remain elastic and exchange carbon dioxide and other poisonous gases in the blood for oxygen.

Dr. Claude Burnett, one of the surgical residents in the training program for Chest Surgery at the Hospital in 1954, '55 and '56 had become acutely interested in emphysema. He was particularly concerned about pulmonary resection for these patients. He inflated a lobe of the lung taken from an emphysema patient and photographed it. Dr. Burnett reasoned that we were taking out not only the emphysematous bullae but too much good functional lung.

"These patients need all the lung we can leave them," he said.

We decided to attempt a different type of operation in an effort to conserve lung by decapping the cysts or bullae and repairing the lung base on our next surgical emphysema patient.

A year and half earlier, I had seen a 34 year-old truck driver as an outpatient, who had bullous emphysema in both lungs.

"You are a very sick man," I had said. "My advice is to operate and remove the upper lobe of the right lung."

He could barely function with his shortness of breath but he refused and went on his way. If I had operated at that time, I would have taken out the entire lobe, so maybe he wasn't so dumb. After about 30 months, the truck driver returned and his emphysema was much worse. He looked bluish, needed constant bed rest, and certainly could not live much longer.

I advised surgery again (although he was a poor risk) to start on the right most involved lung. We planned to decap the cyst and repair the lung base. The truck driver agreed.

Once anesthetized, I started the incision. The blood from the chest wall vessels appeared very dark—almost purple . . . a certain sign of oxygen lack. I proceeded as swiftly as I could, opened the chest cavity and found a giant bulla filling the whole space, with the lung compressed under it. The wall of this emphysematous cyst was thinner than a toy balloon. I punctured it quickly and deliberately. There was a swish of compressed air into the chest space.

Using a long surgical scissor, I trimmed away the walls of the deflated sac as near the remaining lung bed as possible.

"Apply more pressure."

The anesthesiologist turned his gauges.

The lung that had been pressed almost flat under the bulla began to inflate—better than I had hoped for. The blood color changed from a wine hue to a good red.

There was much more to do and all proceeded well. His post-operative condition was more satisfactory than I had expected it would be. I savored the feeling—it came so seldom after surgery for these emphysematous patients.

Seven months later, I did the same procedure on the man's left lung. He gained 50 pounds in six months and is now working full-time as a truck driver. This man had been a chain smoker—three or four packs a day. He promised to give it up after surgery. I wonder if he did.

There are 2.1 million Americans known to have emphysema and it is the third most frequent disability among American adults. Most of these people are not suitable surgical candidates. The surgeon general has repeatedly warned us about the destructive effects of cigarette smoking but the Federal Government subsidizes tobacco growers to this day!

* * * *

My friend, Dr. John Towey, superbly trained, intelligent and skilled, had been a long-time smoker. Predictably, he had emphysema and he did very little about it. In spite of being short of breath, he worked long hours. I worried about him, even when our paths didn't cross.

Once I sat in a surgical conference at John's hospital, Pinecrest Sanatorium, in Powers. He presented the case of a male patient who had had extensive tuberculosis, healed by fibrosis. Unfortunately, fibrosis produces much scar tissue. This had stretched the remaining good lung, and in a complicated pattern, produced emphysema. He was a chain smoker but in this case smoking was not the lone culprit.

"I propose we accept the patient for your decapping technique,"John said, looking directly at me.

I examined the patient, who was then hospitalized and cyanotic. He would be a horrendous surgical risk. I'd have to operate in Lansing at the Chest Hospital and I doubted he could even tolerate the flight by ambulance plane.

"John," I said later that day, "I'm sorry, I can't accept your patient for surgery."

A month later in Powers, John brought up the same case in conference. Again, I turned him down, feeling uncomfortable but justified.

John brought the case up again two months later. I was astounded the patient had survived that long.

"What gives, John?" I said. "We have a lot to do today and you've urged impossible surgery for this man three times."

"Well, he is still alive," John grinned, "and you didn't think he'd last a week. I have heard you tell your young residents never to refuse a patient if there is a chance." He switched on a serious face.

"I believe this man has a chance if you operate on him using the lung saving technique you described when you published . . ."

"The results of this procedure," I finished for him. "Yes, I know, it's the most important surgical technique I ever developed, but come on, John, would you submit *yourself* to major surgery if you had as slim a chance as this poor guy?"

"Sure—if you accept him and if he survives, and I think he will, then I'll come down for surgery too."

I stuck to my philosophy and refused. It was almost becoming dangerous. John Towey was six foot four inches tall and towered over my five foot seven inches. I went back to Lansing marveling at the tenacity of both the patient and the doctor.

John had his patient's x-rays right back on the viewing box at the next monthly conference.

I gave up.

"Send him down to the Chest Hospital by ambulance plane," I said. If he is alive when he gets there, I thought, surely my friends on the staff at the Chest Hospital would talk me out of doing the surgery.

They didn't.

I heard Dr. Stanley say to one of the residents, "The Chief got himself into this impossible situation—now let's see how he gets out of it."

Dread lay heavy on my own chest, and I felt even worse when I looked at the frail figure being slid onto the operating table.

Yet during anesthesia, unaccountably, his color appeared to improve. He needed hardly anything to put him under.

217

Because of the anoxia he was practically anesthetizing himself.

I cut through the chest wall and entered the lung space. I was struck by the color of the blood. It was much better than I expected. I cut, trimmed, sewed, inserted a drainage tube, and when I stepped back to signal the end of my labors, the patient actually appeared to have improved in color and respiration.

Naturally, I felt pretty ambivalent about this poor soul who, judging from my many years of experience, had no chance to live more than a few days.

The human spirit never fails to amaze me. He had not only hung on several more months, he had survived the trauma of major surgery. The small leaks in the lung resulting from suturing, healed up and the drainage went well. I took a lot of kidding from my own hospital colleagues. John, particularly, laid it on me whenever I saw him after that.

Our rejoicing was a little premature, however, for when I checked the post-operative x-rays I could see residual air in the pleural space. This means there wasn't enough reexpanding lung to fill the space following the removal of the cyst.

Usually when this occurs, the patient would need a thoractoplasty, which would partially collapse the chest wall and thus reduce the size of the space so that the expanding lung can fill in the remaining area. But this patient couldn't tolerate more surgery. I'd already pushed my considerable luck more than I wanted.

Dr. Claude Burnett wondered aloud—"Could we force up the diaphragm by instilling air into the abdomen?" he said. "This would help obliterate the space."

"Good idea." I was grateful and scheduled the procedure for the next day.

It worked! The diaphragm lifted and within a week the pleural space had disappeared. The patient was less cyanotic and continued to breath easier.

A few days later he returned to the hospital at Powers and subsequently was discharged to his home. I have always been thankful my friends forced me into action. I hope the patched-up gentleman used his additional years well.

CHAPTER 31

BIG WHEEL TURNING

The 1940's and 1950's were frantically busy years for me. I wonder now why I didn't buckle under to one or another stress-related disease. I often caution my surgeon sons not to work so hard.

For example, at one time in late summer, I was General Chairman of the Pembine Conference. We were gaining, and justifiably, a national reputation for making great strides in medical and surgical treatment of chest disease. I also had been elected President of the Board of Trustees for the Michigan Tuberculosis Association. These two organizations had scheduled meetings simultaneously and I was expected to be there—in Lansing and in Pembine, chairing the proceedings.

I fretted a while, loath to miss either and at length worked out a plan. Two of us who were "double booked" would stay for the trustee's meeting in Lansing; two other doctors with whom I wished to confer about Pembine, would wait for us in Lansing.

But the small plane I sometimes used to fly north wouldn't hold all of us. I threw the whole transportation mess into the lap of Theodore Werle, Executive Secretary of the Michigan Tuberculosis Association.

Ted got cracking.

"Oh, Chris," he waved some hastily scratched notes in my direction, "There's a plane out of Grand Rapids for Milwaukee at 4 p.m. You can connect with the Milwaukee Railroad "400" for Pembine at 5 p.m. You'll get to Pembine about 11."

"That's great, Ted, thanks." I collared Bill Tuttle and Roger Hanna, foot-loose for the afternoon until our plane left at 4:00.

"Wait at my house. Ruth's not home but it's open because there are workmen there. Go on over—you'll be more comfortable."

At a few minutes after three, I dashed into my house with Leonard Howard in tow. Bill Tuttle, after discovering my liquor cabinet, was making himself unpopular trying to direct the stone masons adding to my yard wall.

"Come on," I yelled. "It's sixty miles and we have less than an hour to catch that flight."

The plane was apparently late in Grand Rapids so we made it. I could hardly believe our good luck. I turned to the young woman who helped guide us through the airport.

"It looks like you held the plane for us."

"Yes, indeed we did," she flashed a smile.

"In that case," I said jokingly, "will you arrange for a limousine and police escort from the plane to the train in Milwaukee?"

"Of course." She gave me another gorgeous smile, a little wave and retreated.

I glanced about, grinning inwardly. My three companions were out of earshot. I might just have a little fun with this.

We tramped aboard and settled ourselves in the old DC-3.

"Good news, Bill," I said in a low voice to Dr. Tuttle. We were wedged side by side in the well-worn seats. "Capitol Airlines held the plane for us and we'll have a police escort in Milwaukee."

"You're a damn liar," he grunted.

I thought I was too.

I wondered what would happen in Milwaukee—if we really could make connections.

In Milwaukee, its engines clattering, the plane taxied to

the ramp. The others gathered briefcases and suit jackets, as the engines whined down. We stepped into the late afternoon warmth. There, gleaming in the sunshine, sat a black limousine, flanked by two officers on motorcycles. My mind boggled. That charming little lady in Grand Rapids hadn't been fooling.

"Dr. Stringer, sir, over here!" the driver called.

I raised my arm in reply and my three friends gaped at me as he trotted over in full uniform.

"Get right in," the driver said. "The attendants will bring your luggage.

As one, our heads swiveled toward the belly of the plane as two men sorted baggage from the cargo hold. In minutes, we were streaking through the 5 o'clock city traffic. Motorcycle sirens screamed as we sped through yield signs, stop streets, and red lights to the Northwestern Railroad station.

I sat back and tried to look unimpressed. In unison, my friends demanded how in hell I had arranged all this.

"You just have to know the right people," I said, wondering who had arranged it all. I decided to throw caution to the Wisconsin winds.

"I've arranged for the train to wait if we're late." I put on a smug face. Oh, this was getting better and better.

"Not the crack 400," Len said. "That engineer doesn't wait for anyone, not even you." For the first time in our long acquaintance, he looked non-plused.

"Fine thing! Look what I've arranged so far," I said, feigning hurt. It seemed that the more outrageous my lies, the sooner they came to life. Yet I didn't really believe the 400 would be there, and I certainly didn't think it would wait! With sirens dying and the blinkers of the limousine still flashing, we arrived curb-side at the railway station. I leaned from the deep, plush seats and tried not to stare. A solicitous, clean shaven, middle-aged man in an expensive business suit, with several red-capped porters buzzing about him, met us as we climbed out of our expensive speed wagon. I was bewildered. Where would it all end?

"Is this Dr. Stringer's party?"

The proper, dark-haired man nodded when I identified myself, then took a few steps back to briskly supervise our luggage removal. I didn't dare look at my three friends. I could barely hold my face straight. I turned quickly when Mr. Business Suit motioned and we followed him through the station, red caps trailing us, to the "Famous 400". It lay along the track, posed for Pembine, grumbling in protest but waiting. A porter stood by our pullman car. We hopped on board and Mr. Business Suit gave me a little salute with one hand and his card with the other.

"Thanks so much," I called. Should I have tipped him? I thought vaguely, but the train began to move. I wondered how long I could keep up the deception. In the meantime, I basked in my false supremacy.

"This is only the beginning, fellows," I boasted. "You may expect more deluxe treatment for the remainder of the journey."

For once, Bill Tuttle had no response. He shook his head and went directly to the club car. Len Howard asked who Mr. Business Suit was.

Giddy with success, I didn't bother to dig in my pocket for the card. Pulling words out of the air I said, "He's an official of the railroad." He believed me, and with hunger reminding us what time it was, we made our way to the dining car.

Steaks, I thought, would round off my luck, but none appeared on the menu. So I asked the waiter if he could get them anyway. Sorry, but there were none.

"Will you send the steward over, please?"

Len raised his eyebrows but said nothing. When the steward leaned over, I went into my pitch. Tugging the card from my pocket, I read, "Superintendent of the Milwaukee Division of the Northwestern Railroad". No wonder he had a good tailor.

"This gentleman, " I said brandishing the card, "will appreciate anything you can do for us."

That steward found steaks somewhere. Bill Tuttle wolfed his down with little comment, definitely out of character.

Bill always expressed his opinions freely, whether you asked for them or not.

To complete the trip, which had taken on an unreal quality for me, the Four Season's stationwagon met us at Pembine.

Bill Tuttle came out of his partial stupor as we drove toward the club. "Now, everybody, let me handle this when we see John Steele (John was from Milwaukee)."

How would Bill describe our trip? I didn't have to wait long.

In the lounge at the club Bill zeroed in on the hapless John Steele. "John, my boy, we flew into Milwaukee this afternoon, went through your town's 5 o'clock traffic with police escorts and caught the train in ten minutes. Brother, when I go the Milwaukee, that's the way I like to do it!"

I've had some rewarding times in my life but none gave me as much fun. That big wheel just kept turning. It had gotten to the point I was even beginning to believe I was in control.

Back in Lansing, Ted Werle sought me out. "Were your travel accommodations O.K.?" He stood, almost stiffly, his face unsmiling above a correct white shirt and uneventful tie.

"Would you believe ... " I began. Then I saw a tiny flicker of warmth in the cool blue eyes. It grew until it thawed out his face and a grin appeared.

I burst into laughter. "It was all your doing! Now, Ted, do me another favor, don't tell anyone. That was the most fun I've had in a coon's age."

We had a final good laugh when the State Journal and the Milwaukee Globe Newspaper ran an article saying that four doctors from Lansing were being rushed to the Upper Peninsula to stop an epidemic!

Maybe the stresses never overwhelmed me because my sense of humor did!

CHAPTER 32

MICHIGAN STATE POLICE

I was presiding at a meeting of the Michigan Thoracic Society in the elegant, old Book-Cadillac Hotel in Detroit and the meeting was nearly finished. Sensing someone's eyes fixed on me, I looked up from my notes. A big state policeman stood in the doorway of the conference room definitely staring at me. I raised my eyebrows and pointed discretely at myself. The trooper nodded.

I excused myself and asked the vice-president to take over for the remainder of the meeting.

I hurried off the podium and down the aisle. All eyes were on me.

"Your secretary told us where you were, Doctor. You're needed as a witness at a criminal trial in Charlotte. I believe the prosecutor talked to you about the matter and you agreed to testify later this week. However, the case is moving along faster than anticipated and he would like to have you there today. Will you come? A scout car will take you."

"Of course," I said, glancing back hastily at the roomful of my friends. They were buzzing and straining their necks. "Let's go."

I would just let them wonder—it might be fun.

The trial involved the prosecution of a man for assault with a deadly weapon with intent to kill. The defendant claimed self defense. I had treated the victim who required major surgery to control the near fatal bleeding due to a bullet which had passed through the left chest tearing through a major artery en route.

Another officer drove my car back to East Lansing at the proper speed. I went, by relays, with sirens and blinking lights. At each relay—Redford, Brighton, and East Lansing, I changed vehicles. It was exciting, for at each transport the officer opened the back door of the squad car, carried my bag and ushered me into the waiting relay car. Unaccountably, at each one of the transfers, an acquaintance from Lansing passed by, nearly losing control of his own vehicle while he ogled at me. Word quickly got around that the State Police had Stringer and there were various speculations as to why. I just let it go, and laughed inwardly at the quizzical stares cast my way the following week.

I met the Eaton County prosecutor outside the court room in the old county building in Charlotte, where the court was in recess waiting for my arrival. The prosecutor told me that the defendant had already testified that the victim had come toward him with an open knife and he had fired in self defense.

The court reconvened and I was called to the witness stand. The prosecutor qualified me for the court as an expert witness and began his questioning.

"Did you see Mr. Stanford Rutledge as a patient Saturday evening, July 2, of this year?"

"Yes."

"Why?"

"A Charlotte physician called me and told me Mr. Rutledge had been shot in the chest and needed help."

"What was your response?"

"I asked the doctor for a brief description of the extent and nature of the damage."

"What was his response?"

The defendant's attorney objected on the basis that any response would be "hear-say". The court sustained the objection.

"After you learned as much as you could from your consultation with the doctor in Charlotte, what did you do?"

"I requested that the patient be transferred immediately by ambulance to the Chest Hospital in Lansing."

"What happened next in your care of this gun-shot victim?"

The defendant's attorney objected again on the basis of the question being too inclusive. He maintained that many things could have happened unrelated to my treatment of the patient and that I had not even seen the patient yet. The court sustained the objection and the prosecutor rephrased his question.

"What did you do, specifically, relating to the care of Mr. Rutledge after you requested that he be transferred to the Chest Hospital?"

"I called the Chest Hospital surgical supervisor and directed that an operating room be made ready for major surgery if such was found to be necessary when the patient was brought in from Charlotte."

"What did you do next?"

"I went to the hospital and supervised preparations while waiting for the patient."

"What was the condition of the patient when he was brought in?"

"He was semi-conscious and bleeding profusely from a wound in the front left chest. He was markedly short of breath. His color was bluish. The pulse was rapid and thready."

"What did you do for him?"

"Blood transfusion was started as soon as blood could be typed and cross matched. We obtained a portable x-ray of the chest and the patient was taken to the operating room while still being transfused."

"At what time did you first physically examine the patient's chest?"

"When he was brought in I noted a wound in the front of the chest which was still bleeding. When he was placed on the operating table, I was able to and did examine the left chest—front and back and lateral."

"What were your findings?"

"I saw a wound in the back of the left chest just below the tip of the left shoulder blade and another in the front chest wall at about the same level. There was continued bleeding from the front wound."

"Were these openings in the chest caused by gun shot?"

The defense attorney objected on the basis that the witness had not personally observed the production of the wounds. Objection was sustained.

"Did the openings or wounds in the chest wall have the appearance of gun shot wounds?"

"Yes."

"After you examined the chest, what did you do?"

"With my assistants, we surgically opened the chest, identified a bleeding branch of the pulmonary artery, clamped this blood vessel and repaired it."

"Did you recover a bullet?"

"No."

"Why?"

"There was no bullet in the chest. A bullet had entered the back of the chest and passed through the chest wall and lung and exited in front."

"In your opinion doctor, was your patient shot in the back?"

"Yes."

There was a rustle in the courtroom. This testimony was in obvious conflict with prior testimony of the defendant.

The prosecutor addressed the court.

"No more questions your honor."

The judge referred the witness to the defense attorney.

"When the injured party in this accident was approaching the defendant with an open knife in an upraised hand and the defendant fired his revolver in self defense, could the bullet thus entering the chest have caused the damage you have described in direct questioning?"

228

The prosecutor objected.

"The counsel has qualified his question by assuming the witness is familiar with the relative position of the parties in this case when in fact he is not—he wasn't there."

The judge sustained the objection.

Defendant's attorney asked, "Could the damage you noted in this man's lung when you operated on him, have been caused by a bullet entering the front of the chest and exiting from the back?"

"Yes."

The jurors snapped to attention and the judge looked up quizzically. It appeared I had given testimony conflicting with my testimony on direct examination. I knew, however, the prosecutor was well prepared and he would straighten out the apparent contradiction. Elated, the defense attorney thought he had discredited the witness and told the court he had no more questions.

In redirect examination the prosecutor asked:

"Doctor, you have testified that the bullet could produce the same kind of damage to the lung if fired into the back or front of the victim. Can you tell the court on what basis you have determined that the accused shot your patient in the back?"

"Yes."

"Will you please do so?"

"The entry site of a bullet produces an altogether different pattern on the subject's skin and adjacent tissue than the exit site. The entrance is clean and sharp and usually no larger than the caliber of the bullet, whereas the exit is larger and more ragged in appearance. Dr. Lemoyne Snyder," I said, "Medicolegal Director of the Michigan State Police, recognized this and discussed and illustrated the difference in a text he authored, *Homicide Investigation.* I have recognized this fact in other cases as well as the current one. The well-circumscribed hole in the victim's back was clearly the location of the entry of the bullet and the ragged defect in the front of the chest was clearly the exit."

During this lengthly answer to the question, the defendant's attorney tried to stop me two or three times with objections and the judge finally broke in.

"The witness has been asked a simple and proper question, now let him answer it."

On recross examination, the defense attorney asked:

"If the defendant was grappling with Mr. Rutledge, isn't it possible that with his arm holding his revolver around the injured man, the gun could have been accidentally fired into his back?"

"No."

"Why?"

"The character of the bullet wound in Mr. Rutledge's chest was such that the gun could not have been fired from such close range."

The prosecutor had no more questions and I was excused. A state police officer drove me back to my home in East Lansing.

The following day the jury returned a quilty verdict and the accused was sentenced to prison.

* * * *

One of the fringe benefits those days when I was driving madly all over Michigan was a state police courtesy card. It told the state police officers, in effect, not to give this guy a ticket. (I also had a permit to carry in my car a loaded revolver, which I never had to use.)

I was stopped once for speeding west of Detroit somewhere. The state policeman, when I discovered I'd forgotten my courtesy card, gave me a citation and I paid the fine. I never misplaced this card again.

About a year later, I had an urgent call from a doctor at Sparrow Hospital to see a police officer who had been shot in the chest. I was able, fortunately, to go at once. The patient was the same officer who had so courteously given me a speeding ticket.

He had lost a great amount of blood and was in shock. X-rays showed a partially collapsed left lung and the pleural space almost filled with blood. The bullet had entered through the front of the left chest and could be seen in the x-rays, near the left lung root. A touch-and-go case.

We started pumping blood and gave him five units, wheeling him to the operating room while the fifth unit still ran. Without waiting for the family to arrive to give permission to operate, I bronchoscoped and placed a tight gauze plug in the left stem bronchus to keep him from drowning in his own blood.

I opened the left chest. It was as bad as I expected. Progressing toward where the bullet lay, I saw that it had just barely missed the aorta. A little higher and he wouldn't have needed me. I removed the bullet, repaired the remainder of the damaged lung and placed a drainage tube in the pleural space. The anesthesiologist re-expanded the lung and I closed up.

"He's going to make it," I said confidently. And he did. The officer recovered nicely and when I checked on him post-operatively, we chatted pleasantly. I never mentioned the ticket but I am sure he remembered!

* * * *

The Ed Freeman family and the Stringers had become good friends. Ed was command officer of the Cadillac State Police Post and I went hunting in that vicinity whenever I could get away from my work during the deer season. Ed provided my lodging and if I didn't get my buck, the troopers always shared their meat with me. Ruth had learned to prepare venison the year we were at Stony Wold in the Adirondacks and she put on marvelous meals using this wild meat. We kept it in the freezer and if we didn't use up the November kill by March 1, we were in violation of a state law. Somehow I can't visualize state police raiding citizens' home freezers to enforce this law.

One evening in late March we served a roast venison tenderloin to a party of close friends including John Dethmers, Michigan Attorney General. As the guests filed through the buffet line, I carved and served.

"Now, John, this is venison from last season," I said when

he came by. "As chief law enforcement officer of Michigan, if you don't think you should eat illegal venison, I'll ask Ruth to cook you some ham and eggs."

John leaned over the table and sniffed appreciatively.

"I'll just have some of that roast beef," he said.

* * * *

The worry wart, Andrew Langenbacker, whom I nearly drove to nervous collapse when I chose to fly to northern hospitals, went along on one of my deer hunting expeditions. He had become president of the Chest Hospital Board of Trustees and a close friend of Ed Freeman, also, for they had both been tuberculosis patients at the Chest Hospital at the same time. Andy wanted to go deer hunting with me, not to hunt—just to experience what he'd heard so much about from his friends.

On the day before the planned trip with Andy, Ruth and I went to dinner at a friend's home, leaving Ruth's young college-freshman sister, Juanita, with our two boys, Jim and John. Juanita had invited some of her school class mates in for the evening. As she was upstairs putting the children to bed, the doorbell rang and one of the girls answered.

The man was a stranger to her, of course, and very unsteady on his feet.

"Is thish where Dr. Stringer lives?"

"Yes, it is."

The man looked as though he were going to weave right off the door step. She grew uneasy.

"Well, thank God! I have been all over thish neighborhood looking for him."

"Doctor isn't home right now and . . ."

"—thash all right, I'll yust wait."

He pushed his way past her and stumbled toward the davenport. The poor schoolgirls nearly fainted with fright. He had a rifle in each hand!

At this point Juanita came downstairs, saw her friends, fear-frozen, across the room, the guns and drunken condition of the stranger and decided it was no time to panic.

"I can't reach Dr. Stringer, right away . . ." she began.

"Oh, thash all right," he said good humoredly

The girls relaxed as they saw he had changed his mind about waiting and headed for the front door.

"I'll just leave these here," he mumbled, stacking the two rifles in the corner of the foyer. He tipped his hat and left. That was all—no clue as to who he was or where the guns came from.

The following morning, our teetotaler neighbors, the Shepards (Edmond Shepard was Solicitor General of Michigan), let us know that the drunk had indeed been all over the neighborhood.

Andy Langenbacker picked me up for the hunting trip to Cadillac.

"Andy, wait a minute. I've something to show you—and Ed too, after we get there," I said.

I ran back in the house and brought the guns into the car. Andy's eyes nearly popped from his head.

"My God, Chris—we don't need an arsenal." He looked again at the guns. "But they are beautiful."

They were truly magnificent pieces, one with a telescopic sight. I hoped that no one would claim them.

Ed Freeman had rooms for us at the Post and after we were settled, I told him the story of the drunk, and brought in the rifles.

His eyes lit up at the sight of the exquisite workmanship.

"But I haven't any idea where they came from either, Chris," he said.

We were sitting around in Ed's office that night, listening to police calls and reports when the Wexford County Sheriff came in.

"Is there a Dr. Stringer here?" he asked stamping the snow off his boots.

"What's he done now?" Ed asked laughing, then introduced me to the sheriff.

"I'm mightly glad you're here, Doctor," the sheriff said. "I guess I should tell you about a prisoner I was taking to the state penitentiary in Jackson three or four months ago.

This prisoner was an expert wood craftsman and he offered to carve some ornamental stocks for my favorite rifles. I talked to the warden at Jackson Prison a couple of days ago and don't ask me how, Doctor, but the warden knew you were coming to Cadillac to hunt."

"So," he went on, "when he checked and found the guns were finished, he told me he'd see that they were delivered to your house and hoped you'd agree to bring them up when you came. Did you get the guns, Dr. Stringer?"

"I'm not sure," I said, avoiding the startled looks of Andy and Ed. "What makes are the rifles?"

The sheriff began to describe them, then abruptly stopped. He flushed, sensing correctly that I had him in an uncomfortable position.

"Now look here . . ."

"Now you look here, sheriff. I have a couple of rifles upstairs that were delivered to my home by an unknown drunk. There was no identification on the guns. What special equipment did your rifles have?"

"One had a telescopic sight." He named the make of the guns. Ed and Andy now recovered from their surprise, sat grinning at the sheriff's discomfort.

"I'll write out a receipt—Ed, give me some paper, thanks—I'm describing here," I wrote rapidly, "the rifles I have. You sign here before these witnesses so I will be protected if someone else later claims the guns."

The sheriff signed and I gave him his elusive treasures. Shaking hands all around, the sheriff left without further fuss.

"You son of a gun. What did you do that for! I have to work with that fellow," Ed said.

We were still chuckling when we went to bed.

* * * *

We stayed two days. A squad car always patrolled nearby on the woodsy trail so I could be reached by radio if necessary. I got my buck, and Andy had a taste of a comrade's

234

successful hunt. No interruptions, good fellowhip and a restful change of pace. I never found out the identity of the messenger.

* * * *

Dr. LeMoyne Snyder, a Lansing surgeon and attorney, was highly respected in both professions for his skill and intellect. Through the years, he built up a warm association with the Michigan State Police as the Medicolegal Director and became known as an international expert on homicide. The state police owe a rather large slice of gratitude to Dr. Snyder for his participation in solving some of their most baffling criminal cases.

During that era beginning in the early 30's, Oscar Olander was the State Police Commissioner. He was a likeable, astute and no-nonsense commissioner. Under his leadership a state-wide network of state police posts were designed and staffs were developed. The buildings had a uniform, efficient and distinctive architecture, easily recognized. They are still in use.

Prior to that time many of the so-called posts were in temporary buildings or a store-front structure. These posts fanned out through the state with the communication and headquarters center in Lansing. Under Commissioner Olander, the Police Department attained national and international stature. The department regularly attracted outstanding new recruits.

Dr. Snyder worked closely with his good friend, Commissioner Olander, and it was he who encouraged the doctor-lawyer to write the textbook *Homicide Investigation,* which is now in its third edition and eleventh or twelveth printing, and is published in several foreign languages. LeMoyne says, "It's plagiarized to the extent that I am flattered."

When the work of the State Police Department attained prominence, politicians who had not thought much about the State Police before suddenly wanted to get on board.

This was contrary to Commissioner Olander's design for the State Police and he resigned.

The Governor appointed Donald Leonard to the post. As a politician his objectives were far different from the effective Oscar Olander. Leonard certainly could not get along with dedicated LeMoyne Snyder and LeMoyne severed his association with the State Police. Leonard later attempted to gain the governorship of Michigan on two occasions and was rejected.

Dr. Snyder and his two friends, Erle Stanley Gardner and Leonarde Keeler, organized the Court of Last Resort, a non-profit, privately funded association whose primary function was to ferret out unjustly convicted citizens, investigate the circumstances, and exert influence or pressure on courts to reopen these cases. Justice, of course, was their goal.

LeMoyne and his wife, Louise, now live in Paradise, California, near their friend Erle Stanley Gardner until his death.

When our eldest son, Jim, was killed in a climbing accident in California's northern mountains, Ruth and I and the younger boys were devastated. We felt an over-whelming sense of loss, deepened by the incomplete reports we received regarding the circumstances surrounding Jim's accident.

I phoned LeMoyne, who had been a valued friend and colleague when we were both surgeons in Lansing. I could have wept when I heard his warm, familiar voice.

"Chris, come on out and be our guest. We'll discuss what we should do when you get here."

I left a tearful Ruth and our other sons with a heavy heart, lightened a little by the prospect of being with understanding friends, and perhaps learning more about the death of our strong, adventurous first-born son. LeMoyne and Louise met my plane and drove me to their beautiful home in the mountains, as near Paradise as I have ever been. I slept well for a few hours—the first rest I'd had since the terrible news reached us.

For a period of several days, beginning the next morning, LeMoyne and Louise took me to the various places up through northern California, including as near to the scene of the accident as we could get. The tragedy was made so much more bearable because of the Snyders and I shall always remember their kindness with bittersweet pangs.

* * * *

A young trainee candidate for the Michigan State Police appeared to be physically below par and was sent to the Chest Hospital for examination. He was found to have tuberculosis, and the unfortunate fellow was hospitalized for several months. When he recovered, he could not re-enter police officer training and had to change careers.

His case got LeMoyne to thinking. Dr. Snyder suggested that each class of recruits for the Michigan State Police, be sent to the Chest Hospital for a tuberculin test and chest x-ray.

We initiated the policy and later were asked to do the entire physical examination program for these recruits. We soon noted that a relatively large number of these other-wise healthy young men had a high blood pressure. These candidates were going into work which would be demand-ing and stressful, and hypertension could become a danger-ous problem.

Why did so many of these healthy young bucks have high blood pressure? It gnawed at me. I called the commissioner to inquire if this finding had been noted previously.

"Not so far as I know," he said. "But Chris, I don't believe we have routinely taken blood pressure in the past. You people initiated it along with the chest x-rays."

On the way home from the hospital that day, I pushed a sphygmomanometer and a stethoscope into my pocket and stopped at the police post. I repeated the blood pressure readings on these same young men, who were engaged in routine study and prepatory training.

ALL BUT ONE HAD A NORMAL READING. It was easy to figure out then. The excitement and the desire to pass the examination made for a tense situation which elevated their blood pressures temporarily. All but the one, who had persistent hypertension, became competent state police officers.

* * * *

At the close of World War II, American occupying forces in Japan sent a distress call to Michigan State Police. They needed someone to set up a Japanese law enforcement agency amidst the rubble of the defeated country. Commissioner Olander and Captain Harold Mulbar traveled to Japan to study the situation and make recommendations. Captain Mulbar stayed on to implement the program and spent the rest of his life, happily, in Japan.

* * * *

The Michigan Upper Peninsula town named L'Anse is pronounced "Lawnse" and has one of the distinctive state police posts. A police officer stationed at this post was injured in a three car accident while trying to apprehend a man in a stolen car. The attending doctor, Henry Winkler, of L'Anse, phoned me describing the injuries—multiple known fractures, including five ribs, the right hip, and the right femur and clavicle.

Unfortunately, the little town had inadequate surgical facilities.

"You can get him down here as fast as I can come up there," I said when Dr. Winkler finished his description. "Besides, he needs surgery, which we are equipped to do here."

"OK," Dr. Winkler said, "what should I do before I send him?"

"Insert a drainage tube into the right chest through a trocar. Start transfusing blood and continue en route."

"Consider it done," he said.

Good old pilot, Walter Carr, flew the patient south to Lansing, accompanied by a nurse and another L'Anse trooper.

Remarkably, the patient survived the plane and ambulance ride. We received a desperately ill young man, short of breath and cyanotic. I saw that we must re-expand the right lung immediately. The drainage tube was not keeping up with the air leaks in the lung. I had to do a thoracotomy and repair the shattered lung without delay.

I started by removing a segment of one of the fractured ribs. The surgery became more and more difficult, and the condition of the patient became more desperate. I found that rib ends had torn the lung in three places. I repaired these defects with several mattress sutures and the lung re-expanded. During the chest surgery, Dr. Herbert Harris, an orthopedic surgeon, had been operating on the compound fracture of the right femur. We finished about the same time.

"All the other fractures can wait for another time, if he lives," Herb said, as the rest of the team smoothed the cast on the patient's right leg and hip. They took him gently to the recovery room and notified his family of his critical condition.

For 48 hours he did surprisingly well. Then the nurse reported that he was having difficulty clearing the tracheo-bronchial tree. I did a tracheostomy then, so that the nursing staff could use suction to keep these passages clear.

The fifth day there was more trouble. His body temperature began to rise until it reached 105 degrees. He had a headache and he became irrational.

I nearly shuddered as I examined him. In severe multiple skeletal fractures and muscle trauma, particularly involving the long bones, the surgeon must always be mindful of the possibility of fat emboli. My patient was in mortal danger from this complication which is usually fatal within two or three days. Worse yet, no specifics exist for such a complication—just supportive measures, antibiotics and intravenous fluids.

I remained with the trooper every free minute I had for five days and nights. He sank very low at times but on the sixth day he improved and began a slow recovery.

What a magnificient reward!

"Don't send a statement for this man's care," I said to Elvi. I bounced out to the hall to go on my rounds. I earned payment enough in knowing I helped save this young man—and having a good night's sleep for the first time in a week.

The State Police Commissioner wrote me a nice letter.

CHAPTER 33

FORGOTTEN PEOPLE

Late one afternoon in 1953, as I was retreating to my office from surgery, Elvi said, "Dr. Newitt is waiting for you."

She gave me the "I-don't-know-either-look" as I passed by her desk.

Old friend and colleague, Art Newitt, Chief of the Tuberculosis Control Division of the State Department of Health, sat quietly, a half smile hovering under his black moustache. Motioning to the conference table across the room, I sat down; Art rose and repositioned himself across from me. This was obviously an important matter to Art so I just returned his smile and waited.

"Hi, Chris."

He acted like a kid trying to screw up courage to ask Dad for the car. I suspected I was about to be conned again. I looked at him and waited.

"Look here, Chris. I have a little problem"

I didn't need to look here or there or anywhere. I was experiencing deja vu of the first rank. Art and I had been through this whole scene previously in regard to tuberculosis in the Upper Peninsula.

"You and your problems, Art. The problem really is that they are never little problems. Why do you pick on me for your pigeon?"

241

"Now, Chris I wouldn't do that."

"The hell you wouldn't. You know I'm loaded to the neck with the consequences of helping you with your last little problem."

"Yes," he said. "But you did it and I know you well enough to believe that you will help me with this one if it can be done."

What a con artist. I almost knew what the scenario would be after Art's opening pitch, which, succinctly, was his concern about the high morbidity and mortality rate for tuberculosis of the lung among inmates of state hospitals and prisons.

Art came armed with charts, graphs, and figures.

"A state x-ray survey shows there are hundreds of institutionalized patients ill with lung diseases of all kinds."

He pawed through some dog-eared papers.

"See, nothing is being done except a pitiful effort to isolate really infectious cases."

He plowed on and I saw quickly enough that it wasn't Art's problem, but he was assuming responsibility for the horrible situation. Two hours later, in spite of myself, I was worn down.

Olive Henderson brought us coffee and doughnuts, discretely ignoring the fact my lunch hour had come and gone.

"Art, hold up a minute. What do you think I can do? It seems to me you need a full-time surgical team."

"Well, my department doesn't have any money for it; in any case, surgeons and assistants are not available for a surgical team."

I wasn't surprised.

"There are no funds at all," he said, "so I thought you could start a pilot program in one of the hospitals near Lansing, using Ingham Chest Hospital surgical residents as assistants . . ."

"And I would need to take my own nurses and supplies," I finished for him. "And who would pay for such a program? I couldn't do it with Chest Hospital funds, you know that."

"Yes, I know that, but then how did you manage when you started the surgical program in the Upper Peninsula?"

I didn't answer. He knew damn well I'd paid those initial costs from my own pocket. And I was beginning to wonder if helping would propel me to empty pockets. I had a family to raise and educate—two of my boys I hoped would elect to go through medical school and surgical training.

"Chris, if you don't do this, it won't get done. No one else has the pathfinder experience, the surgical expertise and concern essential for this new effort."

He plunged on. "Bill Tuttle once told me years ago that you were the one of his trainees who could approach the frontiers of surgery and conquer."

Bill was still living then, and I had indeed heard that he had made such a comment. Bill Tuttle was a favorite teacher and friend even before he had puffed me up with praise.

I was hooked.

"OK, Art. This is going to take some planning."

Art stared at me a moment. He began to glow as if someone had turned on a switch inside of him activating a pink neon sign. His eyes misted over and I swear his lower lip trembled. He stood up suddenly, grinned and sat down again.

"Where's that map!" he said blinking rapidly. "Yes—Ionia State Hospital for the Criminally Insane is closest to Lansing. Now if we . . ."

* * * *

I asked that Art set up a conference with the director of Ionia State Hospital and the medical staff who might be able to help. I said I would also want to take along our surgical supervisor. We would review the probable case load and the physical facilities available for the program. More importantly, I wanted to talk to the available medical and nursing staff, who would be responsible for patient preparation and essential post-operative care. I hustled Art out then. I thought he was going to kiss me!

A few days later, the director of nursing, the surgical supervisor, Doctor Arthur Newitt, and I drove to Ionia for our first glimpse of the Hospital for Criminally Insane, under Dr. Perry Robertson, director. I had not met Dr. Robertson before but he had once been a Lansing internist. He was a tall, grey-haired man from whom calmness and dignity seemed to flow. I was impressed. From the beginning he offered and provided full cooperation and continually let me know that he was grateful for help for his charges. I am sure he had been indoctrinated by Art Newitt.

The other members of the medical staff were psychiatrists with no recent operating room experience but they were intelligent men, anxious to assist. Early on, an intern from a Lansing hospital who had rotated through the Chest Hospital service joined the Ionia staff and he made a positive difference. My director of nursing from the Chest Hospital took time off to evaluate hospital personnel and equipment. She found no adequate instruments and scant supplies. The sterilizer was questionable. There was no anesthesiologist available, and we would have to bring one from the Chest Hospital until one of the psychiatrists could be trained in anesthesia. The surgical supervisor, Stella Hillman, and I took prodigious notes for our guidance at the Chest Hospital in preparation for the first operation on the criminally insane.

When we finished our conference and had toured the facility, Dr. Robertson invited us to his home on the hospital grounds for lunch. The large white brick colonial home sat on a bluff at the edge of the grounds overlooking a valley and the Grand River below. The town of Ionia lay beyond. The Ionia Reformatory (another state penal institution for young offenders) could be seen slightly up stream to the left. Further upstream a truck farm stretched as far as I could see. We sat on graceful white wicker furniture on the veranda, which ran across the full front of the high columned home.

Mrs. Robertson came out and joined us. Dignified and pleasant, she greeted us warmly and remembered each of our names while we were there. She was obviously a pro in entertaining Dr. Robertson's professional and political guests. I suspected this gracious wife may have been a factor in many hospital appropriations.

A young, white-coated male house servant called us to lunch. As we entered the dining room, I tried not to gape at the splendor of the room and furnishings. The silver, crystal and china were obviously of high quality.

Mrs. Robertson seated me at her right facing the buffet across the room. The hot food arrived from the kitchen carried by the two uniformed waiters and placed on the buffet. One waiter lifted the dinner plate from in front of each guest and the other carved the lamb and served the food. I was intrigued by the long, sharp carving knife he used skillfully and with some abandon.

We were hungry and the plentiful food tasted delicious. When we finished, Mrs. Robertson nodded to the white-coat standing at attention facing her. He removed our plates with the help of his assistant. They brought in steaming apple pie which was also cut and served from the buffet with a sharp, pointed knife. When we had finished this delicious dessert, the plates were removed and the water glasses filled. For the first time our group was alone without an attending servant. We sat and visited a bit, planning and getting additional information from Dr. Robertson. As we were ready to leave I commented on the excellent food and service. "Where are you able to get such good help?" I said.

I had silently wondered about the opulence of this home and service provided by the State of Michigan when they were unable to pay the expense of a chest surgeon. Mrs. Robertson smiled.

"Perhaps you'd like to hear a humorous story." Mrs. Robertson offered obliquely. "It really happened to me."

We all encouraged her.

"A patient I had trained as a cook served in our home for many years. During this time, she had come to regard the home and the Robertson family as her personal property.

"However, she mentally regressed and it was necessary to put her back in 'lock-up' in the hospital. I had become attached to this lady who had served so well. I knew the patient liked lemon meringue pie, so I baked a pie to take to her.

"The concrete walk from our home to the hospital was a little slippery from a light rain that had frozen, but I thought I could negotiate the distance to the hospital. So, carrying the pie, I started to the hospital. The former cook was watching over her beloved former home from a window at the end of the hall on the third floor of the hospital where she had stationed herself each day. She saw me fall on the icy walk, splashing pie up over my face and front."

She sang out, "The old gray mare ain't what she used to be—ain't what she used to be—many long years ago."

"The servants are incarcerated patients from the hospital. My wife trained them," Dr. Robertson said, after we had laughed at the story this delightful lady told on herself.

"What's the crime of the two dining room attendants?" I asked. "They seem to be models of good behavior and training."

Dr. Robertson's voice became a monotone.

"They killed their wives with carving knives."

Our nurse had been sitting with her back to the buffet. She turned pale.

* * * *

I did a thoracoplasty for the first patient operated at the Ionia Hospital for the Criminally Insane. The anesthesiologist from the Chest Hospital accompanied me for the early operations and I also brought a surgical nurse who had prepared packs of sterilized instruments and surgical drapes, and a first assistant. The second assistant was one of the psychiatrists who would take the necessary calls during the post-operative period. Things went smoothly, and the patient was unusually quiet during the post-operative week. There was little pain, or else the patient just didn't complain.

We were not so fortunate with lobectomies for these patients. This operation necessitates placing a drainage tube in the chest cavity and attaching this to an underwater seal with suction to secure re-expansion of the remaining lung. Two patients pulled the drainage tube out and struck the attendant in the head with the water jug on the first post-operative day. One of these patients escaped and was found in a corn field three weeks later. He was brought in and x-rayed. The lung had re-expanded to fill the pleural space and the wound was well healed. The silk skin sutures were still in place so I removed them. The patient who didn't escape did not fare as well. It was necessary to put a drainage tube back in place and he developed a small empyema. Both patients recovered.

The program developed nicely and was subsequently reported by two of the residents in the *Journal of the Michigan State Medical Society.* Other mental hospitals were subsequently added to our program.

Some years later I was invited to Dr. Robertson's retirement dinner in Ionia attended by many doctors, state officials and other friends. Entertainment was provided by a quartet of lovely young women and an accompanying pianist. All were stylishly dressed and sang beautifully, followed by much applause. I was seated next to the senior member of the medical staff and asked him where they had secured the group of entertainers.

"They are all criminally insane," he said, "and still patients in the hospital."

"For what particular reason are they here?"

"All five of them killed their husbands," he said.

* * * *

"Pulmonary arteriovenous fistula" is a shunt or hole between the pulmonary artery and pulmonary vein or branches of these vessels, as they traverse through the lung.

Normally, the artery delivers blood from the right side of the heart to the lungs to pick up oxygen for the needs of the body.

When there is a shunt the blood crosses over and back to the heart without picking up oxygen.

The shunts vary in size producing different degrees of cyanosis and shortness of breath. Clubbing of the toes and fingers develops. The abnormality is congenital.

The first case in any medical literature was reported in 1939 with very few reported cases since. Dr. John Summers, one of my residents, and one of the most conscientious and able surgeons I have ever known, sent inquiries to all of the chest surgeons certified by the American Board of Thoracic Surgery and collected only 139 cases in all of the United States. Most of these were never operated.

Obviously, most of these patients are never properly diagnosed. The first previously diagnosed case of P. A. F. had been seen in many places. He was in the Army at age 23 suffered through many years and improper diagnoses, ending at the Mayo Clinic at 40. He was diagnosed as having polycythemia and was treated by opening a vein and draining blood. In 1939 at age 47, the diagnosis of pulmonary arteriovenous fistula was finally made by Smith and Horton and reported in the American Heart Journal. He was not operated and expired from right heart failure.

Dr. Summer's contribution to the diagnosis and treatment of A. V. fistula was subsequently published in the annals of surgery and has been quoted in surgical text books. I have encouraged and at times insisted that my residents prepare scientific material for publication and I have often published with them. I have encouraged my sons to publish and they have. When they were in medical school I was gratified when they came upon a textbook reference to one of my publications and called home to be sure the work being quoted was their dad's work and that of my resident's in training. On other occasions when a surgical nurse would refer to a Stringer instrument, one of my sons would call to be sure I had designed the instrument.

During my residency years lung forceps were straight across the serated jaws with two sharp corners. The lung could be and often was torn by these sharp square ends. With the help of a surgical instrument company I designed a rounded lung forceps. I also designed and the same manufacturer built neck retractors more suitable for working deep in the neck through a small incision. Similarly I designed a self-retaining rib retractor with swivel and changeable multiple blades. It was not my intention that the manufacturers apply my name to these instruments but apparently they did.

* * * *

Our first case of pulmonary arteriovenous fistula involved the right middle lobe artery and vein. The man had the above described symptoms and, in addition, he had had severe headaches for as long as he could remember. He also had "blacked out"several times.

The patient had served in the Army with these symptoms. I removed the right middle pulmonary lobe and all of the symptoms disappeared.

Our second case was a woman committed to the Traverse City State Hospital for the insane as a catatonic. X-ray of the chest on admission for tuberculosis screening revealed what was described as a tumor in the right lower lung. However, an examination revealed the characteristic murmur over the right chest and the diagnosis of pulmonary arteriovenous fistula of the right middle lobe artery and vein was established.

I removed the right middle lobe surgically and the patient promptly recovered mentally and physically. She had suffered from cerebral anoxia and had never had a mental disease!

If all the patients in the mental hospitals had a good physical examination and an x-ray, one wonders how many could be cured by the treatment of their physical problems.

The most significant deterrent to adequate medical and surgical care in state mental hospitals and penal institutions is a lack of qualified medical staff. Cases like the above two are often missed in private practice, but the chances for a proper diagnosis and treatment for people incarcerated in state or federal institutions has been practically nil.

I believe our work in such hospitals in Michigan has opened some doors. The woman with arteriovenous fistula at the Traverse City State Hospital had been there for several years at public expense when she didn't need to be there at all. However, Dr. Chester Koop is now Medical Director at that hospital and I am sure the same mistake would not be made now. Hopefully, similar improvements will ensue at other such facilities.

CHAPTER 34

BABY BRENDA

I stood by the hospital crib of a little girl named Brenda Towsley. With a pull at my own heart, I saw symptoms of a hopeless heart ailment drawn on the tiny, pinched features of the two-year-old.

The face of the frail, wizened child seemed alive. Her eyes were bright, alert, dancing with good nature.

I loved this child on sight. Don't trust me so much, I wanted to say. Dear baby, I'm not God.

Instead, I forced a smile.

"Has she learned to talk yet?" I asked her parents, as they hovered in the background.

"She has said a few words—and I know she understands everything that's said," her mother replied. "She never whines."

"I think she feels worse about not being able to keep up with her playmates than anything else," her father added.

I turned back to Brenda. She was watching me solemnly now. She knows, I thought. Children know when they're sick and maybe dying.

"We'll have to take x-rays of your chest," I said. "And do some testing to see what is happening with your heart." I patted the bony, little leg. She looked lost in the sea of white bedding.

I conferred with her parents. They could give me no clue regarding any inflammatory disease or injury that could have precipitated the illness. None of the great amount of medical records accumulated during her short life suggested adhesive paricarditis. Yet, the symptoms were all there. It had to be congenital.

"You can see from her records," my friend, Dr. Bob McGillicuddy said when I consulted with him that day. He waved a hand over the thick medical folder. "She's had a lot of diagnoses, including congenital heart disease and cardiac failure."

"Yes," I said, "and one which says she'll outgrow the problem." I shook my head. Bob was concerned and not a little disgusted.

"I'll take the case, of course," I said. "You concur then, that it is adhesive pericarditis.

"The symptoms are clear," he said. "If you operate, Chris, maybe she'll have a chance."

I went back to the Towsleys and told them what Dr. McGillicuddy and I had decided was Brenda's problem and that I would operate. I knew they saw me as their last hope. It wasn't a comfortable feeling.

"I'll see you again in a couple of days," I said.

X-rays, fluoroscopy and tests confirmed our diagnosis. I was gratified at my colleague's expertise. Sir William Osler, father of modern medicine wrote, "Constrictive pericarditis is the most often missed of all serious illnesses." The surgery meant that we had some grueling, dangerous moments ahead.

"Brenda is a poor surgical risk," I told her parents. I was finding it hard to be objective about this sweet little child. "It's a long operation and she may not survive." They flinched at my honesty. I plunged on.

"The disease is well advanced and won't get better by itself."

The parents managed small smiles. "We want you to operate. We understand the risks, but we believe you can bring her through if anyone can." They had made a decision and were relieved to have taken action.

They hurried over to a small, tense figure.

"Dr. Stringer is going to operate and you're going over to his hospital. You'll be all right."

I just wished I had as much confidence as they.

* * * *

In the short time it took to prepare this tiny bit of defective human organism for surgery, Brenda endeared herself to everyone on the hospital staff. I was already too fond of her. She never whimpered at the considerable pain from the disease, which had already affected her other organs, especially the liver and kidneys. She had a smile for everyone, and when the nurse injected the mild sedative before wheeling her to the operating room, she remained cheerful and trusting, and began to talk! Her first sentence was spoken non-stop, to people taking her to what might mean death! How ironical, I thought, that she learns to express herself at this particular moment in her young life. I wanted desperately to succeed. I pushed away the uneasiness.

"I'll give you my best, little Brenda," I promised her silently.

She was ready. When I opened the left chest and my assistants retracted the lung, I could see the tiny, under-sized heart beating feebly in the pericardium. The organ was about the size of a chicken egg.

I proceeded carefully, gratified to see the diagnosis was correct, yet saddened at its severity.

Reaching the coronary arteries, I halted.

"Hold up the pericardium," I cautioned an assistant. He reached down and with hemostats tenderly lifted up the heart sac.

"Careful. Not too much tension." I was trying to free the imbeded arteries from the pericardium. This was a tricky resection and I consciously slowed my movements; willed my fingers to proceed with extreme care. The little heart continued to pulse rapidly.

Just a bit more, I told myself as I snipped and cut above the minute arteries which lay just beneath the epicardium, and directly on the heart muscle.

The heart stopped! The surgical nurse, Christine Howe, said, quickly, "I have the shock paddles in, do you want them?

"No, not yet." I released the hemostats the assistant was using for retraction. "We'll massage the heart first. I don't want to use shock unless we have to." There was dead silence as I massaged the exposed little heart ever so gently.

It started beating again! I watched the heart pulse for two minutes. The action was vigorous and regular. I looked at the wall clock. The heart had been arrested for not more than three minutes; part of that time I had been massaging blood from the cardiac chamber. There was probably no brain damage from anoxia. However, the clock also told me I had been operating on this little girl for three hours and was only about half way through. I started work again, lifting the pericardium away as the dissection progressed toward the base.

I had anticipated even greater difficulty in the next stage of the operation. Not allowing myself to think back over the death and revival of this brave little body, I finished stripping away the pericardium at the end of the atrioventricular groove. This was unusually easy or maybe it just seemed easy after operating around the coronaries. At least it took less time, and time was beginning to be very important. We had been working over her for five hours.

But the last stage was the most difficult and tedious— stripping away the area where the pericardium continues out over the great vessels from the heart. If the pericardium is not removed from around the veins entering the right atrium, the surgery will be a failure, since one of the effects of constrictive pericarditis is to prevent adequate blood return to the heart. The vena cava, however, is very thin and if inadvertedly broken through, will kill the patient. The procedure went better than I expected. I put a drainage tube in the pleural space and removed the retractors.

"You may re-expand the lung," I said.

The anesthesiologist's eyes shone above his mask. My surgical team was all smiles below their masks. A spirit of celebration swept over the room as my assistants closed the incision. It was all over but the cheering. But weren't the clink of the instruments, the restrained elation in the voices of my operating team, the steady rhythm of that small, brave heart—were not these the cheers of victory?

The surgical team, except myself, had yielded to a relief team during these long hours.

I was exhausted, but strangely elated.

I shouldered open the exit door of the operating room and pulled off my gloves and mask.

* * * *

Little Brenda not only recovered quickly and was able to keep up with the most energetic of her classmates, but she decided while in high school, to become a nurse. I inquired of Brenda through her principal, Benjamin Leyrer, at Everett High School whenever I saw him at church.

When Brenda graduated, Ruth found an announcement invitation and a lovely photograph of Brenda in the mail. At the bottom of the picture was written, "Remember me?"

Ruth handed it across to me, a puzzled look on her face. "I don't seem to recall who this is," she said. "Do we send a gift?"

"We sure as hell do," I said. Did I remember that little darling! I'll never forget her. She's a nurse now and very likely an excellent one.

CHAPTER 35

FIRST LADY

Dr. Theodore Bauer, or "Ti", as he is called by his many friends, has asked me through the years to see all of his patients who needed or might need chest surgery. His patients have always been interesting cases with a built-in challenge. I enjoyed the mystery, searching for clues to the patient's illness and coming up with a solution that meant using my hands and brain the best way I knew how.

One fascinating case was the wife of the Governor of the State of Michigan. I had met Governor John Swainson, but I had never met his wife. She was hospitalized at St. Lawrence Hospital.

I drove to the hospital, wondering just how difficult an experience this might be. I was used to dealing with influential people, but being responsible for the loved one of a powerful political person might require unusual finesse.

The first lady was in a small, ordinary single room on the fourth floor. There was nothing at all unusual, or luxurious about it. The Governor's wife, however, was not at all ordinary. She looked much younger than I had expected—a beautiful woman with shiny blonde hair.

I was most impressed, however, by her warm, pleasant manner, which in spite of a noticeable shortness of breath, never varied. She answered my questions intelligently.

Yes, she told me, sharp pains in the chest had begun the

day before, and had become worse during the night. Breathing became increasingly labored.

I examined her chest. There was a left thoracotomy surgical scar and it was well healed. I wondered about it. Aloud I said, "Tell me about your chest operation".

"Well, it started several years ago." She had a soft voice.

"I developed some unexplained chest symptoms and my doctor referred me to chest surgeons Doctors O'Brien and Tuttle in Detroit. They advised me that my left lung was partially collapsed."

"What specifically was your treatment?"

"They withdrew the air from my chest that was producing the collapse of the lung and advised complete rest."

"Did you go to the hospital for the rest?"

"No, I went to my parents cottage on Higgins Lake. After three weeks my left lung was found to be more completely collapsed and Drs. O'Brien and Tuttle admitted me to Herman Kiefer Hospital for surgery."

Air that is trapped in the pleural space tends to be absorbed just as it does in artificial pneumothorax but if the leak of air from the lung into the space is greater than the absorption rate the degree of collapse increases. Sometimes the tear in the lung will heal spontaneously or if it can be pulled out against the chest wall it can seal itself.

Mrs. Swainson was admitted to the hospital in September 1952 and Drs. O'Brien and Tuttle apparently considered the escape of air into the pleural space to be of sufficient severity to warrant surgical correction. At that time surgeons were not using continuous suction with an electric pump in a further effort to avoid major surgery.

Following surgery Mrs. Swainson recuperated at home and had no further difficulty until the present illness.

She was almost exhausted now. I patted her shoulder. "I'll need x-rays, so you just take it easy. I'll move as fast as I can—let's see if we can pinpoint the cause of your pain and breathing trouble."

The x-rays did indeed tell an interesting story. Her right lung was about fifty percent collapsed. There were several cystic-looking areas of lessened density in the upper part of the partially collapsed lung. They looked like pleural blebs. I reasoned that one of these congenital blebs had ruptured, allowing air from the lung to escape, thus deflating the lung.

This is not a common occurrence, but it is frequent enough and too often not recognized. I would have to start with certain staged procedures which I had worked out recently and reported in medical literature. Hopefully this approach would avoid major surgery.

I phoned Governor Swainson whom I considered to be one of Michigan's finest, and arranged for him to meet me in the x-ray department of St. Lawrence Hospital. He came at once with his retinue: two state troopers and his male executive secretary.

Leading him to the x-rays on the illuminated viewing boxes, I explained what had happened to the First Lady and why. Then I outlined my proposals for treatment.

"These procedures are somewhat risky, but there's an even greater risk in allowing the lung to remain collapsed," I said as kindly as I could. "If the lung is not re-expanded promptly, the pleural space might become infected and this compounds the problem. If you wish additional consultation, I will be happy to expedite the arrangements."

"No," he said, "I understand you have had considerable experience in managing this type of problem. I leave her in your capable hands."

His words should have given me some comfort; perhaps they did. But I knew the measured approaches I planned to use might not be enough.

I began the procedures, which would take about five days. The first step was to attempt to remove the air through a large needle inserted through the chest wall under local anesthesia. This is very likely what Drs. O'Brien and Tuttle first did several years before when the left lung was treated for the same problem. The procedure is a simple one and if it works, fine, but if it doesn't, I proceed to the second step, which is somewhat more complicated. The first step didn't work in this case, which meant that air was still leaking out of the lung faster than I could withdraw it through the needle and syringe. I prepared for the second step. With my patient propped up in bed and locally anesthetized, I made a short incision just beneath the clavicle using a #11 scalpel blade and introduced a trocar. However gently one does this, it is always the most uncomfortable part of the operation, not because of pain but because of the feeling of pressure as the trocar is pushed through the muscles of the chest. I intended to put a rubber tube down the trocar, pull the trocar out of the chest leaving the tubing in place, then draw the air out from her pleural space, which was still leaking through a tear in the lung. The electric pump used for this purpose is attached to the tubing in the chest through an underwater seal. The amount of negative pressure produced by the pump through the underwater seal must be carefully calibrated. Just enough to keep ahead of the leak but not enough to pull a larger hole in the delicate lung surface. I usually start with the equivilant of 1 cm. of mercury and regulate the pump just enough to produce some bubbling of the escaping air through the water in the receiving bottle, and oscillation in the manometer tubing when the patient inhales. If successful, the lung re-expands and works normally.

There was a "pop" as the trocar entered the pleural space. From there, the procedure went well with continued suction using the electric pump.

The third option, which would mean major surgery such as Mrs. Swainson had for the same problem in the left lung several years before, was not necessary this time.

*　*　*　*

The press phoned my office every day.

"Elvi—refer them to the Governor's office," I said.

This didn't work for long. The Governor simply instructed his secretary to refer all calls to my office.

"Dr. Stringer," Elvi complained, "they're pestering me to death. I can't get away from the phone long enough to do my work."

"OK, Elvi—enough is enough."

I shut myself in my office and prepared a short statement, got it approved by the Governor's aide and released it.

I was most anxious to see the results of the therapy I had given the First Lady. I ordered post-procedural x-rays taken on the sixth day after there was no more air coming out through the water trap. The lung had fully expanded!

After signing the discharge, I visited my patient to instruct her about post-hospital activities.

"While I was treating you, I ordered a tuberculin skin test," I said.

"Sometimes a spontaneous collapse of the lung is due to tuberculosis but your tuberculin test is negative and in any case you have no other findings suggestive of tuberculosis so that possible cause is ruled out. The other and more frequent cause is congenital pleural blebs or little cyst-like spaces in the lung which rupture spontaneously. This latter is what happened to you. I doubt if you will have any more trouble but I want you to rest for a few weeks then limit your activity for about 3 months. At that time we will get another chest x-ray just to be sure."

"Well, thank you, Doctor."

After the First Lady went home, I got a letter from my old friend, Dr. Chester Koop, who had followed the story in the Flint media.

"Who knows," he wrote, "you may be the next White House physician."

My real reward was in restoring this gracious lady to normal health without subjecting her to further major surgery and the loss of another lung lobe.

CHAPTER 36

TRAUMA!

"Chris, I have Bill Sober in the hospital here in Grayling."

I recognized the name, although I didn't know the victim. The Sobers were a prominent, wealthy Lansing family.

"The sheriff's men picked him up in the woods, south of Grayling this morning," my friend, Dr. Perry Spencer, went on. "He apparently drove into a tree and was catapulated into the woods. No one knows what time it happened and he's still unconscious. We need help."

"Give me some idea of the nature of his injuries," I directed. I had a hunch I was being drawn into a serious case, but I owed Perry the courtesy of listening. Perhaps I could offer advice by phone and avoid the long drive to Grayling.

"I believe one lung is collapsed and possibly the other partially so. Blood has accumulated in the abdomen. There is urinary bleeding."

"Do you know if he was struck in the head?"

"I don't believe so, Chris, but he is unconscious. The pulse is rapid and irregular and he's breathing with difficulty."

"Perry, his condition sounds desperate but I doubt if I could drive the 150 miles and get there in time to do any good."

There was a short interval of background conversation—voices unfamiliar to me. I waited.

"Just a minute." I waited again.

"Mr. Sober, the patient's father, is standing beside me. He says he has his plane here and will send it down to pick you up.

"You will need a general surgeon, too," I said. Elvi would have to juggle my schedule, but she was used to that. I told Perry as much.

"Mr. Sober says please come and bring anyone you want with you. The plane will be at the Capitol City Airport in about 40 minutes.

I hung up and dialed Dr. Robert Combs, an excellent Lansing general surgeon. He agreed to go with me.

Each with our own pack of instruments, Bob and I met at the airport. The Sober private plane, a ten or twelve passenger twin-engine, sat waiting, its engine idling. We arrived in Grayling 45 minutes later where a chauffeured Sober car picked us up. The driver had a stricken look. "He's about gone," he reported.

From the expensive car we trotted into the modest little northern Michigan hospital. Mr. and Mrs. Sober and Dr. Spencer were waiting in the patient's room. They looked strained and tired.

Bob and I examined the youth. He was, indeed, critically ill. Blood transfusions failed to keep up with the bleeding. Urinary bleeding had stopped, but somewhere in the abdomen and lungs there was hemorrhage. The only encouraging sign was that he was still alive after these several hours. A less strong person would have died upon impact.

Bob straightened from his examinations of the youth and his eyes met mine.

"We should open the chest and abdomen," he said.

"Of course," I said, "but we'll need chest-trained assistants and an anesthesiologist experienced in intratracheal anesthesia, who can control the gas exchange . . . "

"That's not available here," Perry broke in, " and it's risky surgery under the best of conditions."

"Doctors," Mr. Sober said, "both of my planes are here

and ready now. We could convert one of them to carry Bill, if Lansing has these facilities."

"Yes," I said. "The Lansing Chest Hospital is adequate." Mrs. Sober's face brightened and she turned to her husband inquiringly.

We really had no choice—the Sobers were willing to take a chance on their boy's survival if we'd move ahead with preparations. So we moved. I stepped over to the room phone, got long distance and gave instructions to my surgical supervisor at the Chest Hospital. She said they would be assembled for immediate surgery when we arrived.

Someone called an ambulance, and Bob and Perry and I began the preparation. Alarmingly, the patient's blood pressure dropped to 50/20. We quickly gave him a mgm. of levophed to normalize the pressure. I noted it went up only to 80/40 so I added more levophed to a liter of 5 percent glucose and water and started an intravenous drip.

Gingerly, attendants transferred the lad to a stretcher on which he would be transported in flight. Tubes, which would prove to be his lifeline on route, were connnected to both of his arms and he was moved onto a hospital cart. The four of us trailed after the cart and followed the stretcher as it was placed in the ambulance. As we sped toward the airport, I would not have been surprised if the young and reckless Bill Sober had expired before we got there. Yet, he clung to his life.

On one side of the plane, the seats had been folded down. Attendants placed the stretcher on top of these seats and secured it firmly while Dr. Combs and I hovered, anxious to check his blood pressure again. We still weren't keeping up with the blood loss, but the patient continued to breathe.

We were airborn over mid-Michigan in a few minutes, and I could see the second silver plane as it flew along side, carrying the distraught parents.

In Lansing, another ambulance waited. The stretcher was unloaded, slipped inside the vehicle. Bob and I scrambled inside too. A city police escort raced ahead of us; behind followed the family.

The anesthesiologist stood ready and two resident surgeons and two nurses were scrubbed and gowned when we walked into the operating suite. It had been one hour and 15 minutes since we left Grayling.

* * * *

After anesthesia, Dr. Combs started work on the abdomen and I began on the chest. I found the lung torn and about 60 percent collapsed. An artery lay ripped and almost drained, but it started to bleed again when I aspirated blood from the pleural space. I repaired the lung, expanded it and placed a drainage tube in the pleural space. I injected penicillin in a saline solution into this same space. Then I repaired the surgical incision.

"Look here, Chris," Dr. Combs said, when he had opened the abdomen. "Most of the bleeding is the result of the liver being shattered.

He repaired the tears in the organ and closed the abdomen. It was twelve p.m. and we had operated for eight hours.

I was desperately tired, but there was still much to be done. "Bob—you go home and rest," I said, "it's my responsibility now that he's here. You just check in when you come back."

"OK, but his blood pressure is down to 50/20. I don't see how he'll pull through."

I hastened to the surgical floor where the patient had been transferred and ordered the blood flow increased. That made the seventh unit.

Throughout the night and the next morning, his blood pressure stayed so low I had to advise the Sobers that their son would probably die.

"Find another consultant," Mr. Sober pleaded. "I'll fly him from anywhere in the country."

I welcomed the opportunity to share the responsibility and suggested Dr. Chiles, Chairman of the Department of Surgery at the University of Michigan. Mr. Sober quickly agreed.

"Send him down here and we will take care of him," Dr.

Chiles said. Disgusted, I mumbled something about the patient's blood pressure and slammed down the receiver. To move the patient again meant sure death!

Dr. Fallis! I should have phoned him first. Fallis was willing to come, and Mr. Sober, grateful to have something to do, sent one of his planes to the old Detroit Airport near Ford Hospital where Dr. Fallis was Chief of the Trauma Division.

Dr. Fallis was competent, courteous and understanding. He reviewed the records, x-rays and examined the patient within minutes of his arrival.

To the parents he said, "Everything has been done that could be done. Your son is lucky to be alive. I must say though that he has no more than a 50 percent chance of surviving."

Standing beside this fine man, I couldn't help but think he was an optimist. Anyway, he charged and received $1,000 for the one hour consultation. He should have.

The next five days, the patient fluctuated drastically. One of the doctors remained with him constantly.

On the seventh day, he had improved enough so that I was encouraged to tell the parents I thought their son would make it.

I know people say strange things under stress, but I could hardly believe her response.

"Isn't it too bad," she said, "he let his medical insurance lapse a month ago."

I was so tired I could hardly stand upright. I had labored day and night and hardly slept these past eight days. I turned and walked slowly back to my office. Young Bill Sober did recover, but both he and his sister died rather young from cancer. Sadness darkening his face, Mr. Sober told me recently, "They were both heavy smokers."

CHAPTER 37

OUR FOUR SONS

Our oldest son Christopher James Jr. was born in Detroit while I was still in training. He was a healthy, good natured child and became a tall, athletic, serious young man whose objective was a life of service to humanity. "Jim" chose graduate school in the Social Sciences at Michigan State University, and when he was 25 years old he served a summer internship at the Mendocino State Hospital in Northern California. One weekend he and three other graduate students happily left their books and patients to climb in the Sierra Nevada Mountains. Jim was in the lead and called back to his friends that he would try to find a easier path down from the top. Without warning, Jim fell from a ledge which was hidden by brush. He never regained consciousness. Officers from the California State Highway Patrol, the Hambolt Country Sheriff's department and the California Forestry Patrol assembled at the scene of the accident but somehow four hours passed before our injured son was taken to a hospital for emergent care. I felt that any two of the patrolmen could have done it in less time. One of the several conflicting reports was more concerned that "Officer Miller's clothes were soiled and sweaty at the finish and a change was necessary." Jim was finally transported to a poorly equipped and staffed hospital in Garbersville after which there was an unfortunate attempt to transport him via a small plane to the University of California Medical Center in San Francisco. Jim died en route and the little plane turned back to Garbersville. Dr. John Summers, a former Resident of mine, was in Sacramento where he had established his practice. I called John, and he and his wife Lee spent several days in Northern California researching where Jim had been, how the accident happened and what kind of care was provided. Dr. Summer's detailed report was the only significant report I ever had. Three months later I called my long time friend, Dr. LeMoyne Snyder, famed medico-legal expert. LeMoyne asked me to come to his home in Paradise, California. With Dr. Summer's report in hand we went back over the territory gathering information. Where there was alleged to have been an inquest, the county record contained the one word "Inquest" and a blank page. We, of course, had to reconcile ourselves to the tragic loss. It took years for me to master the bitterness at what I saw as negligence.

Our second son, John Wayne, was born soon after we came to Lansing. John never developed as well as his three tall brothers. His muscular body was unusually short. We were concerned about his development and took him for examination several times to the pediatrics departments at Henry Ford Hospital and the University of Michigan Hospitals. We were repeatedly advised that there were no abnormalities and that he was simply going to be a small man. After graduating from Michigan State University with a degree in advertising, he went with the Batten, Barton, Durstine, and Osborn Advertising Agency in Detroit.

We were in Florida when John phoned from his hospital bed in Harper Hospital. "I guess I've got high blood pressure, and I don't know what else." he said.

I was puzzled. "I want to talk to your physician," I said. "Don't go away." He laughed and gave me the name of his attending physician.

I called his doctor and was advised that he had made a diagnosis of fibromuscular hyperplasia constricting the left renal artery, probably congenital! This was producing the high blood pressure.

So far as I knew, John's blood pressure had always been normal. Pediatricians characteristically seldom took the blood pressure of children. It is true that most children do have a normal blood pressure but almost everything else in a child is normal also.

I was advised by the doctor that John was scheduled for kidney surgery at 1:00 p.m. the following day.

"Who's doing it?" I asked.

He mentioned the man—adding that he was a chest surgeon.

"What is a chest surgeon doing fooling around with the kidney! You just unschedule him until I get there."

I was able to get a flight from West Palm Beach that afternoon and reached Harper Hospital about 6:00 p.m. The chest surgeon met me in x-ray and we examined the films. The arteriogram was a good one. There were two principal renal arteries, and there was a marked constriction of one of them. I asked the chest surgeon what he planned to do when he got in there.

"I'll use the splenic vein for a patch of the constricted artery."

This was ridiculous. You couldn't any more do that than you could patch a string with a piece of rope. I clamped my mouth shut and hurried back to John. I checked him out of the hospital that evening, angry and worried, and with the Harper Hospital films we drove to Ann Arbor where we spent the night in a hotel. The following morning I called Dr. William Fry, a good friend and professor of surgery at the University of Michigan. Dr. Fry was primarily interested in vascular surgery and had reported on his surgical treatment of renal artery abnormalities.

He admitted John to the University Hospital for observation and further studies. He also secured the old records and we learned for the first time that when John was examined in the pediatric department as a teenager about ten years before, he had a blood pressure of 150/80, which was high for a teenager. We had never been told! It is very probable this had something to do with his growth pattern. While in the University Hospital, John's blood pressure came down to near normal and Bill Fry decided to observe him as an outpatient to see if it stayed down. However, on the third trip as an outpatient the blood pressure was back up.

"It's time to stop playing Mickey Mouse and get the thing corrected surgically," Dr. Fry said firmly.

So John was scheduled for immediate surgery. When Dr. Fry opened the kidney area and exposed the blood vessels, he found that the constriction of the artery extended out into the arterial branches in the kidney parenchyma. Bill had perfected a dilitation technique, which he had used on children but never on adults. He decided to attempt this procedure for John using graduated steel bougies. He was able to accomplish a good increase in the lumen of the arteries and the post-operative condition was good. The kidney was saved by this new technique. Bill Fry immediately reported the case in the journal, *Surgery*.

John's younger brother, Ted, flew to Florida to bring his mother and the car back home.

One afternoon, about a week after John's surgery, I went down to get the car and pick up my wife in front of the hospital. We had been with John everyday since his hospitalization and he seemed to be recovering nicely. But when Ruth ducked down beside me, she was anxious.

"Dr. Fry came in to see John just after you left and told him the blood pressure had not returned to normal as he expected, and the kidney would have to be removed after all. More surgery is scheduled for tomorrow."

Forgetting I was parked at the loading zone, I bounced out and took off running to catch Bill Fry before he left the floor. I wondered as I hurried through, how in the world blood pressure could be expected to return to normal in one week, after it has been elevated for 29 years!

The important thing it seemed to me, as I squeezed into an elevator, was whether or not the dilated arterial branches had stayed dilated. I wasn't sure whether or not a post-operative arteriogram had been done to determine this. I reasoned that if the dilitation had held, we should expect the blood pressure to come down over a period of time. I intercepted Bill on the floor. No, he said, a post-operative arteriogram had not been done. Bill agreed to cancel the proposed additional surgery and obtain the arteriogram the following morning.

I slept so poorly it was easy to be at the hospital early the following morning. When I saw Bill at the far end of the hall, he waved me up to him.

"I have something to show you."

Hardly daring to hope my suspicions were correct, we walked to the x-ray department and saw the arteriogram done that morning. The renal arteries and all of their branches were perfectly normal!

We brought our son home. Over a period of about six weeks, the blood pressure returned to normal and stayed there.

If the diagnosis had been made when it should have been made, treatment would have been undertaken during John's early years and he probably would have developed normally.

In reporting the case in *Surgery*, Dr. Fry says:

It is distressing that hypertension in children is rarely discovered during physical examination. Routine blood pressure evaluation has been an unfortunate error of omission.

We were to have our John only eleven more years . . .

* * * *

Quotation from Ruth's journal:

"Our first knowledge that winter that John's health was out of control was the telephone call from the hospital, March 2, 1969, when he said, 'I thought I had better give you my new address. I am in Harper Hospital.' John never lost his sense of humor, and in addition he wanted to spare us worry, but there was apprehension in his voice as he told us he was scheduled for surgery the next day.

I know he was relieved when his father appeared in Detroit. John shared his hospital room with a big black man, and they had joked together when his father left the room. John chuckled and rolled his eyes as he quoted his roommate. 'Your daddy sure do take charge!' "

When Jim and John were ages 11 and 9 it appeared that we would not have more children although we wanted a bigger family. We therefore proceeded with the construction of a new home for a family of four. It was our dream home, an authenic French Provencial. Ruth had carried the tattered plans in her purse ever since my training days in Detroit. We ended up spending four times what the architect estimated the cost would be when we came to Lansing and twice as much as his estimate when we did start construction. But it was unique in its European style and attracted favorable attention from several architects and builders.

For a time during construction we rented 2 rooms at the Porter Hotel. During that time, Jim became ill with the mumps. I had never had the mumps so I carefully stayed out of Jim's room and out of contact with him. John, who shared his room, and his mother who took care of him, did not get the mumps but I did, and on the very day we moved into our new home. My bedroom was on the first floor and the shades and the drapes were not up yet. A good friend and urologist, Dr. J. F. Harrold, confined me to bed in an effort to prevent a complicating epididymitis. This precaution was a waste because I contracted epididymitis on both sides. I was swollen and miserable and I was satisfied to lie there in the barren room. After my recovery Vera Langenbacker asked if I had the mumps on both sides. "Yes," I said, "on all four sides."

While I was down, people (some we knew and others we didn't know) continued to come to the front door and ask to look through the house. I told Ruth that the next time anyone rang I was going to answer the door in my pajamas regardless of doctor's orders. When the door chimes sounded, I jerked the door open, and emphatically told the people standing there, "The house is occupied." Then I realized that the man apparently leading the group was a physician friend from Mt. Pleasant, Michigan, who referred a lot of chest surgery to me. I invited him in with his party but he declined. He didn't refer any more patients to me either. I estimate that it cost me at least $10,000.00 to open that door.

About three months later Ruth said, "I have this funny feeling." I answered, "Of course you do, you are pregnant." I had also noticed a slight bulge in her waist.

In medical school I had been told the epididymitis usually causes sterilization. I talked to Dr. "Free" Harrold about this and learned that the infection sometimes has the opposite effect. It stimulates sperm activity. So I had been the guilty one in Ruth's apparent inability to become pregnant. A few months later after Dr. Fred Tamblyn confirmed the pregnancy, he assured us that there was only one baby. I didn't believe this. Ruth not only had blossomed, she had ballooned. So one quiet Sunday I drove Ruth and Jim and John to the Chest Hospital and x-rayed her myself. I left her on the x-ray table and took Jim and John with me into the dark room to develop the x-ray. When I put the film up in the view box there they were—two little skeletons! John's eyes grew wide. "Wow! don't they get tired standing on their heads?"

I went back to the x-ray table and told Ruth she was going to have twins. She turned to look up at me and said "Rub that grin off your face." We were elated. With two coming at one time Ruth and I figured that we would finally have a daughter.

At delivery there were three other obstetricians in the operating room with Dr. Tamblyn. Dr. Donald Drolett's only function was to stand in the doorway and keep me posted where I sat at a desk about fifty feet down the hall. After the first baby Don called to me holding one finger up—one boy. Turning back to the room he came out in about five minutes and held two fingers up—two boys. He went back in and came out the third time in about five minutes and threw both hands up calling, "That is all." Sister Mary Assissium, the hospital administrator, was coming down the hall and the back of Don's hand caught her squarely in the face. She never forget the Stringer twins.

Years later, in our grief over the loss of our two oldest

sons, Ruth recalled Dr. Fred Tamblyn saying, "The Good Lord really wanted you to have these babies." How prophetic "Tam" was. Both of "these babies" have now become distinguished surgeons in their own right.

CHAPTER 38

SCHEMING IN THE WAR YEARS

In the early 1940's no drugs or agents existed which were effective against the tubercle bacillus. And to make matters worse, tuberculosis could be far advanced before it was diagnosed because the disease is often symptomless. Sometimes even in the presence of symptoms, doctors misdiagnosed.

When miniature x-rays were perfected, masses of infectious cases turned up. Credit for this was due to x-ray equipment installed in mobile units, as well as stationary machines set up in hospitals.

The Chest Hospital in Lansing was the first hospital in the United States, and, so far as I know, in the world, to own and operate its own mobile x-ray unit. In wartime, we did considerable maneuvering to accomplish this. We had no provision in the budget for the approximately $35,000 needed to make this purchase. As a wartime measure, all truck chassis large enough for mounting the unit were limited to the armed services. The housing was available only through a small manufacturing plant in Indiana. Miniature x-ray units themselves were being almost totally diverted for military use.

I tossed the issue to my resourceful hospital board member, Andrew Langenbacker. I could depend on him to address one problem at a time.

"Things are moving right along," Andy soon reported. "We've talked seven other businesses into donating all the money."

"Wonderful! I bet I know where the first substantial contribution came from," I laughed. Andrew was more than a hard worker; he was generous.

"Well, yes, but the other good news is that our friend, Henry Hund (President of Reo Motors), has located a truck chassis in Pittsburgh. He had routed it there for the military, but it was too short. He has already sent a driver for it."

Not long after, Andy phoned me again.

"Henry just called. He said the welders are through extending the length of the truck chassis. Reo is driving it down to Indiana and they're going to mount the body housing."

"Great work, Andy. By the time they have it back here, the x-ray equipment should have arrived. We'll be in business."

I put the phone down with a flourish, smiling to myself. I had done some scheming myself. I knew Clarence Carlton, Secretary and Vice President of Motor Wheel, who was also vice-chairman of the war production board. Through his efforts we were able to obtain the unbelievable priority of AA-1.

I discovered, however, one dark day, that there were a hundred and sixty AA-1 priorities ahead of us for these x-ray units. It would take forever for this many units to filter down out of the military need.

I took my problem back to Clarence.

"I'll try again," he said.

It wasn't long before Elvi trotted into my office, smiling widely and holding out an official-looking letter.

Tearing it open, I saw it labeled "prior priority to AA-1". Although I had dealt with a lot of wartime priorities in my hospital director's position, I had never heard of a "prior priority to an AA-1" and I haven't heard of one since.

The equipment was shipped to Lansing and rapidly installed in the shiny new motor unit. We were ready to roll.

At the first factory where employees were surveyed, more than two percent were active tuberculosis cases, only a few of which had been previously diagnosed. This was an astoundingly high figure for the Lansing area and much higher than we found in any of the other groups. Further research showed that many of the employees in this plant were from high tuberculosis rate areas in other parts of the country.

During the late 1940's, more survey-type x-ray units became available for the diagnosis of tuberculosis and other pulmonary diseases. Some were owned and operated by local health departments, others by local tuberculosis societies, and some by hospitals. All, however, were stationary units. The Ingham Chest Hospital owned the only mobile unit. Eventually, the Michigan State Department of Health purchased a mobile unit for operation primarily in the less populous areas of the Northern Peninsula.

I was chairman of a committee appointed by the Governor of Michigan to advise him whether the State Health Commissioner should be reappointed. If not, who should be appointed in his place? A hearing was held in the Governor's office attended by my committee and several local health officers and by the State Health Commissioner, Dr. William DeKline. I gave the report of the committee that DeKline should be replaced. The president of the local health officers' association spoke, supporting the report. The Governor asked DeKline if he had any response. DeKline then attacked me personally, saying "Stringer has gone out into the community without consulting me and raised money for the purchase and operation of a mobile x-ray unit." The Governor who had been facing a window swiveled in his big chair to face DeKline saying, "Is that bad?"

DeKline was not reappointed. He went to his office and gathered his personal things and was coming out the front door with an arm-load of papers when he noted a photographer taking pictures in front of the building. Although it was for another purpose, DeKline thought he was being photographed as the displaced commissioner, rushed the unsuspecting photographer and broke his camera.

After the committee had spent many hours considering possible candidates for commissioner, we finally recommended Dr. Kenneth Altland, the current Deputy Commissioner. A swarm of Senators were upset with the committee for not recommending the reappointment of DeKline, and the Senate refused to approve the appointment of Altland.

The Governor then asked me to take the post. I didn't think I was qualified, and I was deeply involved with other commitments.

The Governor appointed one of the local health officers, Albert Heutis.

As the tuberculosis case-finding program gained momentum, the number of new cases of the disease per hundred thousand population started a steady decline. Through the ensuing years, anti-microbial drugs effective against the tubercle bacillus were developed, primarily by the research departments of the large drug companies. With the effective "cover" provided by the drugs, more sophisticated surgical procedures came on stream. These procedures, such as surgical removal of the diseased lung or diseased part of the lung, could not be done without the prohibitive risks of such massive surgery prior to the anti-microbial era. Eventually, as the drug regimes became more effective, and as the number of far advanced cases became fewer, the indication for surgery decreased. The earlier surgical procedures, drastic and deforming, had long since been abandoned. Eventually, the drug treatment of tuberculosis became so effective that there is now very little, if any, indication for surgery of any type in the treatment and control of the disease. This takes me back to Professor Howard Beye who told us as students, "If any of you ever practice surgery like you practiced surgery three years before, you are practicing malpractice."

As Michigan went forward in its accelerated case findings and treatment program, inevitably more hospital beds were needed.

The state built new ones at Gaylord and Houghton—the latter to replace a county-operated hospital.

My own Chest Hospital again needed modernization and additions, and part of those funds came from earnings derived from its surgical services to other counties and hospitals.

But by the middle 1950's with our high rate of success in case finding and treatment, these additional facilities weren't needed. By 1961 the number of new cases found by surveys became less than .01 percent. Thus, if the cost per examination were $2.00 (a low figure), then the cost of diagnosing one case of tuberculosis became $2000.00.

* * * *

It seemed to me that a good place to begin dismantling the mobile x-ray service program was at the place where it started—my Ingham Chest Hospital. I said as much while I was still director there. It was silly, I explained, to replace the original mobile x-ray unit which was about to die from old age. I had discussions and confirmations from Dr. John Cowan, of the State Health Department, as well as from Mr. Irvin Nichols, executive secretary of the Michigan Tuberculosis and Respiratory Disease Association. The year was 1958.

To my surprise, these suggestions were met with instant hostility by the Michigan State Health Commissioner. Some time had gone by since I had first suggested winding down the program. In the meantime I had resigned as Medical Director of the Ingham Chest Hospital to devote full time to my private practice of chest surgery. I was also chairman of the Ingham County Medical Society Public Health Committee. I believe I was not only in order, but entirely reasonable in hanging on to my views.

Dr. Albert Heustis, who was still State Health Commissioner, as a member, gave me a bad time in these meetings. He vehemently opposed discontinuing the program.

"Dr. Stringer wouldn't have made such a recommendation if he still were responsible for its operation," he said to the committee members.

They were embarrassed for him. The health commissioner apparently was the only one who had not taken the time to read the records. If he had, he'd have known that I had, indeed, advocated discontinuing the mobile x-ray unit while I was still responsible for operating the case-finding program.

* * * *

Evidence accumulated during these mobile x-ray years showed that excessive x-ray exposure is a health risk. Interestingly, the multiple miniature exposure is more of a risk than standard-sized x-rays.

To nobody's credit, Ingham Chest Hospital did purchase a new mobile unit at the cost of many thousands of dollars. It was used only for a short time, then garaged after persistent urging from the Michigan Tuberculosis and Respiratory Disease Association.

Today, diagnosis is done by standard x-rays and tuberculin skin tests, followed by laboratory testing. Usually a patient is treated in a general hospital, like one with any other illness, started on anti-tuberculosis drug therapy and sent home. Most are able to resume their daily work after three or four months. In the past, such patients would be disabled for several years.

CHAPTER 39

THE CASE OF THE
DESPERATE DERELICT

The Volunteers of America, a charitable organization, has operated a home for destitute persons in Lansing for many decades.

One beastly cold morning, Dr. Hurth phoned. He was at the Volunteer Home.

"I know it's two o'clock in the morning but one of the inmates here is bleeding profusely. Can you come?"

I dressed quickly and drove to the shelter. Dr. Hurth met me at the door and led me to the cot of the poor creature, who lay, weakly coughing up blood and spitting into a dented, rusty bucket. His rag-tag clothing was encrusted with an accumulation of filth, old blood, and alcohol, and his emaciated body was just as dirty. He stunk. I would have been repelled but for his pitiful condition and his obvious need.

I examined the man's chest and found, surprisingly, that there was no gurgling. Yet, at the rate he was expectorating blood, I feared he would bleed out before I could do anything for him.

"Call an ambulance," I said. "I'll admit him to St. Lawrence Hospital."

With an appreciative handshake, Dr. Hurth saw me into the ambulance. I rode with Derelict Dan to the hospital emergency entrance.

The emergency room nurses cleaned him hurriedly. One of them rolled her eyes.

"If you hold your breath," she wheezed, "you don't smell how awful he is."

His blood, in the meantime, had been typed, cross-matched and checked for red cell and hemoglobin. This would help determine how much hemorrhage there had been and how much blood we would need. Whatever he had, it appeared to be serious.

Surgery was called and the patient transferred to an operating room. Under local pharyngeal anesthesia, I bronchoscoped the man. He coughed spasmotically when I passed the metal tube between the vocal cords, which made it very difficult to inspect the trachea and the bronchi. But when the area was free from spasms, there were no abnormalities. I was astounded!

I withdrew the bronchoscope and pondered the figure propped up before me. I had the feeling that he had turned himself over completely to us, as if he were an infant who somehow understands that those caring for him were his last hope, and passively accepts the uncomfortable treatment.

Maybe it was an esophageal lesion. That could account for the lack of abnormal physical findings in the lungs.

I introduced the esophagoscope. It is a larger caliber instrument and longer than a bronchoscope. There is a greater risk than bronchoscopy, because the esophagus is not protected by cartilaginous rings. These rings in the trachea and bronchi keep the air passages open for breathing. This is not necessary in the esophagus which is open only when something is passing through it, such as food or liquid.

I inspected the walls down to the esophageal ending. Everything normal—and no blood in the esophagus either.

I was baffled. The great quantities of blood Dan expectorated had to come from somewhere. If there had been an abnormal shadow in either lung, I'd have considered exploratory thoracotomy. But in this case, I wouldn't have known which side to operate!

His red cell and hemoglobin were low, and I ordered transfusions for him repeatedly during the next three days.

The floor nurses used this time to scour his skeletal, vermin-infested body, shave him and clothe him in white hospital pants and gown. The regular meals were extra nutritious and aides brought him more nourishment mid-afternoon and at bedtime. He was on complete bed rest for fear of the activity aggravating the bleeding. He was not even allowed up to go to the bathroom.

Radiology did a gastro-intestinal x-ray series on him—there was a small chance of a lesion there. But it was normal too. The chest x-ray was normal. The tuberculin skin test was negative.

Each morning, when the nurse would step in to care for him, Dan would be coughing up blood. Everyone connected with Dan had seen the distressing occurrence. There was even occult blood in the stool. But from where?

I was challenged. Here was a mystery to test my capabilities. Since Dan was holding his own due to the nurturing watchfulness of the entire hospital staff, I made up my mind to see this weird case through, no matter what.

I enlisted the help of another surgeon. He got no further than I did.

I put Dan through the discomfort of bronchoscopy and esophagoscopy again. Nothing! I could have kicked at the walls. Yet, each time I found myself stalled at a blind alley, the more determined I was to continue the search for the source of the bleeding.

We x-rayed after instilling contrast media in both the bronchial tree and the esophagus. Everything was normal.

I instructed the head nurses on all shifts to have a nurse go into the patient's room every hour, day and night.

After ten days, the bleeding subsided. As Dan's doctor, I was gratified. As a detective I was frustrated. I would probably never know the cause of his problem.

He was discharged and returned to the bleak, crowded shelter. I was sorry but it was better than the streets in winter.

One week later, Dr. Hurth phoned again. This time it was four in the morning. Dan was bleeding again.

"Send him back to St. Lawrence and I'll meet him there."

I know I shouldn't have been pleased, but I was. I had another chance.

Disregarding the cold and snow, I hurried to the hospital. Dan was even dirtier than he was the first time I saw him, but I didn't wait for him to be cleaned. I lost a lot of popularity with the emergency room nurses, I think, but I figured that if I could inspect the bronchial tree and esophagus immediately after the onset of the bleeding, I might find something. I didn't.

I phoned Dr. Tuttle in Detroit.

"Shoot, Chris, if you have 'scoped this man three times and found nothing, what makes you think I can?"

I hung up, feeling blue. Poor Dan was in bad shape and my best efforts were for nothing. I had checked all the other body systems; they were healthy.

I even worried about Destitute Dan at night.

"You talked about him again in your sleep," Ruth would say at breakfast. "I wish you'd get to the bottom of this so I can get some rest!"

"I've got an internist, two resident physicians, a cardiologist and a hemotologist trying to help," I protested, more to myself than to Ruth. "And none of them have come up with a clue."

We persevered. The internist and each resident doctor did a complete physical independently of each other. All they found was the not unexpected low hemoglobin and red cell count.

I hid in my office, at last, and made notes about the case, starting with that which was unusual.

1) Dan had an excellent appetite and relished the hospital food. (Actually, it wasn't all that good.)

2) He revelled in the daily inbed baths the nurses gave him. This, from a guy who had seldom, if ever, given himself a bath.

3) He bore the diagnostic procedures cheerfully, yet many of them have been distinctly painful.

4) He seemed to welcome the idea that I might have to open his chest surgically—a major operation.

5) There was no moisture in the lungs. Some of the great amounts of blood he was expectorating would normally have been aspirated into the lungs.

6) Was he concealing something we should know about his condition? If so, why?

With Dan on a wheeled stretcher, I presented his case to the hospital staff conference; several doctors examined him.

"Are you sure the red stuff you're worried about is actually blood?" one of the physicians asked.

The pathologist answered for me.

"Yes, that red stuff that has Chris in a tizzy, sure is blood."

I threw the case open to the conference.

"Since I have been working for three weeks on this fellow with no results, will one of you take over?"

There was an uncomfortable silence.

I went home and spent another restless night. What was I missing?

The next morning, instead of heading toward my own hospital, I drove straight to St. Lawrence. I would talk to him; perhaps a chance remark would provide me with part of the combination to unlock the mystery that had all but taken over my life.

I walked into Dan's room, my mind ready with questions I hadn't asked before.

He wasn't there!

He's bled to death, I thought, with a sick sensation in my stomach. I flew to the nurse's station. Several white, starched figures hovered around the high counter.

"What's happened to my problem patient?" The words didn't come out as professionally as I would have liked, but I didn't care. As I waited for someone to answer, the women's faces slowly broke into smiles, which widened until they looked like a bunch of jack-o-lanterns.

The supervisor spoke up.

"Nurse Doe will tell you about your patient."

Nurse Doe moved forward and I remembered that she was new at St. Lawrence. She had been on the nursing staff of a hospital in Battle Creek.

"I went into Dan's room right after breakfast this morning. It was my first time on this floor. I started to make small talk about how well he had cleaned up his breakfast tray. When I looked at him straight on, I recognized him and he recognized me. He bounced out of bed, threw on his pants and shirt, and while I just stood there in surprise, he ran down the stairs, carrying his shoes.

"But why?" I almost stopped breathing. The answer was coming. She *knew*.

"We had your patient in Community Hospital in Battle Creek a few weeks ago and under similar circumstances.

While the doctors were trying to make a diagnosis I went into his room unexpectedly and I saw something. He pleaded with me not to tell on him. He said it was a perfect way for him to be in a warm place with good food and a lot of attention during the winter."

I could have shaken Nurse Doe for prolonging the suspense.

Her smile was rueful. "Of course, I had to report what I'd seen and he was discharged."

"Miss Doe," I said, almost croaking. "What did you see?"

"He used a large safety pin to rupture blood vessels in the posterior pharynx."

"And produced hemorrhage right there in his throat," I marveled.

Poor Derelict Dan. We might better have called him Desperate Dan. To think of the self-inflicted torture, besides the not-so-comfortable things I did to him. I had been fooled before, but never like that.

CHAPTER 40

GENESEE

"Thank you for your offer and for your confidence, gentlemen, which I value," I said, "but I can't accept. There's still too much to be done here."

I met the eyes of each of the men. They constituted the Board of Trustees for the Genesee County Sanatorium which later became the Memorial Hospital. The hospital was under construction that year of 1949, and the board had offered me the medical directorship.

"Well," the chairman said, wagging his head, "we really didn't think we could entice you away. But you will help us, won't you?"

"Of course—the Board and your staff will always be welcome at the Chest Hospital. We'll do everything we can to help you get underway."

Another member stirred.

"Dr. Stringer—how about recommending someone for medical director."

I thought a moment.

"I can have three names for you in a couple of days," I said. "I'll phone."

It wasn't difficult to keep my promise. My foremost recommendation was Dr. Chester Koop of Plymouth, Wisconsin. I had known him and been impressed when he was associated with Dr. John Towey (Big John) at Pinecrest Sanatorium in the Upper Peninsula.

The Genesee County Memorial Hospital Board of Trustees did appoint Chester Koop as their Medical Director to what was then, a sanatorium.

Chester was a whirlwind. He spent a lot of time with me at the Ingham Chest Hospital discussing procedures for opening the new hospital. We were hospitalizing some of the Genesee patients, and these people would necessarily be transferred to the new sanatorium.

One day we were going over the details of these transfers.

"Chris, all the surgical facilities will be in place soon—the suite, equipment and supplies . . ."

"I know that, Chester. I conferred with the Board for several months. What are you getting at?"

"Oh, yes, well—I have an idea that the University Hospital in Ann Arbor will still expect us to send chest surgery patients over there." There was a determined set to his jaw. "I intend to have all chest surgery done in my hospital."

"And you want me to come over and do it. Now, Chester, I'd rather not. Major surgery away from my home base is not something I want to be responsible for. I don't want to operate and leave the patient. They need good follow-up."

He was persistent. "You've done it with mental patients where they couldn't be transferred."

I was finally persuaded. Chester joined me and my staff when we made grand rounds and he quickly learned our post-operative procedures. I was gratified with his perceptive organization when the hospital was completed and I began my trips to Flint to operate.

About this time, Chester found a home to buy in Flint and his contribution to the family move was to drive the children to their new home. His pregnant wife and the furniture preceded him.

Chester had built up the back seat of his car to make a good-sized bed. And to be sure the children wouldn't be fussy, he gave each one of them a dose of phenobarbitol when he started out. It worked well and the children were still sleeping when they reached Chicago.

Since Chester planned to drive straight through to Flint, arriving very late, he foresaw a problem finding drinking water to administer another sleeping pill. So he woke them up, gave each of them another tablet and they dozed off again.

Several hours later Chester began to be a little apprehensive. He saw no sign pointing toward Flint and he felt that they should be close, anyway.

By that time, it was 4 a.m. He came to a small town and checked at a gas station. They were in Clare—100 miles off course.

Chester and children got to Flint early the following day. I wonder how much trouble he had finding his new house.

* * * *

Dr. Koop was right about keeping his surgical patients "at home". Everything went well in the sparkling new hospital. It was a handsome building; entrance steps of wide, smooth granite and a foyer gleaming with white marble.

The top floor surgical suite was unusually spacious. It, too, shone with newness.

In the beginning, I proceeded cautiously. I took the entire operating team from my hospital each time I was scheduled there for surgery.

It was obvious after a short time, that this was unnecessary. Since the staff there was well trained, I only needed to go over procedures initially. Soon, I worked along as well with my Genesee team as with the Ingham team, and post-operative care was the best in both hospitals.

* * * *

Marie was among those I trained as part of the Genesee surgical team. She was an excellent surgical nurse, witty and always jovial. She was also obese and had to field occasional pointed remarks from her colleagues about her weight. I know she tried a lot of regimes to reduce, but all had been unsuccessful. Mostly, she was kidded about not being able to get close enough to the operating table to see what was going on. She did well in spite of her bulk, and even devised a useful place to hold the Bovie cautery—a tool I used often to coagulate small bleeding areas. She fashioned a pocket in the sterile drapes where I could thrust the cautery handle and blade when it wasn't being used.

This kept the instrument from slipping away or off the table, and it was handy for me to find without having to ask for it. This pocket was across from me and directly in front of my nurse. The cautery itself was electrically activated by a foot switch conveniently placed on the floor near my right foot. It worked well. I was pleased with her thoughtfulness and told her so. She flushed with pleasure and gave me a smile that would have lighted up a dark room.

Once, when the Genesee team and I were operating on a particularly demanding and difficult case, Marie did her usual fine job. She was across from me, leaning over the patient. I was isolating the pulmonary artery, oblivious to all else. Suddenly, Nurse Marie began to howl. The team froze—it was like the ending on a TV show when the camera stops the action. Nurse Marie began thrashing about beyond the drape sheets.

"The cautery," she shrieked.

The terrible realization hit me. I still had my foot on the activating switch! I jerked it off about the time the Nurse freed herself. The steel cautery knife had sizzled through the drape sheets, her gown, and finally burned a small hole in her belly!

Apologizing profusely, I suggested she leave to obtain first aid.

"Oh, I can finish here," she said, and she did without complaint, ignoring the stifled giggling among the crew at the operating table.

The following week, we were operating on a similar case, but one thing about the procedure was different. There was a glass test tube in the drape fold into which I was instructed by Nurse Marie to store the cautery knife and handle when not in use. I acknowledged the change with a smile. The foot switch, too, was in a position where I had to fish for it.

CHAPTER 41

HEART ATTACK

"You've skipped lunch again," Elvi scolded as I hurried past her to my office. She got up and followed me to my desk. "Operate all morning and then expect to see a waiting room full of people with no food on your stomach."

"I'll be OK, Elvi."

But she was planted solidly, waiting to do battle.

"I'll get you a sandwich from the drug store and be right back," she said trotting out. I didn't answer. Elvi looked after me on the job as well as Ruth did at home. Elvi actually had more time to pursue the project than my wife, for I was spending more of my hours working than not.

I saw the last patient out at 5:30 that evening. At home Ruth was dressed and ready for dinner with Chet and Mary Koop in Flint. I did a quick shower and change and drove the 50 miles to Koop's faster than I should have.

"What do you know," Mary Koop smiled as she welcomed us. "Only 45 minutes late! Better than you usually do."

"Enough of your smart talk, Mary," I said fondly. "Where's Chester and my old-fashioned?"

We settled in the living room for the easy conversation that flows when old friends with common interests gather. I wasn't particularly tired, rather I felt the need to just let down.

I took a couple of sips from my drink and became nauseated. I sat the glass down and waited for the waves of queaziness to subside.

At that point, Mary announced dinner and we started toward the dining room. The table was beautifully set, but the food odors made me wretchedly sick. I excused myself, hurried upstairs to a bathroom and vomited.

I remember staggering to a bedroom, but little else until Chester roused me.

"It's 10:00 Chris; we've been looking in on you thinking you were just overtired. Are you all right?"

I sat up weakly. "It couldn't have been something I ate, Chester. I've only had breakfast and half a sandwich all day."

He looked at me sharply.

"Let's have a listen." He left and returned with a stethoscope. "Did the military detect your heart murmur, Chris?"

"Heart murmur? That's the first I've heard about a heart murmur."

"Here, listen for yourself."

I heard but I didn't really need the stethoscope. I felt the murmur with each heavy beat.

"Promise that you'll take care of it right away," Chester and Mary fretted. They helped Ruth fashion a bed in our car's back-seat and Ruth drove home.

The following day was Sunday and I felt much better. On Monday morning, I did two major surgical cases and after lunch I went to see Fred Swartz, a Lansing internist who had given me routine physical examinations through the years.

"There is a blowing systolic murmur, which wasn't there before," he said. "But I suppose you know this."

I inclined my head, hating the thought. My twins were teenagers; I wanted dearly to see them educated and started in their careers. And Ruth, was she going to be denied the retirement years with me? Still so much I hadn't done! For the first time in my life, I was afraid. Kay Purdy's warning whispered at me, "You'll burn yourself out."

"I want another opinion," Doctor Swartz said. "Will you go see Art Olsen at the Clinic?" (He didn't say Mayo Clinic—all Mayo men assume you know they mean the Mayo Clinic when you say "Clinic".)

"Sure—I'll leave tomorrow. I would like to visit our old friend anyway."

I didn't feel nearly as brave as I sounded.

When I arrived at the Mayo Clinic the following day, Art had pre-registered for me and arranged for Dr. Howard Burschell to see me, too. Art was a pulmonary man and he wanted one of their cardiologist's opinion, also.

Dr. Swartz and Dr. Olsen both thought the chordae tendneae from my mitral valve had ruptured. Burschell was a specialist in cardiac problems, but he had one heck of a time making up his mind about me.

First he agreed with Swartz and Olsen; then he didn't. He felt it should be operated; then he changed his mind. Later, he said it could be the insufficient mitral valve was due to myocardial infarction. But he wavered on that, too.

All were agreed, though, even Burschell, that I was disabled, should take time off, and never go back to the heavy work schedule I had made my life style.

This was the second week of December—1962. Ruth and I discussed my health carefully and decided to take a three month Florida vacation.

"If you stay here," Ruth said, "you'll see patients, and the phone will ring off the wall."

My friends rallied. McGillicuddys recommended a place on Singer Island where they were going soon. And they actually made the living arrangements. Ruth made plane reservations and packed—all the while giving the boys and Nita Frederick, our long-time housekeeper, detailed instructions for getting along while we were away. A neighbor drove us to the airport, and when we got off the plane, a luxury car awaited us, courtesy of Olds Motor Works.

I rested and rested some more, yet fatigue overtook me. It was a new experience—being dead tired.

293

"Hummm," Ruth said when she noticed. "You've always kept yourself so busy you didn't know how tired you actually were—you sort of numbed yourself into keeping going."

* * * *

Back home, I was referred to Dr. Marvin Pollard of Ann Arbor. He in turn asked Dr. Ralph Brandt and Dr. Joseph Morris, a chest surgeon, to see me.

Dr. Morris' consultation report said, "Rupture of chordae tendineae, probably due to trauma." He later altered his opinion concerning the cause of the rupture when the question of trauma became important. Fortunately I had secured a copy of Dr. Morris' original consultation. He was, at that time, promoting a new technique for reconstruction of the ruptured chordae, using a teflon pulley replacement. He suggested open heart surgery at once, using this technique to repair my valve.

"I like to do such operations early," he explained.

I declined and haven't heard anything about the teflon replacement technique for years. I understand that the teflon tended to pull out and defeat its purpose.

Over a period of a year, I saw four other chest surgeons, all friends, and each wanting to operate on my heart by a different method.

"When you fellows agree on one method, I might let one of you operate," I said. I was exasperated and worried. I knew right cardiac enlargement usually follows rupture of the chordae.

"OK, Chris. We give you about two years without surgery." That they agreed upon!

* * * *

The two years passed. I had given up my practice of surgery and felt fine. The right heart had not enlarged as my friends predicted.

One day I kept a dental appointment in the morning and a legal deposition in the afternoon.

294

The dentist injected my mouth with novocain and, unknown to me, it was laced with adrenalin. I would have refused it if I had known about the added drug, for adrenalin is capable of producing constriction of the coronaries. Nowadays, most dentists don't use it.

About an hour after my dental work was finished, I felt the onset of substernal chest distress. I skipped lunch, trying to deny its seriousness, and kept the legal appointment.

My chest pains began again.

"I cannot continue the deposition, gentlemen. I don't feel well." I rose to leave.

"Dr. Stringer, you must stay and see this through. We have an important case here," one of the attorneys said.

I left the lawyer still talking at my back and drove to Dr. Swartz's office, forgetting that it was his day off. I called Dr. Bauer's office. There was no answer. Then I remembered most of us closed our offices on Wednesday or Thursday afternooons. I knew I had some nitrostat at home so I turned homeward, took the drug and lay down. It relieved the pain, and confirmed the probability of angina.

My son, Tom, drove me to Ann Arbor the next day and Dr. Brandt admitted me to Saint Joseph Hospital. Tom says I insisted on carrying my own bag into the coronary intensive care unit.

I had a decent night, but about 6 a.m. the next morning, I awoke with terrible, grappling chest pains. I knew it was a severe coronary occlusion and I was scared. I rang for a nurse and asked for Dr. Brandt at once. I knew he was in the hospital early each day. The minutes dragged by and it was an hour before he appeared. I was semi-conscious but extremely angry and told him so. "It took longer to get a doctor at my bedside than it would have if I had been home."

"I'm sorry, Chris. An intern got the message instead of me. It won't happen again."

"I would probably be dead," I whispered.

I hovered between death and life for some 48 hours. Then I improved slowly and recovered. The most crucial time was the first 24 hours after the coronary occlusion.

Dr. Brandt's parting words the day I left the hospital were, "You were lucky". I sure was. He didn't even call Ruth, although he knew my condition was critical. He did tell Ted, who had just started medical school in Ann Arbor. Ted called home and reported to his mother. Tom had not yet left for medical school so he was there. It was agreed that he would drive his mother to the hospital the following morning; Tom, suspecting that the problem was more serious got to another phone and called his brother back to get more information. Ruth and Tom came to the hospital the next day and Ted met them there where the three of them had a conference with Dr. Brandt. *This was more than 24 hours after the coronary attack.*

Some seven or eight years later Fred Swartz told me he couldn't hear the murmur any more. Ralph Brandt claimed it was still there. So what else was new?

Florida cardiologist and chairman of the coronary care unit of the Miami Heart Institute, Dr. Richard Elias, examined me about ten years ago.

"You've done a better job on your heart than any surgeon could do. The mitral insufficiency due to the ruptured chordae has improved."

No one seems to know why or how. It just is not supposed to happen. I am not about to argue with the gift of additional years though.

The week following the graduation of our twin sons from medical school, I was driving with both boys from our East Lansing home to the Olds Hotel in Lansing where plans were being made at the City Club to celebrate the event of their graduation from medical school and introduce their recently acquired brides to about 200 of our Lansing friends. It was an opportunity to reminisce with them about my entrance to Lansing to practice medicine a generation before. Much of the area between Lansing and East Lansing had been farmland then and there was a trolly track on Michigan Avenue connecting the two cities. It is built up solid now and the effect is essentially one metropolitan area. The celebration banquet was a gala event and contrasted sharply with our humble beginnings in Lansing.

I lived a moderate life and allowed my heart to fend for itself, which it has done unexpectedly well. I'm grateful I had the means to retire. So I'm alive twenty years after I was supposed to die, and I'm writing this. Ruth is her usual sweet-tempered self, full of projects. What more could a man want? Our sons are now accomplished and successful surgeons. Our daughters-in-laws are lovely and the grand-children are perfect.

*   *   *   *

From Ruth's journal:
"I remember . . . one Sunday evening years ago, a new maid had moved into our home. Later, she said, 'I was feeling lonely and homesick. You had guests that night. I could hear Doctor Stringer's voice, and then the group would laugh. It happened over and over again, and I decided then that I would be happy here, too.'

Story-telling is a talent, and he has it. I am glad he has written some of them down.

I had always said, 'Chris will never retire.' He was one of those persons who never walked—he ran. I am sure that had something to do with a heart problem developing. When there was no choice but retirement, he might have resented it to the point of making life miserable for those of us near him, but he didn't. His mind remained so active; I have felt having sons interested in medicine had something to do with his reading so avidly on medical subjects. His interest and determination to keep abreast of the times, has meant he never seems to run out of something to do—or read.

And, of course, writing HIS book was 'on a back burner' for years. Through it he has met other writers, and that has opened new doors and new fields of interest. He has said, 'If I had known it would take so long, I might not have started it.' But he has made new friends as he has written, and being a perfectionist, has gone over and over his material. In the end, I am sure he will not regret the time spent on it—nor will his family.

Said one of our daughters-in-law, 'Dad never really

297

retired. When he couldn't practice medicine any more, he just moved on to other things.'

I think perhaps one of the many gratifying highlights of Chris' medical career was reached in the spring of 1983. A letter came from the President of the Michigan Thoracic Society, which said, in part: '. . . you have been selected to receive the 1983 Bruce Douglas Award, the highest honor the Michigan Thoracic Society can bestow upon its colleagues . . . for the recognition of your valuable contributions to the field of pulmonary medicine.

Because of the pioneering efforts of men like Bruce Douglas and you, our profession has acheived the stature we enjoy today. We are pleased to honor the results of your career!'

Bruce Douglas was a great friend and inspiration to Chris. He died in a car accident at the height of his career.

The award was made on June 24th. Friends from around the state came to honor him, and many wrote who could not be there. Doctor Chester Koop made the presentation for 'your especially noteworthy contributions to the field of lung disease treatment and research,' and referred to Chris' many scientific publications through the years.

His family is justly proud!"

INDEX

302

O

P

R

S